CW00642169

The Clifton Chronicle

John Kennedy

with an historical introduction by Dr. Alan Crosby

Carnegie Publishing Ltd., 1990

The Clifton Chronicle
by John Kennedy

Published by Carnegie Publishing Ltd., 18 Maynard Street, Preston PR2 2AL.
Typeset in Times Medium and Zapf Chancery by Carnegie Publishing Ltd.,
Printed by Mather Brothers Ltd (a member of the Pindar Group of Companies),
1 Garstang Road, Preston

First edition, September 1990

ISBN 0 948789 54 9

The Clifton Chronicle

John Kennedy

with an historical introduction by Dr. Alan Crosby

For Doreen

Contents

Chapter Two

The Colonel

Chapter Three

John Talbot

Chapter Four

Harry

Preface

An historical account of the Cliftons of Lytham from the 12th to the 18th centuries, by Dr. Alan Crosby

HE Clifton family derived its name from the village of Clifton, in the township of Clifton with Salwick between Lytham and Preston. Here they owned land, and eventually the manor - a property which they retained for several hundred years until it was sold in 1917. The first of the line to be recorded is Osbert, whose son, Walter, held lands in Clifton, Salwick, Westby, Plumpton and Marton. In about 1170 Walter was one of the witnesses of a charter involving the exchange of lands in Lonsdale and Hutton, and his presence at such a transaction suggests that he was recognised as a major local figure and important landowner.

He was a thane of Saxon origin, perhaps a grandson of one of the few Saxon landowners to keep their property after the Conquest. It is interesting to note that already, in the twelfth century, the family lands were spread among the townships of the south Fylde. Although they later acquired other properties in adjacent townships - most notably, of course, in Lytham - it was not until the middle of the eighteenth century that they looked further afield for the purchase of land, and throughout their existence the family wealth was predominantly in the Fylde lands. This Walter is also recorded as being a benefactor of Cockersand Abbey in the period 1190-1217.

By the end of the thirteenth century the line had adopted the surname 'de Clifton', in consequence of their connection with the village. The 'de' form remained in use until the late-fifteenth century, but as was the case with most such names the simple form, without 'de', eventually became standard, and so the surname Clifton arose. There is very little detailed documentary evidence about the family in these early years: not until the late-fifteenth century do wills, estate records and official papers begin to appear in any significant quantity. We do know, however, that by the end of the thirteenth century the family was well-established in Lancashire society. The Cliftons were becoming major landowners, with extensive properties. They were among the upper rank of county gentry families, and so served with their equals and peers in filling the various positions expected of, and the perquisite of, their number.

Thus, in the fourteenth and fifteenth centuries, they appear as MPs for the county: William de Clifton was Knight of the Shire (M.P.) for Lancashire in the Parliament of 1304, for example. They were also members of royal retinues (especially those connected with the Dukes and Duchy of Lancaster) and, in consequence of the latter role, they were given minor offices in the gift of the Crown. We learn that various members of the family, at different times, served in the French wars.

All this might suggest that the Cliftons, as with many other high-ranking gentry families in medieval England, could ultimately have been expected to rise into the ranks of the nobility, either by favourable and fortune-bringing marriages, or by the grant of titles and lands as a result of service to the Crown.

But this did not, with one short-lived exception, occur: in 1900, just as in 1300, the Cliftons were simply untitled gentry. The reason, it can be postulated, is that they were devoutly Catholic. Their wise policy was to keep a low profile, to court no ostentation, or connections with London, and to avoid, as far as possible, the persecution and suffering which could result from such strong Papist beliefs. It did not always work, but this reticence helps to explain the lack of elevation in status.

Although details of the family's early activities are scant, some colourful incidents have found their place in local history. In 1337, for example, Sir William de Clifton of Clifton was involved in a heated and acrimonious dispute with the Abbot of Vale Royal in Cheshire over the question of tithe rights. This has always been a touchy matter between Church and laity, and Sir William claimed that he held some of the tithe rights in Kirkham parish which were exercised by Vale Royal (which owned the manor and parish church of Kirkham).

The Abbot accused Sir William of a series of offences, major and minor: that he had thrust with a lance at one of the brethren; that he had retained twenty marks which he owed the Abbey; that he had allowed tithe corn to rot in the fields, instead of conveying it to the barn as was the custom; that he had left a cart, laden with hay belonging to the Rector's tithes, in the field, for a month, to the damage of the hay; that he had used the Rector's mare as a hunting palfrey, and thus derided the Rector; that he had failed to keep tithes of calves, pigeons, huntings and hawkings, and had threatened the procurator with death if he ventured on Sir William's land to collect what was due to the Rector; that he and his companions irreverently entered the church at Kirkham and impeded the priests, disrupting their services and duties; that he did not allow his tenants to be punished even if they were living in open sin; that he had, in contempt of the Church, had his child baptised elsewhere than in the font at the church; and that he had ordered Thomas, Clerk to the Abbot, to be publicly scourged in the market place at Preston, even to the effusion of blood.

It is clear from this lengthy catalogue that William was in deep trouble, and he was ordered to appear at Westminster to answer the charges: he refused to attend. Eventually, he was compelled openly to confess his guilt, to ask for pardon, to seek absolution for himself and his followers, to pay the twenty marks owed, and to make financial settlement with the Abbot for the tithes that had been lost or destroyed.

The scourging of poor Thomas had been approved and accepted by many of the bystanders (suggesting that William was not alone in his attitude to the monastic houses!). Their names were recorded - there were thirty-one of them, including Adam the Harper, and they were ordered to buy, at their own expense, a large wax candle which was carried round Kirkham Church on the Feast of the Palms, and offered to the patron of the church, the Blessed St. Michael - which doubtless taught them not to suck up to the gentry and perhaps provided Adam with a new lay for appropriate harp accompaniment!

In 1372 Robert Clifton, grandson of this Sir William, was charged with having siezed a certain William Garlick at Little Singleton and carrying him off to Westby where he imprisoned him for a fortnight, also having taken his corn and other goods. In defence it was pleaded that Garlick was a villein of Robert's manor of Westby who had absconded. In 1382 this Robert Clifton was returned as a Knight of the Shire for Lancashire; he later went to Ireland with John Stanley in the service of the King, and was appointed Chamberlain and Receiver of Caernarvon; he died in 1401.

Robert's father, Sir Nicholas Clifton, had been appointed as governor of the castle of Ham in Picardy by John of Gaunt in 1383, and in 1394 was made deputy to the Earl of Huntingdon as Admiral of the West. In 1396 he became Keeper of the Lordship and Castle of Bolsover in Derbyshire. These appointments, granted to father and son, were not of major political importance and gave no great power: but they did reflect the connections of the Cliftons, in this period, with the service of the Crown. They were the sort of minor sinecure posts granted to those who had supported and assisted the Crown in its various ambitions, foreign and domestic.

Such support was shown in the early-fifteenth century, when Thomas Clifton, the eldest son of Robert, accompanied Henry V to France and was present at the Battle of Agincourt, as was his son, John, who was one of the retainers of Michael de la Pole, Earl of Suffolk. Thomas was knighted after the battle - the stuff of drama and romance, perhaps, but that his family still had their roots firmly in the lawless soil of the Fylde is shown by the accusations made against his two sons, Richard (the heir) and the same John who was at Agincourt, that they had waylaid Henry Fleetwood in Kirkham and attempted to kill him. The family might have been in the outer circles of courtly life, but chivalry was not the rule in fifteenth-century Lancashire!

Thomas had married Agnes, daughter of Sir Richard Molyneux of Sefton. The alliance forged by their marriage was very significant. It marked a further stage in the social advance of the Cliftons. They had married into a very important, powerful and influential south-west Lancashire family, a family which was to be one of the leading dynasties in the county almost to the present. Hitherto, they had tended to form marriage alliances with similarly placed old gentry families in north- and mid-Lancashire. Thus, the William Clifton who disputed with Vale Royal married Margaret, daughter of Sir Robert Shireburne of Stonyhurst; previous generations had married into the de Samlesburys of Samlesbury, and the de Cantsfields of Cantsfield in Lonsdale, among others. The Molyneux family was more important, and its connection with the Cliftons was to be a long-standing one. In later generations the cousinship resulting from the marriage ties was to be reinforced by further alliances, and it is apparent that of all the family links it was the one with the Molyneux, eventually to be ennobled as Earls of Sefton, that counted the most.

In 1512 Cuthbert Clifton died, leaving only a nine-year-old daughter, Elizabeth, as his heiress. By this time the family held extensive lands, including the manors of Clifton, Westby and Salwick, and property in Kirkham, Newton with Scales, the Plumptons, Warton, Wrea, Elswick, Greenhalgh, Esprick, Goosnargh and Preston. Elizabeth Clifton's position was a very difficult one. As a child, and a female, she was prey to the manoeuvrings of male relatives and to others who had ambitions to gain all or part of her inheritence, either by marriage or by seizure. In particular, she had her uncle, her father's brother, William Clifton, who was not content with the property which he would receive under earlier agreements made in the lifetime of his brother.

Elizabeth became, as was customary for a child heiress, a ward of the Crown. Her uncle William immediately seized most of the lands which were rightfully hers. Shortly afterwards, at the age of just eleven years, she was married to Richard Hesketh, the king's attorney for the County Palatine. Such marriages were quite commonplace: the Crown obtained fees and commissions for arranging and consenting to the marriage, the husband (in this case a middle-aged man) obtained great wealth and fortune, and the bride, if she was fortunate, acquired a powerful protector who would fight for her inheritance in order to keep it himself. In Elizabeth's case this happened: her new husband took steps to reclaim the properties and manors, and eventually forced William Clifton into arbitration.

The case was judged by the Bishop of Ely, who chose to divide the Clifton estates into two portions, and to offer the first choice to Richard Hesketh and his wife Elizabeth. In 1515 the decision was made: the Hesketh chose to have the manor of Clifton with Salwick, the tithe rights and Ribble fishery rights, the lands in Salwick and Preston, and various other lesser properties. William Clifton, therefore, obtained the other part: the manor of Westby, and property in the Plumptons, Wrea, Elswick and adjacent townships. In effect he gained the western part of the Fylde properties, the Hesketh the eastern half. The ancient family estates were, therefore, from 1515 onwards, split into two different parts.

William Clifton continued the male line. Elizabeth Hesketh was a childless widow after the death of her husband in 1520 - and still only seventeen years old! Her second marriage reinforced the links with the Molyneux family: her new husband, who was perhaps attracted not so much by the sentiment of marrying into the Cliftons as by the prospect of a seventeen-year-old with two fortunes at her disposal, was Sir William Molyneux of Sefton. They had three children, but only one of these produced an heir: their elder daughter, Anne, married Sir Henry Halsall of Halsall near Ormskirk, a lucky man indeed - by marrying Anne he obtained half of the Clifton estates, Richard Hesketh's portion of the Hesketh properties, and William Molyneux's part of the Sefton estates!

William Clifton died in 1537, leaving a son, Thomas, as his heir. William's will survives and gives fascinating detail about the family and its estates. He asks to be buried in 'ye p[ar]yshe churche of Kyrkham in ye place wher my ancestors are buryed', and makes complex arrangements to ensure that the property is well managed after his death. Included among his bequests is the provision that 'all my servants dwellynge w[i]th me shall have after my decease every of theyme their [whole] wag[e]s truly payed for their servyce done and this their halffe wag[e]s over to helpe theyme to servyce'. Care for the welfare of servants and retainers is a feature of all the Clifton wills during the next one hundred and fifty years or so. William was a major landowner, but was still very conscious of the connection with the land: he came from a long line of men whose wealth derived from the soil, and he was well aware of the detailed business of farming: he leaves his son Thomas 'vi of my best Incalffe qwyez [cows] and vi bullocks whyche wer pastured in the Pele last sommer'.

The second half of the sixteenth century saw serious problems for this line of the family. After the Reformation they adhered devoutly and fervently to the Old Religion. They staunchly refused to turn Protestant, and in 1577 were formally registered as recusants. This was in itself troublesome, although they escaped the very heavy penalties inflicted upon Catholic gentry outside Lancashire. As in so much else, Lancashire remained to some extent a law unto itself. But matters were made worse by the fact that for several generations the family suffered the early death of the head of the family, and the succession of a minor. Thomas Clifton died in 1551, his son, Cuthbert in 1580. On Cuthbert's death the heir was his son, Thomas, aged eighteen.

Thomas was also registered as a recusant, as a fine for which he had to provide a light horseman for service in Ireland in 1584. He married Anne, daughter of Sir John Southworth, and died only four years after his father, in 1584, aged only twenty-two. The sole heir was his son, Cuthbert, who was three years old. Cuthbert became a Ward of the Crown, under the guardianship of William Norris of Speke. The documents by which guardianship was granted describe the lands held by the child Cuthbert, including the manor of Westby, fifty-five messuages (dwellings), thirteen gardens, ten orchards, three hundred acres of mossland, two hundred acres of meadow, two hundred acres of pasture, and three hundred acres of arable land, all in Westby and adjacent townships. There were other properties, in places such as Freckleton, which were not part of the ancestral estates, but had been purchased by Cuthbert's father and grandfather comparatively recently.

Cuthbert Clifton grew to manhood; he is the first member of the family of whom a portrait has survived. It was painted in the early-seventeenth century, and shows a slim handsome young man with curly hair, wearing an elaborately padded and embroidered doublet and hose and a fine ruff. It was this Cuthbert who may be regarded as the founding father of the Cliftons of Lytham, for in 1606, when he was in his late-twenties, he negotiated the purchase of the great estate of Lytham from his Molyneux relatives.

The Move to Lytham

IN all the property purchasing and inheriting of the previous five centuries, Lytham had been passed by. The reason is clear: every square inch of the township was, until the dissolution of the monasteries, the property of Lytham Priory, a daughter house of the Benedictine cathedral priory of Durham. The priory was founded in the reign of Richard I by Richard Fitzroger, a local landowner. He granted it lands which included the whole of the township of Lytham, and the possession and rights of the parish church of St. Cuthbert. Throughout the medieval period, therefore, the monks of Lytham Priory were the sole landowners, and no secular landowner was able to obtain property in the parish.

At the Dissolution Lytham passed to the Crown, and was then rented out to tenants. There were serious difficulties because of the 'rage of the sands', the blowing of sand from the shore and dunes inland: in the 1540s it seems that there was serious encroachment by the dunes across agricultural lands behind, as a result of which Sir Thomas Dannett, the Crown's tenant of the manor of Lytham, successfully petitioned for the reduction in his annual rent from £48 19s 6d to £26 8s 2d. He claimed in his petition that almost 1,000 acres had been engulfed by sand between 1540 and 1549, and that it threatened the manor house itself.

The manor house was a conversion of the former priory buildings, and was on the site of the present Lytham Hall. Dannett was the first of a succession of tenants, but in the 1570s the entire property was purchased outright from the Crown by the Molyneux family, who added it to their already extensive Fylde estates, but themselves let it out to further tenants. From the point of view of both the Clifton and Molyneux families, the distribution of their estates left something to be desired. The Cliftons wanted to increase their Fylde landholdings, and to be rid of various minor properties south of the Ribble, while the Molyneuxs had the great bulk of their estates in the Liverpool-Formby-Ormskirk triangle, and were not really directly interested in the Fylde. The families were closely related and on good terms, and so Cuthbert Clifton, on reaching his majority, was able to begin negotiations for a redistribution.

On 14 February 1606 he signed an agreement for the purchase from Sir Richard Molyneux, for £4,300, of the entire manor and estate of Lytham. As part of the agreement lands south of the Ribble were handed over to the Molyneuxs: a tidying-up of the estates of the two families thus took place. Cuthbert had a very good bargain. There were almost 5,500 acres of land, including a great park and a fine manor house; there were great tracts of grazing land, there were expanses of moss, there were fisheries and mills, and there was the village of Lytham itself. From this point the centre of Clifton activity shifted. Although the family retained, and indeed continued to develop, its Westby properties, their main house and permanent residence was, from 1606, Lytham Hall, and they were known as the Cliftons of Lytham.

As befitted a young and prosperous gentleman, Cuthbert, having bought his great new estate, proceeded to improve it. He pulled down much of the old priory, and on the site erected a new manor house in the contemporary Jacobean style. Some parts of the old manor and priory were retained, but most was reconstructed. And in 1616 he came to an agreement with his tenants for the enclosure and improvement of the large tract of land known as Lytham Hawes. This lay across what is now present day Ansdell and Heyhouses, and on to the edge of the modern Blackpool Airport. It was an area of open grazing land and pasture. By the agreement of 1616 this land was fenced and ditched, turned into fields, and improved in quality, and soon afterwards a series of farms was founded at intervals across the land, which thereby became much more valuable for agriculture and produced a much larger rent return for the lords of the manor, the Cliftons.

Cuthbert Clifton was knighted by King James I in 1617, when the king was visiting Lathom House. He, and his family, remained staunchly Catholic, a faith which in the later years of the century was to cost them dear. Sir Cuthbert Clifton died in 1634, having transformed the family fortunes, and having produced a large family by his first wife, Ann, daughter of Thomas Tyldesley. That family was to be decimated by the vicissitudes of the Civil War.

As Catholics the Cliftons were, almost automatically, royalist. Sir Thomas Clifton, the eldest son of Cuthbert, was one of the leading Lancashire royalist gentlemen, and was among those who, in 1642, were deprived of arms by adherents of parliament, and who in consequence petitioned the King at Chester to be allowed to arm themselves in defence of his Majesty and, they added as though an afterthought but no doubt in reality at the front of their minds, in their own defence as well. No fewer than three of Thomas's brothers, Lawrence, Francis and John, Captains in the King's army, were killed in action during the Civil War.

When the Earl of Derby made his ill-executed foray to a Spanish ship that had been driven ashore on Rossall Point, early in 1643, he spent the previous night as a guest at Lytham Hall. He forded the Ribble at Hesketh Bank and arrived with a small troop of cavalry. The expedition to Rossall was a fiasco: he set fire to the ship, the crew scattered, and he could not find any arms or cannon except those which he seized from the nearby mansion of the Fleetwood family who, unusually for Lancashire, adhered to the cause of parliament. He returned, frustrated, to Lytham Hall, and there no doubt sought solace in the company and hospitality of Sir Thomas Clifton. And then back, in failure, to Lathom House.

But not for long . . . hearing that the ship's cannon had been removed to Lancaster by parliamentarian forces before he had even reached it, he decided to attack the castle. Back across the Ribble he came, and made his headquarters at Lytham, holding a forced muster of able-bodied males at Kirkham the next morning. On reaching Lancaster Castle he found it heavily garrisoned by regular troops, for whom Fylde peasants were no match, so instead he set fire to the town and burned about 170 houses.

At the siege of Bolton in May 1644 the town was stormed by Prince Rupert, to whom it surrendered after a gallant defence. One George Sharples of Freckleton had received a commission in the parliamentarian army, and had been ordered to raise a company in Lytham, which had not been successful: it was said that the people 'reflected the loyal sentiments of the Lord of the Manor, and could neither be coerced nor seduced from their allegiance to the King'. Sharples, despite this failure to persuade the Lythamers to change sides, became a Captain, and was present at the siege of Bolton. He was taken prisoner by the royalist forces and was dragged, almost naked and barefoot, through the miry and blood-stained streets to the place where Cuthbert Clifton, the eldest son of Sir Thomas Clifton of Lytham was standing, having been the leader of one of the successful royalist assault forces. Clifton, and others nearby, 'caused him [Sharples] to stand in the dirt to his knees, jeering upon him, and put a Psalter into his hands that he might sing them a psalm to make them sport'.

Cuthbert was elevated to the rank of colonel, in acknowledgment of his services at Bolton, and returned to the Fylde for a few days to raise a fresh detachment of men – they flocked to his standard, unlike that of the luckless Captain Sharples. Cuthbert made provision for his men by appropriating cattle and sheep from Layton Hawes, regardless of ownership, and by relieving some of the Puritans of Kirkham, Bispham and Poulton of their bedding! The author of *A Discourse of the Warr in Lancashire,* one of our main sources for information about this period of the county's history, was a Fylde man and supporter of parliament. He was hostile to the Cliftons, and notes sourly and cynically that 'for provision of his soldiers, as also for their lying, made a prey of his own country, for he caused many poor man's stock of sheep to be taken out of that Common belonging to Layton called the Hoos . . . Such wise counsel he had, and such a kind respect he bore his own country.' But, after all, this was wartime . . .

He then marched to Liverpool to join Prince Rupert, and was involved in the capture of the town in June 1644. In reward for this he was made Governor. But a few days later the town was regained for parliament, Clifton was taken prisoner, and died in jail in Manchester a few months later – yet another Clifton had died for the royalist cause.

Cuthbert, the second son of Sir Cuthbert Clifton and uncle to the Colonel, had entered the Society of Jesus in 1630, and is said to have reconciled the Earl of Derby to the Roman Catholic faith on his way to his execution at Bolton in 1651. Thus, of the sons of Sir Cuthbert, three died for King and faith and one served the faith as a priest for most of his long life (Father Cuthbert died in 1675), while the eldest grandson also died in fighting for the King. It was indeed a difficult time, when the devotion of the family to the Catholic cause showed even in the hardest moments.

Sir Thomas Clifton was inevitably punished for all this. The victory of parliament meant that his enemies were in power. His estates were confiscated and put up for sale, the proceeds to be used for the benefit of the Navy. Ultimately, they were compounded for – that is, the family kept a part of them in return for paying a fine. The family's properties were handed over by the Parliamentary Commissioners for £4,523 7s 9d to John Fleetwood of Penwortham, a Protestant, and others, including John Wildman, 'a greate manager of Papists' interests'. Blackwood suggests, in his work on the Lancashire gentry in the Civil War and Commonwealth, that it is likely that Fleetwood and Clifton came to a tacit understanding: that the former would simply protect the estate so that eventually it could be returned to its rightful owners. Certainly by the mid-1650s the estate was again granting leases to tenants, in the name of Fleetwood but apparently on the instructions of the Clifton family.

Returned it was, on the Restoration of Charles II in 1660, although Sir Thomas died in 1657 and did not live to see the property regained. His successor was his surviving son, Sir Thomas, who initially seems to have had serious financial difficulties – scarcely surprising in view of the sequestration of his estates by Parliament. His brother-in-law lent him money, and in March 1658 wrote asking for its repayment:

> I sent unto you not long since about the thirty pounds due at Christmas, but your father's unexpected death it seems retarded the payment for that time, for by that you desired a respite for a month or two to give answer because you was then not satisfied how to act in the estate, my occasions are now so urgent as they require a speedy account . . . so

hoping to receive satisfaction concerning my just desire, I rest, your very loving brother in law and faithful servant, R. Whalley.

In 1661 Sir Thomas was made a baronet in recognition of his and his family's services and steadfast loyalty to the royalist cause since 1641. This second Sir Thomas, once the family estates had been returned, was a very wealthy man indeed, for by the marriage of his parents the Clifton estates had been reunited. The first Sir Thomas (died 1657) married his distant cousin, Ann, the daughter and co-heiress of Sir Cuthbert Halsall of Clifton Hall, and hence the direct descendant of Elizabeth Clifton who had inherited half the ancestral lands in 1515. Ann Halsall, as co-heiress to her father, obtained the Fylde estates of the Halsall family, and so on her marriage to Sir Thomas brought with her Clifton, Salwick and their attendant properties. All the ancestral lands were reunited, but the great Lytham estates were now also part of the Clifton property. They were now, without any rival, the greatest landowners and the greatest family in the Fylde.

But the second Sir Thomas, despite the restoration of the fortunes of his family, and his elevation to a baronetcy, had a tragic life. He married twice, firstly to Bridget, daughter of Sir George Heneage, and niece of the Earl of Cardigan, and secondly to Bridget, daughter of Sir Edward Hussey of Huntington, Lincolnshire. By his first wife he had four sons and four daughters, all of whom died young without issue except a daughter, Mary, who married the sixth Lord Petre. There was only one child of the second marriage, a son, Thomas, who was the great hope and joy of his parents, and to whom the great family estates were due to descend . . . but this son also died, in 1688, aged twenty. He is commemorated by a tablet in Kirkham Church: 'To parents obedient, kind and moderate, All other virtues he did celebrate'. Of Sir Thomas' nine children, only one lived to marry. He had no male heir despite such fecundity.

And Sir Thomas' misfortunes were not confined to his dynastic failure. The Restoration of the King and the restoration of his fortunes were not enough to free him from the continued threat of persecution for his faith. All was well until the downfall of James II and the great fear of, and suspicion of, Catholics which accompanied the Glorious Revolution. Catholic gentry such as the Cliftons were, in the years after 1688, again the object of great hostility. Under James II the Catholic gentry had enjoyed a brief period of good fortune. In 1687 the King purged the bench of Justices of the Peace of its Protestant members, and replaced them by Catholics. Hitherto the Catholics were excluded from exercising the magisterial rights to which their status would otherwise have entitled them. Sir Thomas

Clifton was one of the number admitted to the Bench at this time.

But in 1688 the King was deposed, and the Protestant ascendancy was restored. Out went the new Catholic magistrates and back came the former Protestant ones. And in the following year, 1689, Sir Thomas, by then an old man, was suspected of conspiracy in the 'Lancashire Plot', a half-imaginary conspiracy said to have been aimed at the restoration of James II. He was absolved from guilt, but in 1694 a much more serious charge was levied against him.

Acting on 'evidence' provided by one Lunt, an informer, the authorities arrested a number of Lancashire Catholic gentry and nobility and put them on trial for high treason, accused of plotting the overthrow and assassination of King William III. Sir Thomas was arrested at Wrea Green, held under house arrest for a short time at Lytham Hall, and then sent via Wigan to Chester, where he was imprisoned in the castle. From there he was moved to London, where he and the other accused were lodged in the Tower of London. Clearly, his very life was in danger. But the trial proved to be a disaster - from the point of view of the Government. Plenty of evidence was brought, from reliable witnesses, to show that Sir Thomas and the others arraigned with him had not met, to conspire at the places and times which the informer had indicated. It was soon apparent that Lunt was a congenital liar, and that much of the 'evidence' was pure fabrication. The accused were all acquitted, and the trial collapsed in shambles.

But all this had been too much for a man of Sir Thomas's age. Imprisonment, repeated removal from one place of confinement to another, and the stresses and strains of the trial itself, proved fatal. Only a couple of months after the end of the trial, and his release back to Lytham, Sir Thomas died, a broken man.

The only light-hearted interlude in the surviving record of the family during the late-seventeenth century comes in the letters of Sir Thomas' brother, William Clifton, a great traveller. In 1676-1677 William made a very long pilgrimage to Jerusalem, with the most devout and worthy of aims - to worship and offer prayers at the holy shrines. He did, however, manage a good deal of entertainment on the way, and spent some months unashamedly as a tourist, travelling from court to court through central and southern Europe, and reporting back home in letters which survive and which are of great interest. He had intended to travel from Venice to Vienna and then down the Danube to Constantinople, but he failed to get the required pass, and so had to go by sea from Leghorn (Livorno) in Italy.

His first letter was sent from Vienna and is dated 3 June 1676, and he then made a lengthy tour through the upper Danube valley, southern Germany, Switzerland and Northern Italy, before returning to Leghorn. His letters report gossip and information about the places he visited – sometimes apparently culled from guide-books rather than his own observations, but sometimes, as in his description of Dresden, more from personal experience: he says:

> [They] are all Lutherans here . . . and its ye drunckest coorte in all Germany, ye ducke him selfe, though seventy years of age, goes never sober to beed, not doth hee care for the company of any, but those who will drink of ye silver and gould cuppes, which upon perticular feasts hee causes to goe round, houlds three full quarts a peece!

Before leaving Venice for Vienna he had received a letter from the Rector of the English College in Rome, reporting the death of his nephew Cuthbert, one of the many children of Sir Thomas who died in childhood. It caused him great distress, and as it came soon after other deaths in the family, he said:

> little did I thinke at my leaving England to have hard of the death of soe many of my relations in soe short a time, probably I may bee the next, for besides that I am of the famely, the dangers that I am now going into both by sea and land are by most estimed very hazardus. I will not bee unmindful of ye all att the holy Sepulcher, if it please God to bringe me thither safe; not small is my grife that I must leave Venice and Europe without receiving the least syllable from you.

Eventually he sailed from Leghorn in the English ship *Advise* of Yarmouth, commanded by Captain Spooner. It was 'a stout shipe and 320 tons, twenty gunns': the latter were a great source of comfort, as the Eastern Mediterranean was infested with Algerian pirates. He is next heard of from Aleppo in Syria, where 'within five days I am to begin my pylgramidge by waie of Damascos, being ye only European in ye whole Caravan, itt being chiefly composed of Percians, Armenians, Graecians, Maronits and Turkes . . . I hope by God's Assistance in twenty-five or six days to bee in Jerusalem, where I will not be unmindful of ye and my friends'.

Whilst there are no more of his letters preserved, William must have returned safely, as – rather ironically, having gone through what he had – he was among those arrested with Sir Thomas Clifton for plotting in 1689. His portrait survives – a tall, middle-aged man of distinguished appearance, dressed in Middle Eastern or Turkish robes with a background of an imaginary foreign landscape. William Clifton was the first of the family, as far as we know, with a taste for travel to exotic places, but he was by no means the last, as later chapters in this book make clear.

From the late-seventeenth and early-eighteenth centuries there also survive fragments of correspondence and diary entries which show the Cliftons in a more light-hearted vein. Despite the trials and tribulations which the family went through, it was wealthy and well-connected, part of a complex web of family relationships woven among the Lancashire gentry families by ties of blood and marriage, and mutual adherence to the old religion, which gave them common interests. This is one example:

Honrd. Sir.
tis Mr Tyldesleys earnest desire and my particular request to ye will pleas to give my cosen Cuthbert leave to come to stay three or four nights hear a fox hunting. Mr Molyneux is hear w[i]th all the rest of the company joyns in the presentment of their Humble sarvises to yr. self and lady and I am to ye both

yr. Most Affectionate
Cosen and Humble sarvant
Eliza Tyldesley

Mr Tyldesley begs yr pardon that he writes by my hand for he went a hunting this morning by day.
These for Sr Thomas Clifton att Litham

Elizabeth was the second wife of Edward Tyldesley of Fox Hall in what is now Blackpool. In 1707 Nicholas Blundell recorded in his diary that he had been to stay at Dukenhalgh with the Walmesley family: Sir Thomas' heir, his nephew Thomas, had married one of the Walmesley daughters, and as part of the house party the family came to stay at the same time as Nicholas (1 July 1707):

Mr Livesley and one of his Doughters came to Dungenhall just when we had done dinner. Mr Clifton of Lithon and his Lady and four or five of their Children came to Lodg at Dungenhall as did also Mr Walmeslet of the Lower-hall and his Lady.

Nicholas, Thomas Clifton and William Walmesley went, a couple of days later, over to Stonyhurst to dine. It was all part of a large but intimate circle of well-to-do gentry families, usually related to each other and with a common bond of Catholicism.

Sir Thomas Clifton, as we have seen, left no living children apart from a married daughter, Mary, Lady Petre. The family estates had to descend in the male line, and so the inheritence, apart from ample provision for Mary, who had married very well in any case, descended to the eldest son of Thomas' younger brother, John Clifton. John had married Isabel, daughter of Thomas Blackburne and widow of George Parkinson of Fairsnape in Bleasedale. By this marriage the extensive properties of the Parkinsons in the Goosnargh-Bleasdale-Chipping district had passed to the Cliftons. The baronetcy became extinct with the death of Sir Thomas in 1694, and so the younger Thomas, his nephew, was plain Mr Clifton of Lytham. It was he who went to Dunkenhalgh in 1707, with his wife Eleanor, née Walmesley.

Thomas Clifton was implicated in the 1715 Jacobite rebellion. As before, his Catholicism made him an automatic target for suspicion, and government agents posted in Lancashire to watch the Catholic gentry paid him special attention. In 1716 one such agent reported that:

> the family of Thomas Clifton Esquire of Lytham a Roman Catholic of very considerable estate seems to have been very deeply engaged in the late rebellion, George Clifton his brother is actually outlawed on account of that rebellion . . . the eldest son of the said Thomas Clifton has absconded ever since the action at Preston and is also said to be fled to France . . . and I have been assured by a clergyman of the Church of England in his neighbourhood a very zealous man for the Government that was there but proper encouragement given there might be a cloud of witnesses produced that would fix the matter plainly upon him.

In other words, sufficient bribery or persuasion might result in people coming forward to testify as to Thomas Clifton's involvement: but, as was so often the case, the Cliftons commanded great and often fervent loyalty from their tenants and workers, and were held in the highest respect. Nobody came forward – the people shared the religious views of the family, they were employed by them, and regarded them with admiration. Undoubtedly some disliked, feared or detested the Cliftons. Undoubtedly they made enemies. But the general opinion seems to have been that they deserved loyalty, and it seems that, usually, they commanded it from their tenants and neighbours.

Thomas Clifton registered his estates as a papist with the Clerk to the County in 1717, as he was required to do so by anti-Catholic legislation passed in the aftermath of the 1715. The estate was listed in immense detail in the Papist Estate Rolls, and it is interesting to note that among the many dozens of cottages and smallholdings of which he was the landlord, quite a few in Lytham parish paid part of their rent in the form of buckets of cockles and mussels, an indication of the importance of shellfishing in the economy of the township and in the lives of the cottagers, many of whom were part-time fishermen. The list of properties includes Lytham Hall, with its park of 300 acres; the mills of Lytham (which at this date were still in the park, close to the Hall); and over a hundred cottages and about 1,100 acres of rent-producing land in the township of Lytham. There were also very extensive properties elsewhere in the Fylde.

Thomas Clifton's heir was yet another Thomas, the son who fled to France during the 1715 rebellion. The younger Thomas, who was born in 1696 just after his father had inherited Lytham and the other estates, married in 1723 his distant cousin, Mary, daughter of Richard, the fifth Lord Molyneux. Their marriage reinforced, yet again, the Clifton-Molyneux ties which were, by this time, four hundred years old. In Nicholas Blundell's diary is a charming insight into this wedding. The marriage was at Woolton, the family seat of the Seftons, and on 18 November Nicholas recorded that 'Mr Standish and I rode out to the Sea-Side in Expectation of Meeting Mr Clifton and his Lady in their way home to Litham they being Married upon the 16'. They did not appear, and Nicholas rode out again on the following day, but once again the happy couple failed to come by, so 'I sent Robert Weedow to Wooton to wish them Joy and we three went to see Mr Molineux of the Grange who is dangerously ill. I began to cover my Asparagus'!

Why did Nicholas and his friends ride out to the seaside to see the newly-married couple ride home from Woolton to Lytham? The answer is that they were riding northwards along the coast - literally, for they were using the firm sands of the beach as a roadway, to avoid the foul and muddy road overland through Ormskirk. They would have ridden past Formby and Birkdale to Hesketh Bank, and then across the Ribble ford straight to Warton and Lytham, a faster, better and far more comfortable way than the road.

And three years later their first son was born. Nicholas Blundell again records the occasion, on 11 July 1727: 'I sent to Wooton to see Mrs Clifton who was lying in of her first child'. It was this child, yet another Thomas, who was to increase the status and prestige of the family still more, by marrying into the nobility and by his rebuilding of the old-fashioned Jacobean house at Lytham Hall to give the superb and beautiful mid-eighteenth century house we see today. And it was not to be long before he came into his splendid inheritance, for his father, that Thomas who had ridden home along the coast in 1723, died in December 1734, leaving his son, aged seven, and four daughters.

Foreword

T is now sixty years since I was articled to William Whinnerah, agent to the Clifton estates: straight from the prairies of western Canada - where my father had sought his fortune - I was a raw youth by any standard. For eight years I had made sporadic attendance at the village school, riding a cow pony four miles there and back to the farm. My classmates were the assorted progeny - boys and girls - of parents representative of almost every European country, together with a few half-breed Indians, Chinese and Americans, who had settled in the district. The area had only opened up about the turn of the century when the railroad came and the settlers, lured by the prospect of fortunes to be made from the growing of wheat, ploughed up the virgin soil where once the buffalo grazed in their hundreds of thousands - the hunting ground of the Blackfoot and the Cree.

How different, then, to find oneself in an environment where the toil of a thousand years had sought to wrest a living from the land. The sacred permanent pastures enclosed by quickthorn hedges made cattleproof by inherited skill in trimming and laying, instead of vast windswept areas of ploughland enclosed by barbed wire. Solidly built brick farmsteads that reflected the prosperous days of farming in the mid-1800s - ironically devastated by the import of cheap grain from North America later that century - instead of buildings and houses of 'two by fours' and 'ship lap' roofed with shingles or tar paper.

Fortunately, I had always had access to books at home, as my parents both loved literature and history, a love which I inherited and which responded and grew in this new atmosphere.

The estate office itself was the repository of letters, documents and plans relating to matters as far back as the sixteenth century, many of which were kept in a small room off one of the drawing offices. When a lull in my work permitted, I would steal into this little room and take down the dust-covered leather-bound books of accounts, lift the lids of boxes containing bundles of old letters and deeds, and lose myself in the past. William did not approve of this 'idling' and considered I could be better employed. Adjoining his office was the strong room or muniments room, the iron door of which he would open with a huge key and disappear inside with a candle in a pewter candlestick. Here were kept the more important documents and private family papers. No one else was permitted to enter and as time went on I ached to see what treasure this Aladdin's cave contained.

It was not until many years later when I, myself, became agent to the estates, that my wish was fulfilled and, upon my retirement, settled down to write this story and release the voices from the past so long held captive.

John Kennedy
Lytham, February 1989

Introduction
The Office

AN you read?'

'Yes, Sir.'

'Can you write?'

'Yes, Sir.'

'Can you add up?

'Yes, Sir.'

'You can start on Monday at nine o'clock and don't be late.'

And that was how I commenced my career at the estate offices, Lytham in March 1929.

The rather grim, grey, elderly man sitting on the opposite side of an enormous desk piled high with papers was William Whinnerah, resident agent to the Lytham estates of Henry Talbot de Vere Clifton, squire and lord of the manors of Lytham, Westby-with-Plumpton and Marton.

I had been taken to Lytham as a last resort, as upon my arrival in England from Alberta, the problem arose, 'what is to be done with him?'

I was sixteen years of age, six-feet tall, and whilst my prairie schooling had enabled me to reply in the affirmative to William's very basic questions, further enquiry would have revealed a somewhat barren field of scholastic ability. True, I could drive a team, ride a cow pony, throw a lariat and chew tobacco, but these accomplishments, excellent as they may be in their own way, are not such as to open the gates immediately to the world of commerce or the professions in England. With a view to remedying this lack of knowledge, I had been interviewed by the headmaster of a well-known north-country public school, which went somewhat in this wise:

'Ah yes, now, have you any algebra?'

'No, I guess not.'

'Any Greek?'

'No, I guess not.'

'Any Latin?'

'No, I guess not.'

'Oh dear, I'm afraid he's rather backward – any geometry?'

'Well, just a little I guess.'

'French?'

'No, I quit school back in Viking on account of that.'

So it appeared that if I were to be enlisted into this emporium of knowledge I would have to be with the very small pupils and, as the head said, 'Really, I don't think it would do.'

I wanted to go to sea but, as shipping was at rock bottom, we were dissuaded from having me apprenticed.

Forestry and mining engineering were explored next, but without success, and finally Edmund Whinnerah, brother of William and land agent to the Dalton Hall estate of Penrhyn Hornby in Westmorland, who had married my aunt Maggie Kennedy said; 'We had better go and see William.'

William Whinnerah was Victorian in manner and appearance. His favourite expression was 'God bless the Queen'. He was tall, over six feet, very spare in body, had a rather high querulous voice and, being bald on the top, he combed his hair from the back of his head forward and then turned it back from his forehead in order to give the illusion of a reasonable coverage. His teeth were black and irregular, so that when he laughed, throwing back his head as he always did, one had a view of a dark stump-lined cavern, the inner recesses of which he used to explore with a gold toothpick after meals. He wore dark grey tweed suits, hard turn-down collars over flannel shirts, black boots with thick soles, dark overcoats and Burberrys that reached down between knee and ankle and, of course, a bowler hat. He always carried a rolled umbrella or a good thick walking stick with which he would probe, man, beast or other object that aroused his interest. He was a fellow of the Surveyors Institution and Land Agents Society and, prior to taking over the management of the Lytham estates, had acted for Lord Wilton.

He was in many ways a relic of the past, practised rigid economy in business and his home, but was the most generous of hosts to guests under his roof. He would not use pads for making notes but would select suitable used envelopes from the morning post, fishing them out of the wastepaper basket by his side and carefully slitting them open with a paper knife. He always used steel pens as he did not believe in fountain pens and a ball point would have been anathema to him. The envelopes upon which his notes had been made were carefully stacked in date order against the ink well in front of him, and he would flip through them as if using a card index.

He was an ardent diarist, his office diary being fully entered each day, recording visitors and interviews; sometimes including physical descriptions of the people and always the weather, a.m. and p.m. He also carried a pocket diary in which he recorded his daily out-of-pocket expenditure. One day he asked me, 'Do you keep accounts?' As I was in receipt of five shillings per week pocket money, I replied, somewhat naturally, 'No, I don't have enough money,' and was smartly told, 'Don't be impertinent.'

William would never swear, but could deliver the most frightful verbal dressing downs I have ever heard. He hated Scotsmen and fat men and could reduce the latter into a state of steaming perspiration in a matter of minutes if he fell out with them. Oddly enough, he rather enjoyed a dirty story, and one old tenant who would come to see him about paint for the buildings, a new field gate, land draining tiles or other matters for which the landlord was liable, would come prepared with some crude and earthy tale which would have the old man in stitches, and his high crackling laugh would penetrate into the drawing office. Sure enough, the voice pipe whistle would sound, 'Give Mr Blacoe an order on Henry Alty's for nine hundred three-inch tiles.'

Each office was equipped with heavy round ebony rulers with which the older members of the staff could rule lines - such as cash columns - with great dexterity. It was such a ruler that Mr Micawber had projecting from his waistcoat when exposing the odious Uriah Heap and with which he disabled Uriah's right hand. William always had his ruler on the immediate right hand of his blotting pad and one day explained to me that it was a useful weapon of defence in case of personal attack by a dissatisfied tenant or other disgruntled party.

He had never seen a film show until, when on his annual holiday in London with Gerty, his wife, they ventured into a News cinema because it was raining, and saw 'Mickey Mouse.' This apparently reduced him to near hysterics and was subsequently referred to as 'the best thing he had seen since Punch and Judy.'

When eating a piece of fruit pie, he would devour the hard marginal crust first and work down to the last succulent morsel at the apex of the wedge, which was downed with audible satisfaction. This apparently, was the only approved method of pie eating in his younger days, and those who started at the apex and worked towards the marginal crust (which they might leave) were beaten and sent, pieless, to bed. He always had his lunch in the office, which invariably consisted of a chop, a small steak or a piece of fish, with no vegetables, accompanied by one slice of dry bread and washed down with a glass of water. This repast was served by the office caretaker and cooked by his wife.

The estate office stands in the centre of Lytham on what was originally the site of the main gates to the Hall, which were moved brick by brick and stone by stone to their present position in Ballam Road when, in 1861, the railway connecting Lytham to Blackpool severed the main drive.

When I started in 1929, the general office was on the right of the stone flagged entrance hall, wherein was the agent's secretary, a girl junior and an office boy. Vast cupboards stood against the walls in which were kept the letter books of fairly recent vintage, the older ones going back into the early-1800s being kept upstairs. A prominent feature of the room was the letter press in which the letter books were compressed after the day's correspondence had been typed and laid between the thin tissue sheets interspersed with damp cloths. Whilst the system was laborious and sometimes the letters went into the envelopes in a somewhat damp and blurry condition, the resultant copies were contained in a bound volume and could not be detached therefrom without damaging the book and making it obvious that it had been tampered with.

The cashier's office was on the left side of the hall and, there, Thomas Alfred Dean presided over his rental, cash books, lease registers and ledgers. Thomas was very old and had been with the estate for so long that he seemed to have merged into and become part of the furnishings. His office had originally been upstairs, but in view of his age, he and his books were moved downstairs to save his legs, but force of habit was so great that almost invariably he walked upstairs each morning and went into his old office, and so had to trudge downstairs again.

Under the counter was an ancient revolver, for when large sums of cash were handled on rent days, it was apparently considered that there might be a security risk.

If Thomas Alfred had ever to use the gun in defence of the squire's rents it would have been problematical as to who would be in the greater peril, the marauder, the office staff or Thomas himself as he had never - so far as I could learn - fired the thing and had the utmost trepidation of such an emergency arising. The rental was completely rewritten each year, as the names and number of tenants and lessees changed from time to time and also increased as new building leases were granted and the town grew bigger.

The two drawing offices were upstairs and had the greater part of their floor area taken up by large drawing tables. A great deal of surveying work was done as the comparatively new towns of Ansdell and St. Anne's-on-the-Sea were still developing and accurate surveys had to be made prior to the preparation of layouts and the planning of roads and sewers.

Around the walls were cupboards with shelves and drawers filled with plans, documents, books, surveying equipment and drawing requisites. The mantelpiece in each room was covered with bottles and jars containing pounce, drawing ink, paint water, alum water, chloride of lime and ox gall; there were also sticks of Indian ink and water colours for rubbing down, in shallow china dishes. The purpose of some of the foregoing items would probably puzzle a modern draughtsman, but they served very well once one knew what they were for.

William Gregson was the chief surveyor, as had been, from time to time, his father and grandfather, the latter being schoolmaster and estate surveyor in the early 1800s. William was an easy-going, plump, rather cherubic looking man who had served his time in the council offices in St. Anne's on the Sea when it was an urban district. He left the council offices to become a public works contractor and came to the estate only a few weeks before myself. He was a first-class practical surveyor and engineer, and knew better than anyone how to lay sewers and construct foundations in the running sand and alluvial silt that underly so much of the Lytham St. Annes area. William was also an accomplished yachtsman and honorary secretary of Lytham lifeboat. He was invariably good humoured and had great patience in teaching the articled pupils the mysteries of surveying. He always wore a black Homburg hat and smoked a pipe, never buttoned his jacket, which flying open displayed a generous expanse of waistcoat, the pockets of which contained pencils, rubbers, penknife and watch tethered by a leather strap.

As photocopying plans was not so general in those days as now, a great deal of tracing had to be done, and this was the principle function of John Bagot. John was then, I would say, in his mid-fifties and had been with the estate since leaving school at fourteen. He was a tallish, heavily built man, rather bald, very florid complexion, wore glasses all the time, always wore respectable suits and carried himself with considerable dignity and gave a first impression of being a person of some consequence. He had, in fact, a small private income.

In addition to tracing plans, writing out orders to local tradesman for goods and materials and answering the shrill summons of the voice pipe whistle, John used to collect the cottage rents every Monday morning. Equipped with his rent book, a small float for change, overcoat or raincoat with deep pockets and his bowler hat, he would sally forth to the east end of the town where the cottages lay.

As when John was ill or on holiday, the rents still had to be collected, the pupils had to be shown the procedure and would accompany him at least once on his rounds. This was not so simple as one might imagine:

Mrs Parkinson of number three is out cleaning, so the door will be open

> and the rent and book are behind the clock on the parlour mantelpiece – Mrs Smith at number ten also goes out on a Monday morning, but she likes to lock up, so the rent should be under this piece of slate – Don't believe Mrs Jones at number twenty, she'll say that her husband hasn't given her the rent, she's got it alright, but wants to put it on a horse.

Matters of arrears had to be sternly but justly dealt with, and, as the round continued, John's air of importance would grow as he was greeted with considerable deference by the ladies who knew early attention to the matter of repairs depended upon his goodwill and prompt reporting to the surveyors.

Upon his return to the office it was noticeable that his usual ruddy countenance was slightly intensified, and a gentle aroma of malted liquor would emanate from his person. It might also be noticed that reconciling the entries in his rent book with the neat piles of notes, silver and copper coins on the table in front of him seemed to require great mental effort, with repeated adding up and searching of pockets before he descended the stairs and handed over the proceeds to Thomas Alfred.

Adjacent to the drawing offices was the holy of holies, the agent's office, or 'Boss's room,' wherein sat William at his huge desk upon which, in addition to the used envelope daily record already mentioned, were stacks of used deed envelopes, each being inscribed by his own hand in bold lettering, with the title of the matter inside. This was his filing system, and the carbon copies of the daily correspondence were inserted, loose, with plans or other documents in the appropriate envelope. The letter books, of course, provided the master filing system for correspondence, which was infallible as no copy could be removed or tampered with. When the matter was closed, or by effluxion of time became redundant, the by now battered package would be placed in one of the large black deed boxes stacked two and three deep round the walls. Each box had its title in white lettering: 'Ribble Navigation', 'Lytham Church and Tithes', 'Trustees of Thomas Fisher', 'Railways', 'Kildalton Castle', 'Lytham St. Annes Corporation', 'Mortgages', 'Fylde Water Board', 'Lady Drummond' and so on. Upon first entry into the room one was reminded of the memorial plaques on the walls of a church or mausoleum and there was the faint, musty smell of age and dust about the place; callers would remove their hats and gaze about with apparent reverence for the past.

I do not think that the office has been altered in any way since it was built. There were open fires in every room, which were kindled each morning in winter, and when we arrived at nine o'clock would still be spluttering, crackling and emitting puffs of smoke into the room. All lighting was gas, and the suspended fittings over the drawing tables gave a pleasant greenish light, a soft hissing sound and probably more warmth than the fires.

One dark winter afternoon, William Gregson was lying half across the drawing table plotting a large survey we had just completed. His balding head was a foot or so below the twin mantles illuminating the table; the day after, feeling queer, he went to his doctor, who, after carefully examining him said;

'I know it's the middle of January, William, but you appear to be suffering from sun stroke.'

William, the agent, refused to have the gas replaced by electricity, and his own residence at Westby was lit by oil lamps. He said he did not believe in electricity as he once had a greenhouse with electric heating which failed in winter and all his plants died.

Inter-office communication was by means of voice pipes, which could also be used for listening in if someone had been called into the boss's room for a good wigging, which was always worth hearing. On one occasion, a light-hearted pupil blew down to the general office and, quickly pouring in a bottle of green ink, blew again; the office boy down below, replying, and putting his ear to the tube, got the lot!

There had always been a lot of horseplay in the office, and for years John Bagot had been the principal butt of what the pupils considered to be humorous; such as putting a dead mole in the pocket of his overcoat, filling his suitcase with lead weights from the drawing tables when he was going away for the weekend, so that the case could hardly be lifted off the floor, and other somewhat childish pranks. This legacy of horseplay survived from the days when the agency was with Thomas Fair and Son, who, apart from the Clifton estates, had a large land agency and surveying practice, and usually three or four young gentlemen as articled pupils, some of whom were being trained with a view to managing their own estates.

At the rear of the office was the stable yard with four-stall stable, coach house, hayloft and groom's quarters overhead. The yard was then cobble paved and had the usual mounting stone for equestrians. Before the coming of motor transport the stables had housed the agent's saddle horse and harness horse for his trap. Some of the pupils had their own mounts and one young man was said to have raced a passenger train from Lytham to Moss Side, jumping the hedges and ditches on the way, a distance of about three miles.

Jim Shorrock was the estate foreman in charge of the workmen who did ditch cleaning, drain laying, hedging, planting, felling, mowing, road making and all the usual outside tasks necessary to estate maintenance. Prior to William Whinnerah taking over as agent, there was the estate yard at the east end of town comprising sawmill, carpenters and joiners shop and smithy, with painters, slaters and bricklayers, in fact, all the equipment and tradesmen required for building new houses, cottages and farm buildings and repairing and maintaining the existing ones. After William took over, the yard was closed and all building work was done by contractors.

Jim Shorrock was a large, heavy man with droopy whiskers, trousers usually tied under the knees with twine, waistcoats, jackets and overcoats in season and a pork pie hat. To go his rounds of the estate to see that all was well and that his men were carrying out their tasks, he rode an ancient bicycle that was so solidly built of iron that it must have weighed close on a hundred-weight. To mount, he used a back step, and it was an impressive sight to see him take off. He sometimes wore an old raincoat fastened up at the back with safety pins so that the flaps would not get entangled in the rear wheel, and to mount he placed his left foot on the back step, leaned forward grasping the handlebars and pushed off with his right foot. Having gained initial momentum he reared up on his left leg and plumped down on the saddle, a few erratic wobbles and he was underway at an incredibly slow speed, which he seldom exceeded, and which gained him the name of 'The Ballam Express'.

Each morning Jim arrived at the office and reported to William, the agent, who, because Jim was rather portly, took a delight in conducting an inquisition by interrogating him as to the progress of the various jobs in hand, invariably chiding him for being dilatory, was critical of the manner in which the work was being done, and generally chivvying him up and attributing all delay to Jim's stoutness.

After a session lasting about fifteen minutes, poor Jim would come out of the room in a high state of perspiration and proceed down the stairs, which, having steel nosings on the treads, and Jim's boots being clogged (or shod with steel), would sometimes result in him losing his feet and shooting down five or six steps at a time with a clatter like a shire horse slipping on wet cobble stones. The old man's door would fly open and he would shout over the bannister,

'What are you doing now, you fool, making all that noise?'

Tom Mathews was the gamekeeper who also had to report to the office on matters of rearing, apprehending of poachers and prospects of the shooting season. Like all good keepers Tom was a somewhat secretive, taciturn person, who was always filled with foreboding as to the expectation of life of his feathered charges before the shooting season commenced, due to the depredations of weather, disease, poachers and predators. He usually carried a sack from which, sometimes, came mysterious rustlings and muffled squeaks, and out of which he one day produced an adder.

A small source of revenue for Tom's beer money was the sale of golf balls picked up in the woods which surround the Fairhaven Golf Course. Sometimes, if there was a scarcity of lost balls, he would lie concealed in the undergrowth with one of his springers, and if a ball arrived in the near vicinity, driven by a golfer at long range, the dog could quietly slip out of cover, pick up the ball and bring it back to Tom, who would add it to the contents of the mysterious sack.

The office staff also included Alice Kenworthy, who had the distinction of being the first female to be employed in what had previously been a wholly male establishment, and who assisted Thomas Alfred in the cashier's office. When William first took over, Alice was foolhardy enough to take him a cup of tea at eleven o'clock,

'God bless the Queen, what's that for?'

'It's for you, sir,' said Alice tremulously.

'Take it away, there's no time for tea drinking in this office!'

Louis Lomax, like John Bagot, had been with the estate since leaving school, and acted as personal secretary to the squire when in residence at the Hall. An assistant surveyor and usually two articled pupils, of whom I was one, made up the complement.

Lytham lies within the borough of Lytham St. Annes on the north side of the Ribble estuary, and is some seven miles from Blackpool to the north west. The town, like Blackpool, grew from a tiny fishing village into a holiday and residential resort with the advent of sea bathing at the end of the eighteenth century. With the coming of the railway in 1846, the residential development was increased by the erection of good-class houses for the newly wealthy cotton manufacturers of industrial Lancashire, and in 1876 the sister town of St. Anne's on the Sea was born amid the sand dunes and rabbit warrens that stretched along the coast between Lytham and Blackpool.

Big sister Blackpool raced ahead to become the largest seaside holiday town in Britain as she had no scruples about lifting up her skirts and dancing a merry jig to the jingling music of hard-earned 'brass' pouring into the coffers of the Golden Mile, providing as she does, the fabulous, the thrilling, the classical, the vulgar and the naughty; all wholly delightful to the fun hungry proletariat from the grim cotton towns, who, during their Wakes Weeks, rushed into her welcoming arms in ever increasing numbers. Lytham and St. Annes, however, were brought up under the watchful and protective eye of the estate to be, seemingly, strictly respectable, as becoming to Victorian young ladies. The towns were carefully laid out with wide carriage roads, and plans of all buildings had to be submitted to the Squire's agents for approval. The building leases contained covenants whereby:

> nothing was to be done on the premises that might be considered to be as partaking of a nuisance or annoyance to the locality;

furthermore, the lessees were to

> perform suit of court at all courts to be holden for the Manor of Lytham.

As there were a vast number of such leases, this last covenant was patently ridiculous!

Each town had its pier on which respectable entertainments were performed, and Lytham Green and promenade provided ample space for young and old (and dogs) to disport themselves; but no sideshows, organised games, public meetings or religious services were allowed thereon. Ultimately, in 1922, the two towns were united and became the Borough of Lytham St. Annes. It was unique in that it contained five golf courses and twenty churches and chapels with a population of 23,000.

An old Blackpool resident was heard to say,

'We Blackpoolers always like to come to Lytham because it's such a well laid out town, which is not surprising as it's been such a long time dead.'

Whilst the young of the borough were brought up in an environment that should have put them beyond all temptation, there on the horizon, only seven miles away, the beckoning finger of Blackpool tower promised delights forbidden by the teachings of home, chapel and church. Parents might frown and lecture, but a taste of the gay life on a Saturday night probably did lad and lass little harm, and perhaps made them better able to cope with some of the realities of life when they grew older.

After I joined the estate office staff no time was lost in getting me to work. The production of plans for building agreements and leases, farm tenancy agreements and for the construction of new roads, sewers and buildings went on continuously and, coupled with the outdoor surveying work, kept us all busy.

Under the careful instruction of William Gregson I soon learned how to run a chain line, take offsets, set up and use level and theodolite and how to book the data thus obtained. I found it all utterly fascinating and those who have not experienced it can hardly appreciate the real pleasure of plotting a survey, as one begins to see the shape of buildings, fields, roads and other objects picked up during the survey, appear on paper. Similarly, such a one might be surprised at the frustration and mortification if it does not fit together as it ought. The frantic checking of measurements and anxious conferences with one's assistants,

'Are you sure you were on the right peg?'; 'Do you think those kids moved one of the rods?'

I have always agreed with Usill, who, in his well-known work on surveying, says that the young surveyor should be properly clad and in his right mind.

When I had gained some proficiency in the work, William Whinnerah one day summoned me into his office and explained that as the main road from Lytham to Preston was to be widened by the County Council, an old pair of thatched roof cottages attached to one of the farms would have to be pulled down. In these circumstances the County was obliged either to build a new pair or make a lump-sum payment in lieu. William had plumped for the latter and agreed a fairly handsome settlement of which he proposed to spend about half on two new cottages. I was to draw the plans. Feeling as Vanbrugh must have done upon receiving instructions for the plans of Blenheim, I spent some days in a state of concentrated inspiration and finally produced a drawing showing a pair of dwellings, each of which had a bathroom on the ground floor, which I considered a stroke of genius. The children would hurry home from school and the happy mother would lovingly bath them whilst keeping an eye on the evening meal cooking in the adjoining kitchen in anticipation of her good man returning from the plough. He, removing his boots in the porch – by now covered with rambling roses – would lave himself in the bathroom and then sit down to his meal, having first kissed and dandled the infants on his knee. An imaginary scene of domestic bliss that almost brought tears to my own eyes.

Upon presenting my creation to William, however, he took one look and said:

'God bless the Queen, what's that?'

Feeling slightly hot, I replied: 'It's a bathroom, sir.'

'A bathroom in a farm labourer's cottage? They use the dolly tub, man!'

I replied: 'This is 1931, sir, and people bath their children regularly.'

'There's far too much bathing these days,' came the reply, 'do you know the Squire sometimes has three baths a day? I don't think I have three baths a year!'

And so they were built without bathrooms.

The first rent audit I attended was held at Bartle, to collect the rents in respect of a neighbouring estate which William also managed. I entrained at Lytham and was joined by William at Wrea Green. Proceeding a few miles we descended at Lea station and walked through the quiet country lanes, calling at farms and cottages, noting necessary repairs and complaints of various kinds. This being a very minor audit not involving a Rent Day dinner, we lunched by ourselves at the 'Sitting Goose'. It was a wet, showery day in May and the landlord ushered us into the best room where a bright fire was burning and a clean white cloth was spread. Photographs of previous generations glowered at us from the walls, but the general atmosphere was one of cosiness as a heavy shower lashed on the windows outside. The landlord himself, wearing a white apron, waited upon us, bringing first some fish and then a dish of fresh asparagus which, never having seen before, I was about to attack with a knife and fork, when to my amazement William picked his up in his fingers saying,

'God knows why, but this is the only acceptable way of eating asparagus in polite company.'

Then came a whole roast chicken, which he dissected with surgical skill, and I had my first lesson in carving 'which you must learn to do if you're going to be a Land Agent.' Upon the arrival of a crisp and golden apple pie I was instructed 'Take some of that Lancashire cheese with it; apple pie without cheese is like a kiss without a squeeze.

The Lytham rent audit was a much bigger affair. Held in May and November, it went on for five days, the farm tenants coming in from the Lytham district, Westby with Plumptons, Warton and Marton. Wooden benches were set out in the estate office hall for the tenants waiting their turn to enter the rent room. There was much shuffling of feet, subdued conversation and occasional muffled bursts of laughter. The rig of the day was suits of heavy tweed or blue serge of such enduring quality as to last a lifetime; white collars, some turned down, some with wings but all bone hard and secured in front with a gold or brass stud which some considered the only adornment necessary; though silk ties and even stocks might be worn. Most wore massive black boots so burnished up with black lead and spit as would have won approbation from a sergeant-major in the Brigade of Guards. There was a general creakiness and faint smell of moth balls about the gathering, which was known locally as 'Lytham Races'; a satirical inference as to the unlikelihood of people racing to the office to pay their rents.

Upon entering the rent room, which was normally the general office, the tenant would find himself facing a long table, at the centre of which sat William, his usually rather grim visage lightened by the kind of smile one usually associates with a dental surgeon inviting a client to take the chair.

In front of him were two large slop bowls, one containing small change and the other full of florins, on his left sat Thomas Alfred with his rental, on his right Louis Lomax with the Repair Book, Alice Kenworthy had charge of the cash, and as the money piled up a pupil counted the notes into bundles of one hundred pounds.

'Good morning, Mr Morris, I hope the family and yourself are in good health. Not been the best of harvest weather, I fear. Now, Mr Dean, what does Mr Morris owe us this time?'

Usually the bigger farmers paid by cheque and very often would hand him a blank cheque ready signed. William would explain how the amount demanded was arrived at, which might be increased by the cost of items properly chargeable to the tenant or reduced by sums he had himself expended with the consent of the agent for the benefit of his holding. Whatever the amount was, the tenant would almost invariably say:

'If tha' says it's reet, it's reet as far as I'm concerned, thee fill it in.'

This was the kind of relationship that existed in those days - complete faith and understanding between the tenants and the estate - and when a bargain could be sealed by a handshake. Having received cash or cheque, William would say:

'Do you want a receipt or will you take for a drink?'

If the tenant decided for the latter, a florin was taken from the slop bowl and shoved across the table. Very few receipts were issued.

I only once scored a point over William. We were developing an estate just outside Lancaster which entailed the construction of a number of roads and sewers, and one Friday afternoon the boss told me:

'You are to go to Lancaster tomorrow morning and set out that new road and sewer and give the contractor the levels.

This was the period when I first took up sailing, having proved utterly incapable of playing golf or tennis. Billy Gregson, the chief surveyor, as already recounted, was a keen sailing man and we had arranged to go trawling off Blackpool catching the ebb tide from Lytham about one o'clock p.m. on Saturday, after the office closed at twelve noon. I was furious as it meant catching a train, changing at Preston and taking a bus from Lancaster on to the job, while carrying ranging rods, level and staff and a bundle of pegs. Rushing off to Billy Gregson, I poured out my woe and said:

'Well the fishing trip's off!'

Billy thought for a moment and said:

'I'll pick you up at home with my car at six in the morning; we can easily do the job and be back in good time.'

We got to the site at seven o'clock, finished the pegging out and levelling by eight o'clock and were back in the office by nine o'clock. At a quarter past nine, sitting behind my drawing board, I heard the measured footfalls of William coming up stairs as usual, pausing to crash down the lid of a half-opened deed box which had been left on the landing. He came straight into the drawing office and saw me sitting on my stool with a self-satisfied smirk on my face.

'I told you to go to Lancaster this morning!'

Ah, what a delightful moment;

'I've been, sir, the job has been done, and the contractor given the levels.'

For a moment he looked at me, then walked into Billy Gregson's office and said:

'Has Kennedy been to Lancaster this morning?'

On receiving Billy's confirmation he said:

'Well, that's the first time I've been put in my place in my own office.'

With my somewhat limited prairie school education it was essential that I should attain a higher plane of scholastic ability in order to get anywhere in the profession of estate management. Like my parents, I have always loved literature and history whilst abhorring mathematics and kindred subjects. Now, however, I had to buckle down and swot in order to pass the preliminary examination of the Surveyors Institution, which I passed after two attempts. From then on it was night after night of home study as I was never allowed a single day off for swotting, something that embittered me against William, although I shall never regret the extraordinary experience of working with a man who was so completely Victorian in manner and outlook. A few crumbs of advice fell from his lips:

'Never be obliged to anyone, let them be obliged to you. Never lend money, give it if you must.'

He also had some rather unusual sayings; if there was a slight discrepancy in a plan or measurement and one said 'It's not much, sir', he would say 'Not much! It would be a lot on the end of your nose.' Or, of some problem that might arise, 'Difficult? It'll be easy if you hold your mouth right.'

So began my association with the Cliftons of Lytham and for the next fifty years - with the exception of five minesweeping years in the Navy - the estate became my life. In the following pages I have endeavoured to tell something of the story of the estate, the family and their land agents.

Chapter One

Thomas the Tree Planter

HEN Thomas of Fairsnape died in 1743, his son Thomas – who had hurriedly departed to France after the 1715 rebellion – inherited the estates, which his father had registered, as had many Papists in accordance with an Act of Parliament passed in the reign of George I. He seems to have taken seriously the matter of ensuring the continuance of the family name, as he married three times: first, Catherine, daughter of R. Eyre Esquire of Hassop, Derby, but she died without issue; second, Anne, daughter of Sir Barnaby Haggerston Bart of Reedsmouth Hall, Northumberland, who produced two daughters; and third, Lady Jane Bertie, daughter of the Earl of Abingdon, by whom he had three daughters and one son, John.

It was this Thomas Clifton who built the present Lytham Hall. The old manor house, which had been rebuilt by Sir Cuthbert, was gradually demolished as the new Georgian house rose in front, but portions of the old establishment were retained in the Long Gallery, kitchens, butler's quarters and other domestic offices which enclose the courtyard at the rear. The work was commenced in 1751 but was not completed until 1764. Carr of York was the architect and this was the second mansion designed by him. Commenting on his domestic architecture he is alleged to have said, modestly, that he 'endeavoured to arrange the necessary conveniences with some degree of art'.[1]

John was born in 1764, the year the new house was completed, and Lady Jane was perhaps well pleased to have presented her husband with a son and heir to inherit the estates and beautiful new mansion. She may also have felt gratified at getting her youngest daughter married off to John Talbot, brother to the 15th Earl of Shrewsbury, and whose son, another John, became the 16th Earl.

John seems to have led a quiet life in comparison with his ancestors, devoting his time to the improvement of his estate and his string of racehorses – he won the St. Leger twice. Like his sisters he was baptised in St. Cuthbert's Parish Church, Lytham, and also in the Roman Catholic Church. He was nineteen when his father died in 1783, and when twenty-one married Elizabeth, daughter of Thomas Widdrington Riddell of Swinbourne Castle, Northumberland. She, also, was a devout Catholic, and bore him five sons and five daughters. Whilst he appears to have kept in close touch with matters in Lytham, he bought Pitzhanger Manor, Ealing from Sir John Sloane, the famous architect, in 1815 and lived there until his death in March 1832.[2]

Of John Clifton's five sons, Thomas Joseph was the eldest; born in 1788, he was commissioned in the 14th Regiment of Dragoons and saw service in the Peninsular War, as did his brother Edward, who was a captain in the Coldstream Guards. Details are lacking of the parts played by the brothers during the engagements in which their regiments were involved, but amongst the letters found in the estate office is one from General Minas to Thomas couched in the most affectionate terms. The date is 4th February 1824 and the address 72 Great Portland Street. The letter is written in Spanish and relates to purely family matters which makes it tantalising, as Elizabeth Longford in *Wellington, the Years of the Sword,* writes of the heroic bands of guerillas formed during the war, two of the leaders being Minas, elder and younger:

> The elder Minas in Navarre was held to be a model of humanity because he did not kill his prisoners unless they were badly wounded.

What could have been the connection between the guerilla leader and the young British officer?

It was in Paris that Thomas met and married Hetty Campbell, the young widow of David Campbell of Kildalloig, Argyll. The ceremony took place at the British Embassy and was performed by Henry Pepys, the chaplain. As, however, upon the drawing up of the draft of the marriage settlement, doubts were expressed by the lawyers as to the legality of the Paris wedding, counsel's opinion was taken and a re-marriage in England advised. A special licence was sought from the Archbishop of Canterbury, but was refused: so a common licence was obtained and on 5th May 1817 they were again married in the parish of Ealing, where they doubtless stayed with papa at Pitzhanger Manor.

Hetty was a Christian Jewess, the daughter of Pellegrine Treves (Mr 'Benares' Treves) sometime Gentleman of the Bedchamber to the Prince of Wales - later George IV - and Hetty Stoke Sloper. He is described by William Hickey as 'one of the most dashing bucks of the Metropolis, and the constant companion of the Prince of Wales.' In 1780 he had gone to India as a clerk and subsequently held a number of appointments there including Third Judge of the Court of Appeal and Circuit at Benares, and finally Postmaster General of Bengal. His father was also named Pellegrine and had married the Baroness Bathsheba de Paiba as his second wife.[3]

As Thomas was the eldest son and heir apparent to the estates, adequate provision had to be made upon marriage for the purchase of a residence in which to set up his own 'necessary establishment.' To implement this, he received the sum of £30,000, with which he purchased Hatch Court, Ilminster, in Somerset. He was also provided with an allowance of £3,000 *per annum* out of estate funds.

According to the accounts kept by Mr Benbow, the estate's steward or resident agent, the gross annual income from the estate was over £40,000, with disbursements of £27,000. John Clifton as tenant for life and squire of Lytham had an allowance of £10,000 and Elizabeth, his wife, had £300 per annum pin money. The younger children had their Portions of £250 a year each, and the eldest daughter, Elizabeth, was endowed with £10,000 when she married Charles Conoly of Mitchford Park in Somerset. It was at Hatch Court that Thomas was taken so seriously ill in September 1825 that Hetty had to write his letters, and on 30th October, in replying to her mother-in-law, said:

> My dear Madam,
>
> Supposing I should have the misery of seeing my beloved Husband in the situation you mention, I assure you on my honour I will consult *his* wishes *only* and if he desires to have a Priest he shall be instantly sent for, but supposing I may be reduced to such a state as to be incapable of acting, Mr Iddon will write his assurances to you at the bottom of this letter and after all the kindness, anxiety and attention, he had shown you may have the firmest reliance on him.
>
> Yrs. Affectly,
> H.C.
>
> Mr Iddon presents his compliments to Mrs Clifton and has great pleasure in assuring her he does not consider Mr T. Clifton in any danger, should any alarming symptoms arise Mr Iddon will with the greatest readiness meet the wishes of Mr T. Clifton and his family by furthering so much as lays in his power the promise Mrs T. Clifton has made.

Mr Iddon proved to be right in his assessment and Thomas recovered.

Hetty's letter and her mother-in-law's concern that a priest should be sent for in the event of Thomas's demise is made clear by the remarks of the Rev. G. L. Haydock as recorded in Joseph Gillow's *Haydock Papers*:[4]

> John Clifton died May 23rd, 1832 near London, perhaps still a Catholic, and was brought to be buried at Lytham. His son was zealous for ye

> Protestant Church. He had never been so for ye Catholic Church, though educated at St. Cuthbert's College; and marrying a Protestant clergyman's daughter said to have been a Jewess and both gamblers – probably neglecting a good conscience – easily made shipwreck of ye faith . . . The father of Thomas had formerly suppressed Salwick Chapel. He lived at variance with his wife Riddell and all this tended to his ruin.

Haydock had for a time been the priest at Westby Catholic Church, which was maintained by the Cliftons, and the bitterness of his writing indicates that he probably left under a cloud. He was, of course, wrong about Hetty's father, but Thomas became a Protestant in 1831, the year before his father died, and this caused a great stir in Lancashire Roman Catholic circles.

Like other great landowners of the eighteenth century, the Cliftons had settled down to improve their vast Fylde estates, draining, planting and improving the methods of cultivation, resulting in greatly increased rent rolls. Before the century came to a close it was manifest that with the increasing popularity of sea bathing, and Lytham then having an unsurpassed beach of golden sand, that the development of the village as a seaside resort had possibilities hitherto undreamed of. At neighbouring Blackpool, during the reign of George I, 1747 to 1727 – then a tiny hamlet – a few visitors were attracted each summer, and by 1735, an enterprising person, blessed with a wife who was a good cook, offered accommodation in a specially prepared cottage. By the beginning of the nineteenth century, Blackpool consisted of about forty houses and a few small hotels, but development was hindered by the ownership of the soil vesting in a number of different people, some of whom owned the hotels and repulsed the advances of others with capital which they were eager to invest in building property for the reception of visitors.[5]

No such problem existed in Lytham, where every inch of the land belonged to the Cliftons who were anxious to promote development by every means and to ensure that the income arising from ground rents was secured by good class property. This meant that the building of the future town lay within the control of one authority – the estate – upon the good management of which depended the successful outcome of the intention to create a pleasant and attractive place in which to reside or spend a seaside holiday.

In turn, the successful management of the estate devolved and depended upon the steward or resident land agent, whose task it was to deal with every problem arising out of the ownership of farms and town properties; the sea embankments and watercourses – vital in this low-lying area – the new plantations, the building of new houses and steadings and the repair of old, the preservation of game, the collection of rents and keeping of accounts. He was also responsible for the hall and home farm staff, and was go-between for the squire and his tenants, dealing with complaints, disputes and family feuds referred to him for settlement.

As the surveying work was done by the village schoolmaster and as enquiries for building plots increased, it is not surprising that J. Benbow, steward to Thomas Joseph Clifton, found himself hard pressed and in 1836 he was replaced. James Fair, who was appointed in Benbow's place, began his career at Knowsley, seat of the Earl of Derby. He left Knowsley to manage the earl's estates in the Fylde, which he did until taking up his new appointment at Lytham. The Fairs were of Scottish origin and James's father came from Fife to take up his appointment as land agent to Sir Henry Bold-Houghton.

Though he was absent from Lytham for long periods, Thomas, like his father, took great interest in his estate and his keenness for planting earned him the sobriquet of 'Thomas the Tree Planter,' and the earliest leases of building land contained covenants requiring the planting of a specified number of trees annually. His interest in the estate and his absences from Lytham resulted in a correspondence between him and his new land agent of almost daily occurrence as he wished to know the 'minutest detail' of what went on.

That Thomas reposed great trust in the knowledge and ability of Fair from the very beginning, is shown by the following letter:

St. Leonards near Hastings
May 2nd 1836

Sir,

Presuming that by this time you will have taken possession of your office as agent to my property at Lytham, I write to express to you the hope that the inititation may prove as satisfactory to you as from your high character I cannot doubt it will be conducive to my interest, and that you will not suffer the laborious duties, which want of method hitherto must first entail on you, to discourage your exertions, as both Messrs. France and Rawstrone as well as myself are prepared to place the greatest confidence as well as control in your hands.

I have to assure you that I shall at all times be happy to hear from you on the progress of affairs at Lytham, altho' at present I must request you to look to my friends Messrs. Rawstrone and France for any instructions you may require on matters there, and I am confident you will find in them every disposition to support your authority and to render your situation as comfortable both to yourself and family as possible. I do not propose leaving here until the second week in June, but after that by addressing me thro' my bankers, Messrs. Wright and Co., any letters will reach me.

I remain Sir
Your obedient servant
Thomas Clifton

Rawstrone and France were trustees of the estate, the former being a Preston solicitor, and upon the resignation of France shortly after Fair's appointment, he, Fair, wrote to the squire asking for his confirmation that Rawtrone's firm should not play any part in the management of the estate:

> Altho' Mr Rawstrone gave me a second time an assurance that the Office do not wish to interfere in the management of your Estate still I have a desire to ascertain from yourself upon what footing the Office and I stand, and I trust there is no impropriety in making the application as upon your answer will depend my continuance in the situation I have at present the honor of holding. I wish in making this application not to be misunderstood, my objection does not originate from any dislike I have to Mr Wilson for I entertain for that Gentleman a very high regard, but I object upon *principle* to holding a situation under *any* Solicitor's Office.

There spoke the real old professional land agent expressing a sentiment heard more than once.

In the meantime, Thomas, with his establishment had moved to Faubourg St. Honoré, Paris, from whence he wrote in a conciliatory manner to smooth Fair's ruffled feathers, pointing out that Rawstrone in his capacity as a trustee, held a Power of Attorney given him by Thomas which, however, he was asking him to relinquish. He confirmed that the solicitor's office would only act for him in legal matters and concluded by saying:

> I did not for a moment suppose your objections to serve under the directions of either Mr Wilson or Mr Rawstrone and Wilson jointly arose from personal objections to them, neither of these gentlemen possess much knowledge of rural affairs and I cannot but think Mr R. will be glad to retire from a situation he only consented to accept at my urgent request and on condition that Mr France would act with him.'

After this, the now mollified James, 'as sole manager of my property', applied himself with renewed energy to the improvements he projected for the swelling of the Clifton rent roll.

Apart from the agricultural improvements and town development, James had in mind a market hall, an agricultural society with members drawn from the tenant farmers, and also a fishing vessel to be owned by local shareholders. Thomas, whilst apparently slightly apprehensive about his own possible financial commitment and involvement in the schemes of his enthusiastic agent, promised to subscribe to the agricultural society by donating an amount equal to one half of that subscribed by the farmers. He also agreed to subscribe to the fishing vessel, but sounded a note of caution in one of his letters:

> Her success will entirely depend on the person appointed to command her, on a former occasion, I think I should tell you, in my father's time,

when they had a fishing vessel, the crew carried her into the Isle of Man, sold her there, and declared she had been wrecked, so that I think the subscribers should take care the commander is himself a considerable share holder.'

So commenced an association between the Clifton family and their agents - three generations of Fairs - that was to last for almost a century. On occasion, the agent might be frustrated and furious at the prodigality of his principal, who, in return, would rage at the parsimony of his agent, but, all in all, there was a deep understanding and mutual regard which also existed between other members of the two families.

Thomas Joseph, whilst expressing the greatest affection and interest in his estate, seldom lived in Lytham. Like his father, John, and like the successors to the estate in years to come, the squires of Lytham were, to a great extent, absentee landlords.

As the estate was the well from which the agent had to draw the funds wherewith to finance the squire and pay the younger members of the family their portions - after discharging essential outgoings - they all kept in touch with the estate office, no matter in what part of the world they might find themselves.

Almost inevitably they all overspent their allowances long before the next instalment was due, and the agent was the recipient of anxious letters with requests for advances which usually contained detailed explanations as to the writer's temporary financial embarr-assment. Such letters - penned to melt the agent's stony heart! - often contained confidences that the writer would not have dreamed of divulging to another member of the family, particularly the reigning squire! This resulted in the agent becoming their confidant, and often advisor, on personal problems and crises - not excluding affairs of the heart. The corollary of this was that the agent and 'The Office' became the hub or centre around which the personal family world of the Cliftons revolved; albeit, from time to time, somewhat shakily.

During September 1837, Thomas Clifton and his wife Hetty returned to England, leaving their establishment in Paris and journeyed to Portsmouth where one of their younger sons, Arthur Edward, was waiting for them. Arthur had been accepted for the Navy and was to sail with Admiral Elliot in *H.M.S. Melville.* Three weeks later the family were still staying at the George Hotel, as various circumstances had delayed the ship leaving harbour. Thomas was becoming impatient as it was getting near Christmas and he wished to get to London as soon as possible.

'I am confidently informed,' he wrote to Fair, 'that she will put to sea the end of the week so that I hope to be in London on Monday or Tuesday next. Unfortunately this brings us just to the holidays to that I fear I shall be disappointed in seeing many it was my especial business in town to meet, for having disposed of one son in the Navy I am now anxious to get another into the Army.'

This was Thomas Henry, the second son, who was to become equerry to H.R.H. the Duke of Cambridge, Deputy Ranger of Richmond Park and who died in 1900, having attained the rank of Major General.

Thomas wrote again to Fair on 29th December saying that the Admiral and his family had that day attempted to board *Melville*, now lying off Spithead, but had been forced back by bad weather.

> Arthur is delighted at the prospect of going to sea, but until necessary he shall not go on board, Mrs Clifton will not part with him as she is not likely to see him for some years.

The ship finally sailed about the 5th January and Thomas was at last able to proceed to London where he arrived and put up at Fenton's Hotel, St. James' Street, on 10th January 1838. The main object of visiting London was to have an interview with Lord Fitzroy Somerset about getting Thomas Henry a commission in the army. Unfortunately, his Lordship was out of town with the Duke of Wellington:[6]

> I am thoroughly sick of London, and above all of this hotel, but I do not think it right to allow this opportunity to escape of doing all I can to forward the views of my son Henry as a soldier, who is to be, though I have ceased to be very sanguine that I shall be able to do much.'[7]

While still at Portsmouth, Thomas wrote to Fair saying that he had heard from his eldest son's tutor that John Talbot had to be at Oxford to reside during the next term and that it was necessary to purchase the furniture of his rooms at a cost of some fifty to sixty pounds and provide him with plate, linen, glass, crockery etc., and a horse; to this had to be added his quarters allowance of £150 and the cost of the tutor having resided at Leamington for one month, presumably coaching Talbot. This, Thomas estimated, would cost him not less than £400, which in his present financial position he was unable to pay from the private income he had as tenant for life of the estate. He therefore prayed that Fair would advance this sum from the estate funds he held.

This, of course, reflects the position of a tenant for life of an entailed estate in those days with a large family, who could be held responsible for 'waste' by deliberate acts which might diminish the value of the estate or by 'permissive waste' caused by neglect having the same effect. The eldest son usually succeeded as tenant for life and had the enjoyment of the lion's share of the income, but had the responsibilities of an English landowner to his estate, the community and the county. The younger children were provided for by their 'portions', fixed annual sums payable out of the estate upon their coming of age, and secured on its lands; so, also, was the widow of the late tenant for life provided for by her 'jointure', and the wife of the tenant for life would have her allowance known as 'pin money'. As the estate had also to provide for the survivors of previous generations who were so entitled, these outgoings could be a heavy charge on the property and it behoved the tenant for life to get his sons into business, the services, or to marry well, as soon as possible. This, of course, also applied to the daughters, and resulted in the many arranged marriages of those days.

Thomas had high hopes of obtaining a commission for Thomas Henry in the 15th Hussars in which there was a vacancy, but his hopes were dashed in March and he decided to return to Paris from where he wrote in April on matters concerning the estate, of which he loved to hear 'the minutest detail' from Fair. The latter won his further approbation by having taken some of the tenants to Liverpool to attend an agricultural meeting (or show) as they had previously considered it too far from home to attend. Negotiations were proceeding with the Wyre Railroad Company for land in Clifton with Salwick, for which he gave Fair entire authority to make any bargain he thought right, 'confiding you will protect my interests so far as you can, and the tenants, under your agreement, will be subject to as little annoyance as possible, I detest the whole thing as you know and therefore wish no favour to be shown [the railway undertakers].' His antipathy to the railroad was aroused as he so disliked the severance of his beloved lands by the construction of the line through them.

In Paris, Thomas was again feeling the pinch as he found the cost of living high and he had suffered some misfortunes; Wykeham, the youngest son, had been critically ill; one of his horses had died and another became so lame that he had to part with him for almost nothing, 'and have supplied their places by young fresh horses from England for which I have been obliged to pay somewhat extravagantly, under those circumstances, calculating the necessary expenses of my household and sons, for the next three months, I fear I cannot continue, to use a homely expression, to make both ends meet, without an addition of three hundred pounds, which I must request you to send to Wright and Co. for me in the course of a month of a few weeks.'

During August, Thomas was preparing to leave Paris for Lytham, which entailed the transfer of his establishment, 'my horses will leave about the 20th inst. and I hope will arrive the second week in Sept. at Lytham, that they may be fit for use when we get there. The day we have fixed for leaving Paris is the 5th or 6th of next month, which will leave time for the servants to pass us on the road and have things prepared for our reception before the 20th.'

Thomas had already been back to London staying at Fenton's Hotel, whilst he conducted some business which had resulted in a series of unspecified disappointments, and on his return to Paris had found his wife very ill and 'obliged to submit to a surgical operation both painful and dangerous'. She was, however, recovering well and hoping to derive benefit from the journey home.

They spent the winter of 1838/9 at Lytham, and he doubtless enjoyed himself viewing the improvements carried out, particularly the new plantations, and giving instructions for more tree planting as the weather and season permitted. Land was still being bought to extend the estate in nearby Warton and Blackpool, and enquiries for plots for new houses were constantly being received.

> During April 1839 Thomas and Hetty have again arrived at Fenton's Hotel and he is making all arrangements for equipping Thomas Henry who has been appointed to the 12th Lancers. Talbot's brown horse at Lytham will make him a very good second charger and the coachman is to take him to Preston to be sent to London by train, with a saddle and the best bridle he can find. A friend of Thomas's who is going out to India has offered him a horse accustomed to troops for £60 which he thinks he will accept and hopes to buy the horse appointments from Henry's predecessor at a reduced price: 'so that mounting the lancer will not be very extravagant.'

Thomas was in for a shock, however:

> I am almost ashamed to write what I am about to do, but have no remedy for it. Henry's outfit has so much exceeded my calculations that I find from a visit to my banker today that I have almost exhausted what has been paid into their hands. His commission £850, fees and regimental dues to the agent £26, one horse as first charger £110. His clothes and personal appointments £126 18s 6d – without his horse appointments and common saddlery, horse cloths, rugs, collars etc. His barrack furniture; that is bed, bedding, bed linen, towels etc. £43 10s 0d and other sundries. You will therefore see that the sum you sent up has been entirely expended, indeed far exceed, if therefore you can remit in addition £200 . . .'

Whilst still in London he received 'most unexpectedly and most undesired the intelligence of the arrival of his son, Arthur, in England who had thought fit to leave the Navy!' The young gentleman was at Chatham on board the *Pelican* sloop-of-war, waiting to be paid off. 'The moment I heard of it I lost no time in enquiring for a school to which I could send him immediately and I believe I have succeeded. Mrs Clifton is exerting herself amongst her friends who have influence at the India House to get him an appointment to India when old enough to hold one, and should she succeed I shall keep him at work either at school or the Indian college until he can go out.'

Hetty was successful in getting 'the late sailor' – as his father called him – an entry to the Indian college at Haileybury when he was sixteen, and in the meantime he was sent straight to school with such haste that Thomas regretted he could not get him there 'until tomorrow or Saturday as he has only returned a few hours from Chatham.'

Poor Arthur, he was only thirteen when he joined the navy, and his father referred to him as 'my poor little boy', but no such tender feelings were expressed now. Henry, on the other hand, wrote saying that his horses had arrived and he was quite delighted at all he had seen of his regiment and was doubtless enjoying himself in Brighton, where he was stationed, with other young bloods.

Now that both sons were disposed of, Thomas and Hetty proceeded to Lytham by train, breaking the journey at Birmingham as she was 'quite worn out'. At Preston they would be met by their own coach, as the line to Lytham had not yet been built.

In March 1840, the following year, John Talbot, the eldest son, and heir to the estate, came of age. The attendant jollifications would entail further expense, but this would probably be regarded as a legitimate charge to be paid by the Estate and not out of Thomas's allowance. The United Independent Harmonic Brass Band of Preston wrote asking for:

> a job of playing at your Dinnering Day . . . if you are having a Band of Music at Dinner we shall be very glad to be ingaged for you on that day, it is one of the first bands in the County . . . the Charge or Pay for us for one day is 8s 6d, each man for the number of ten comes to £4 5s 0d, and Meat and Drink as soon as we get there and all the time we stay there. We can come either in uniform or not according to weather.[8]

Just one year after his coming-of-age celebrations, in March 1841, Talbot – now commissioned in the 2nd Life Guards – became involved in a matter of a very different kind. Lord Ranelagh had challenged Le Comte Paul Esterhazy to a duel and Talbot was acting as his friend. This happened in Venice, and Talbot writes from the yacht *Hamite,* in which he appears to have been cruising as a guest.

The following is his pencil draft of a letter he sent to the Count.

> Having called on you today with Lord Ranelagh to ask you to explain the reasons for your cutting him after having sought his acquaintance just a few days previously, you unhesitatingly said you had done it purposely.
>
> Before going to the ground, for Lord Ranelagh's sake as well as for my

own, will you have the goodness to state in *writing* your reasons for doing so.

But if, M. le Comte, you wish to condemn Lord Ranelagh on an ex-Parte statement will you have the goodness to refer me to a friend so as to get the affair over as soon as possible, also – if safe – it would be better to take place here and at once.

Writing from the Palais Morolui on 30th May, the Count replied that he continued to judge Lord Ranelagh with worldly eyes concerning 'the painful adventures with which one is so familiar' and Lord Ranelagh's words had not persuaded him to change his mind and he accepted the challenge.

He agreed to meet Talbot the next day to arrange the manner in which the 'petites affaires' should be settled. He enclosed his card, on which was written the name of a friend who would be his second, Baron Hans of Place St. Angelo, Maison des Engineers, Venice, with time and date /½ 10/1st June.

At the meeting with Esterhazy and the Baron it seems to have been decided that the duel could not safely take place in Venice, as Talbot wrote to the Count as follows:

Monday
Hamite Yacht

Mons. le Comte,

I have just seen Ld. Ranelagh and his intention is to leave Venice tomorrow night for Ferrara where he will be on Wednesday the 2nd either in the middle of the day or evening. I have given as rendez-vous L'Hotel de la Poste at Ferrara. I hope these arrangements will suit; if so will you have the kindness to let me know at my Hotel. I will bring the Promise about not prosecuting with me when I wish yours.

I remain Mons. le Comte
Yr. very obedient,
J. Talbot Clifton.

Unfortunately, the correspondence ends there and we are left in suspense; did the duel take place? What was the outcome?

In Horace Wyndham's book, *The Magnificent Montez,* the dancer appeared at Her Majesty's Theatre, Haymarket on June 3rd 1843. Lord Ranelagh was there, 'a raffish mid-Victorian roué in an omnibus box with a select party of 'Corinthians' in frilled shirts and flowered waistcoats who hissed and barracked Lola's dance'. This demon-stration was occasioned by she having previously spurned Rane-lagh's amorous advances. Also in the audience, though not in the box, was Count Esterhazy; doubtless an interested spectator, and one cannot help wondering if young Clifton was also there.

Ranelagh was six years older that Talbot and to quote again from

Wyndham's book: ' "The peculiar prominence he has attained" remarked an obituarist, "has not always been of an enviable description. There are probably few men who have had so many charges of the most varied and disagreeable nature made against them. The resultant obloquy to which he had thus been exposed is great, nor has it vanished, as it properly should have done, with the charges themselves".'

His Lordship does not sound to have been the most desirable companion for Talbot, and it was about this time that he got into debt, as we shall see later.

In June 1842, we find Mr and Mrs Clifton in residence at 13 Euston Place, Leamington, from where he wrote to James Fair at least once a week and James kept him supplied with news of Lytham and the estate.

Old Thomas Hall, one of the tenant farmers, was very ill and the squire in replying prescribed wine or 'that favourite medicine, old ale'. Poor Thomas, however, died and the squire expressed his deep regret at losing so old a friend. Thomas himself and his wife had not been well, but were improving owing to the change of air and ministrations of the local doctor, and strongly pressed Fair to come and join them as he also had been seriously ill.

Wykeham, their youngest son, received permission to stay at Lytham Hall until the end of the month, 'as he prefers the society of his pony, dogs and Mr Butcher, the schoolmaster to being here, indeed the confinement of this place would not suit him'.

New cottages were being built on the estate and plans were being studied with a view to choosing the most attractive elevational treatment, but as usual on an English landed estate, with scant regard for the convenience and comfort of the occupants. Lytham Hall was being painted internally and on such matters Thomas had very definite ideas and tastes. 'I beg you will on no account allow Richardson to paint the columns under the staircase in imitation of marble. I hold nothing to be more decidedly vulgar, and having moreover seen at Mr Fleetwood's house a specimen of his painting in that style I do not think he at all succeeds in it.[9] I should wish them painted a very light stone colour, infine, the colour of Portland stone, or the whitest Longridge, and if Richardson does not approve of that let them be painted white and varnished which is no bad imitation of the pure white marble.'

Reading the voluminous correspondence that passed between Thomas and his agent creates the impression of a highly intelligent gentleman, well-educated and of a kindly and sympathetic nature. His writing also reveals a nice sense of humour that emerges even in some of the, to him, most annoying situations. He was keenly aware of his responsibilities as a landowner and the principle that 'the ownership of land in England is a sacred trust'; he had the welfare of the tenants always in mind and would not have them evicted until other accommodation could be found, unless they were deliberate wrong doers. Bearing this in mind, one wonders what his real feelings were about the frightful condition of the mill operatives whose resentment, owing to miserable pay, squalid quarters and unbelievably long working hours, came to a climax in the year 1842. On August 4th, riots broke out at Stalybridge and spread to Ashton, Oldham, Manchester and Preston. Thomas and Hetty were still staying at Leamington, and in his letter to Fair of August 16th, he remarks:

> I see by today's papers an account of the Preston Riots and the dispersion of the mob by the military with the loss of some lives, I trust it has all ended there, and that none of their companions have been sent to seduce any of our workpeople. This part of the country is in the same disturbed state, the spinners from Coventry, and miners from the coal district of Dudley are parading the country and the Yeomanry are all called out, but I am happy to say the country people are hard at work on the harvest which as far as bread corn will be finished very generally this week should this fine warm weather continue.

Preston, where the mob had attacked the troops in desperation at their plight, is only twelve miles from Lytham, yet Thomas does not seem unduly perturbed. The landed gentry of that time were, of course, much against the abolition of the Corn Laws, the root cause of the trouble, and had mixed feelings about the Reform Acts, which sought to extend the franchise and reduce the working hours of women and children, who formed the majority of the mill operatives. The comfortable logic of *laisser-faire* and subscriptions to the various relief funds probably were the salves of any pricks of conscience the gentry might suffer.

Of more immediate concern was the management of the new Clifton Arms Hotel at Lytham, which appointment was sought by Mr Mills, butler to Lord Stanley, and the loss of whom his Lordship 'laments much', as he had managed his household affairs for many years most satisfactorily. Thomas wrote to his Lordship that 'nothing could be further from our wishes than to put him to any inconvenience, and that he might rest assured that any arrangements to prevent his feeling the loss of Mr Mill's services we were not less anxious than himself should take place.' Thomas wrote again on 29th August, as he and Hetty were leaving Leamington for Harrogate in pursuance of their 'change of air' treatment. Mr Mills is shortly taking possession of the Clifton Arms and 'Mrs Clifton will with pleasure patronise a ball on the day you mention or do any thing else to forward his interest.' He concludes his letter, 'Will you be good enough to direct the keeper to kill on the 1st September three brace of partridges and a brace of leverets and send them by coach to Preston to be forwarded to The Lady Dalrymple Hamilton, Oak House, Leamington.'

A year later the couple were staying at 82 Marine Parade, Brighton, but found themselves very uncomfortably lodged; the house was inconvenient and extremely dirty and the furniture old and bad, 'however, we have it but for the present month.' He had his eye on another with coach house, stables and good offices, clean and neatly furnished, rent ten guineas a week or £500 *per annum*. They find everything 'most exorbitantly dear, meat 7½d per pound, coals 30s per ton and almost everything required in housekeeping coming from London by Rail road.'

> Brighton is not what it used to be, a very uncomfortable house, and in a place which some of its oldest residents admit is sadly changed within the last fifteen years, in fact, Brighton now is only filled by rich citizens of London who come down in shoals by the Rail road and occupy the whole place.

So little did they like Brighton that Hetty went house hunting in London, as their own town house was let, and ultimately decided to take 16 Hyde Park Gardens on a seven year lease at £600 *per annum* and they moved there in October 1843.

During their sojourn in Brighton, another financial bombshell had exploded – John Talbot, their eldest, and son and heir, was in debt! After finishing his education at Oxford he had been commissioned in the 2nd Life Guards, presumably at a cost to father of as much, or more as getting Thomas Henry commissioned in the 12th Lancers.

The first intimation came to James Fair, who, as agent, was the recipient of all problems and woes of members of the family, who looked to him for advice, help and sympathy, and acted as go-between where papa was involved.

Writing from the Horse Guards, Talbot said he was compelled to ask Fair's advice on the state of his affairs which were in 'such a state of disorder that I see no way of getting out of it except by borrowing money off my father or the Jews.' He was in need of £1,900, but declined to say what for, except that 'they are neither Play debts or debts of Honner – as either might justly alarm you.' He reasoned that, as he would have to pay interest on any sum borrowed it was better that it should go to the estate instead of a money lender. He did not himself dare to tell his father, as having been in debt before, he had broken his word. 'Besides he might write me a letter, which altho' just, might be so severe, that dutiful son, as I hope I am, might not easily be forgotten.' He would make no promises for the future as the present showed what they were worth. If the raising of the money would curtail any of his father's pursuits 'namely planting, improving etc. etc., there is one other way – to sell out of the army which would give the sum required.'

> I have signed *no Deeds* but have given two Bills. I will not even apologise for giving you the trouble to do this for me – as I feel sure you would do me a kindness if you could, I hope to get your answer on Monday . . .'

Father had to be told by Fair and was extremely angry, particularly as Talbot refused to let them see the bills because he believed some of the items absurd.

Then father wrote to him in terms that compelled him to authorise Fair to show the bills to Thomas and, in forwarding them, Talbot said,

> What you told me about my father grieves me very much . . . I cannot see any reason for what he is going to do except perhaps at the moment he is angry with me and fancy this step necessary. Do pray try and persuade him to do otherwise, not only for his own sake but for the reputation of our family in the County.'

Thomas, in writing to Fair said:

> I have not heard from Talbot today tho' he stated he was writing to me – I am glad to find the step I am about to take has made him feel as I expected, and as most assuredly he deserves to feel.'

From this, it is apparent that Thomas was going to pay off the bills and disinherit Talbot. It seems that the former was done; but before the latter, very extreme measure was carried out, Talbot so managed affairs that he was restored to grace in his father's eyes and placed himself in a very favourable financial position.

He wrote to Fair from Windsor Cavalry Barracks:

> I want to know, if, in case I got married, the extra income would come from what my Father allows himself or from what he allows for the use of the property. If the former of course I can't think of it, if the latter, I think the matter can be arranged; this of course is in confidence . . .
>
> If you can't answer my question tell me what you think, supposing my father gives his consent – burn this.'

James Fair's reply must have been satisfactory as Talbot's next letter from Crockford's Club, shows:

> I write to tell you of an event I know will please you, I am going to be married to Miss Lowther eldest daughter of Col. and Lady Eleanor Lowther and of course Gd. Daughter to Lord Lonsdale. I have been to Wigglesworth about the Settlement which my father will let you know. You, I know, will grant every assistance you can to the gentlemen of the Long Robes. As Lord Lonsdale's health is so uncertain we should *like to*

get it over soon.

I await your letter of congratualtion at Limmers' Hotel. I think of leaving the Army and turning the Sword into a Patent Plough.

All this is no secret. [10]

As father approved of the marriage, Talbot lost no time in sending his resignation from the Life Guards to the Commander-in-Chief. His father agreed to an immediate advance of £600 to be repaid out of the sum Talbot would receive for his commission, and an account was opened with Sir C. Scott (the family's London bankers) into which would be paid his allowance of £500 a quarter as a married man. Father also agreed that he should have Clifton Hall - a smallish mansion - in which to set up his establishment and have the shooting there.

On the 15th March 1844, he wrote saying that he expected to be married on the 22nd, but this was delayed by the death of Lord Lonsdale and by the final agreement of the marriage settlement in which he felt the lawyers in Preston were being unduly slow. Writing again, he said:

Write them a note and hurry them as unless they are quick I shan't be spliced for Heaven knows how long. My Brother was very much pleased at the shrimps and we eat them all. My mother begs me to thank you for your letter to her. Pray remember me to Mrs Fair and I hope Grey Emperor is better.

Grey Emperor was a stallion.

A few days later the marriage settlement was signed, though Colonel Lowther would not give an assurance of how he proposed to settle his fortune to his daughter on his death. Colonel Cavendish had lent his villa near London for a week, and Miss Lowther was anxious to go there before travelling to Lytham. The train journey north was to be broken at Birmingham where they would spend the night, leaving at 11.30 the next morning, so as to arrive at Lytham in daylight. As the railroad had not yet reached Lytham, the last part of the journey would be by family coach from Kirkham or Preston.

31 Bruton Street,
London, 22nd April.

My dear Sir,

I am married, bona fide, about ½ an hour ago; direct to Honourable Col. Cavendish, West End, Hampstead; good bye. I have only time to say this as I am going to Breakfast with Lord Lonsdale.

Yrs,
J. Talbot Clifton.

The speed with which these marital arrangements were commenced and brought to a conclusion seems to have surprised even

Talbot's father, who wrote to Fair on 13th April, nine days before the wedding. He expresses his satisfaction, only regretting Talbot's extreme youth - he was twenty-six and she twenty-two years of age. 'In point of connection I could wish for nothing better, but I fear the young lady's fortune will be but small unless Lord Lonsdale chooses to do something which I think they expect, but eventually it may be very large for both Col. Lowther and Lady Eleanor have brilliant prospects, the latter as heiress to her brother Lord Harborough and I need not say how the Colonel is situated.'[11]

Two days after he again wrote:

> It appears to me if you could induce some of the tenants to meet them at the Lea turnpike and escort them to the village of Lytham and then provide them with a dinner at the Hotel it would flatter the bride and her family, but they should all be provided with favours which will cost you a great many yards of white ribbon. Before they go down will you make Francis Fox take down the brick wall of the wine cellar door and let Wilson have the key and when they have gone have the brickwork restored and Wilson will return the key.

He also gave instructions that ale from the Hall was to be made available to the tenants and the poor were not to be forgotten.

The bricking up of the wine cellar door does seem an unusual security precaution but may have been considered wise when the family were away in view of the recent mob violence in the Preston area due to the industrial workers' unrest.

Thomas was suffering so badly from an infection of his legs that he was unable to attend the wedding. To keep Fair fully posted, however, he wrote,

> The ceremony is just over tho' I was not able to attend. The thing went off with great éclat and was most numerously attended; Lord Lonsdale gave a most sumptuous breakfast after it. Mrs Clifton has just returned and the young couple took their departure at three o'clock for Col. Cavendish's villa at Hampstead.
>
> I have been so often interrupted that I have not time to say more, but I hope you may all have a merry party tonight . . .

Everyone seemed very pleased with these arrangements and the happy outcome of it all, especially the bridegroom, who was now in receipt of a handsome income and all the benefits and privileges of an eldest son who would one day become tenant for life of a large and prosperous estate. His father was pleased as Talbot's income came out of estate funds and would not affect Thomas's own. Colonel Lowther and Lady Eleanor were doubtless delighted to have got their eldest daughter off their hands and married to a young north country gentleman with such good prospects.

There was, however, one person whose name is not mentioned as being highly delighted and excited at the match, and that is the bride. Talbot refers to her very briefly; Thomas seems quite satisfied, though in fairness he does not appear to have even heard of her until a few weeks before the marriage. There is the extraordinary uncertainty about the actual day of the wedding – the almost indecent haste in the effort to get it over before Lord Lonsdale dies. The note that Talbot wrote to Fair half an hour after the ceremony and before sitting down to the wedding breakfast – 'I am married, bona fide, about ½ hour ago' – written obviously, in view of the previous letters to Fair, so as to ensure that he 'saw to it' that Talbot's vastly increased income commenced as from the 22nd April 1844, and no later!

Violet Clifton, in her biography of her husband, the grandson of Talbot, says of Eleanor; 'She had been forced to marry him, but after the marriage she had closeted herself for three days in her room, weeping alone. She had come out of that room embittered, with darting tongue and heart of gall. She had never grown to love her teasing, witty man. She was beneficent to the poor, but violent in her angers. Even when he was slowly dying she was harsh to their only son, Harry who never became Squire.'[12]

This assessment of her nature after the marriage seems unduly severe, as her letters to James Fair, of which there are many, reveal her as a very practical, straight thinking person, who was intensely aware of the responsibilities of her position, when she, in turn, became lady of the manor. She did not suffer fools gladly and, while it may not have been a love match, she and Talbot as time went on seem to have had a strong mutual regard and affection, as will be seen later.

While all these traumas and subsequent rejoicings were in progress, the correspondence between Thomas and James Fair continued, regarding the day-to-day running of the estate and other family matters. Thomas's brother John, born in 1790 and a member of Lincolns Inn, was in a perfectly helpless state and not expected to live long. The new establishment at Hyde Park Gardens 'was to be conducted with rigid economy'.

It was proposed that the Roman Catholic Chapel of Westby was to be closed, which caused consternation and anger among those of the tenants who worshipped there, and some demonstrated their resentment by withholding payment of their rents. Thomas considered that the objectors will find the Chapel at Lytham just as convenient, 'Feeling pretty confident that this position has not risen spontaneously from those whose names are attached to it but at the instigation and probably command of the priests, I can only reply, as I have already done, to Mr Dixon that having weighed well the matter before the notice was served for closing the chapel, I still retain the opinion that it is no longer necessary and that they may at no unreasonable distance find accommodation at the Willows at Kirkham, or at Lytham, for attending divine worship.'

The matter of arrears of rent was also raised by Fair, and Thomas wrote that whilst he objected to harshness, those defaulters who were habitually in arrear and made no effort to remedy the matter would have to be severely dealt with, but, 'I will either give up in part, or the whole, those arrears which you may deem to be most likely to prevent that spirit of improvement which I am so anxious should exist amongst all the tenantry.' We also have reference to one of the burning questions of the day – 'I see by the papers that the anti corn law league have at last roused the farmers in most of the southern counties against themselves, and as associations for the support of protection are very generally forming, I cannot help thinking we ought to do something of the same.'

The new main drain recently put through the estate was proving a success – 'I was rejoiced to hear the perfect effects of the drainage, and that it was admitted by the Tenants, who as you know, are not very easily convinced of the benefits of anything new.' Fair had also purchased a new machine for making land drain tiles, as extensive under drainage schemes were in hand for improving the productivity of the farm lands.

The new agricultural society was anxious to purchase a stallion, and, of course, Thomas was immediately interested and suggested a number of horses that he thought might suit. They, however, preferred their own choice and Thomas, who really knew his horses, drily comments 'I confess I would not like to buy for the Society as they approve of such animals as "New Fashion!",' and he goes on to say, 'While on the subject of horses, I am sorry to have to tell you that the brown colt you sent up for me is lame in his fore feet, I presume from having stood long without his shoes being changed for which C . . . deserves to be hanged.'

The name of the unfortunate groom or horseman is illegible.

On February 3rd, 1844, Thomas sent Fair 1,000 handbills with statements from official documents for distribution among the farmers, which were being circulated in agricultural districts, 'refuting very clearly the statements of Cobden & Co.'[13] And, on February 10th, 'It would give me great pleasure to hear that a coursing club of gentlemen was formed at Lytham and I doubt not Talbot would willingly become a member and I beg you to inform Mr Hornby so. For my part as you know, I am no sportsman, it appears to me it would be absurd my becoming a member of such a club.'

The club was formed and a Captain Ridgeway became the organiser; it grew into a well known meeting and was the forerunner of the Waterloo Cup now held at Altcar.

During March, Thomas expresses his pleasure at reading in the Preston papers that there were still hopes of a public meeting being called to form a protective society in conjunction with the metropolitan one, 'or we shall remain the only part of England who dare not defend ourselves against the league.'

Talbot and Eleanor Cecily had been offered Clifton Hall, some eight miles from Lytham, but after inspecting it, did not think it would suit, as it was too small, and not liking the country, which provoked his father somewhat – 'of course he will do as he likes in that respect, as he has been informed it is the only one I have to offer him, and he will scarcely expect I should resign Lytham to him, tho' it would not surprise me. I find too, that he expects a visit from Col. Lowther and one of his sons, had I known they had intended to receive visitors I would have taken care they had been better provided with plate, linen etc., but it appeared to me so unusual that I did not even think of it, however, I presume these things change with time.' The happy couple were, of course, spending part of their honeymoon at Lytham Hall and Thomas apparently was amazed that they should invite company!

One bit of news, however, cheered him up – 'I received the pleasant intelligence from Frederick [the third son], yesterday, that he has taken his degree of B.A. at Oxford for which he has worked very hard the last year.'

The railroad had not yet reached Lytham and letters had to be collected at Preston; as this was an unsatisfactory arrangement Thomas and his agent had been trying for over a year to establish a post office in Lytham. The appointment of a suitable 'Receiver of Letters' was in the hands of the Lords of the Treasury of whom Lord Stanley was one, and he was using his best endeavours to help. It appears that the matter was finally resolved in June 1844, when a messenger or postman named Greaves was appointed to collect and deliver for 16s per week, and Mrs Wilding, as postmistress, was to receive £8 *per annum*, these being the squire's nominees for the position. Thomas considered £8 *per annum* derisory, but discovered that in some places it was as low as £4.

Thomas was still suffering from colds, chest trouble and the infection of his legs and so he decided to try 'the hydropathic or cold water system, and thought of going for that purpose to the neighbourhood of Richmond where there is an establishment of that kind, next week.'

Soon after, he writes from Richmond:

I am happy to say I think I am improving under the cold water system and write with my body bound in wet bandages.

He had earlier told Fair that he was driven to this treatment as he was counselled by many eminent medical men in town that there were no other means to achieve a speedy and radical cure. As the weather was extremely hot he did not find either wet bandages or a wet shirt disagreeable!

While at Richmond he was informed that Arthur, 'the late sailor', had passed his examinations at Haileybury with great credit, and would go out to Bengal as a writer, in September 1844. His outfit – including the sum of £400 with which to establish himself on arrival – would cost about £1,500, and Thomas was advised by an official of the college that, 'what I recommend to you, I did for my own son a few years ago, when he went out in the same capacity, and a liberal outfit prevents young men incurring debts when they first arrive in the country which often seriously injures them in their career there.'

Arthur was to sail in the *Percursor* of the Oriental Steam Company, and in addition to his fare of £113 he was to have £100 to take with him for expenses at the different places where the ship touched, during which he would have to live ashore.

By the end of August 1844, Thomas had returned to 16 Hyde Park Gardens as he thought he was cured of his ailment, but felt so weak and debilitated that he again needed constant 'changes of air' and proposed a tour on the continent. After a previous illness he had written to Fair: 'I am so far recovered from my attack of illness, which was merely bilious, that I only suffer now from the severity of the remedies which I confess have left me very weak!'

Talbot, having resigned from the Life Guards and now a married man, accepted an offer of candidature for Member of Parliament for North Lancashire, which did not please his father at all. Thomas at first refused to advise him except to inform Talbot that he could expect no pecuniary assistance from him; but later admitted having written for him an 'exposition of his political principles'. It is quite possible that the 'exposition' drafted by Thomas, with his immaculate phraseology and knowledge of current affairs, clinched the matter of Talbot's eligibility and which, being confirmed by Lord Derby, resulted in the present contretemps.

Thomas and James Fair now joined each other in praying that there might be no contest and that Talbot be returned unopposed. Thomas's last words on this occasion were: 'the die is, however, now cast and he must abide by the results, we can only hope amongst his many follies, this will not prove the most costly one'.

Now that Arthur was safely embarked for India and with Talbot's political future hanging in the balance, Thomas and Hetty departed for the Continent. Writing to Fair from Milan in October 1844, Thomas expressed his joy and relief at receiving from Talbot the glad tidings that he had been returned as M.P. for North Lancashire without opposition. Once again, however, he rouses his father's ire: 'I cannot refrain from telling you of a request Talbot has made to me thro' his mother, because I confess after all I have done for him it has hurt me very much . . . he wishes me to give up Lytham to him as a residence. This, I have just written to him: "I most decidedly decline". As he did not choose to accept the house at Clifton, when offered, I could not give up my own home, for such I should consider Lytham, so long as I live.'

At Genoa they were held up for several days by the sickness of one of their servants and by two bridges on the road to Nice having been washed away during violent thunderstorms with torrents of rain. The journey to Nice might have been taken by sea, but Hetty strongly objected as they would miss the most beautiful route in Europe, the road being along the Mediterranean shore the whole way. After three days of postings they arrived, but their stay did not exceed one day, 'for tho' a beautiful spot there is nothing to be seen. This is certainly a splendid town for its size and the country and bay most lovely and climate most enviable, but I am still sufficiently a John Bull to prefer England, even the Banks of the Ribble which are not considered the most beautiful parts of it.'

They embarked the carriage and themselves on the Rhöne and in two days expected to arrive at Lyons and then on to Paris, being back in England about the end of November.

Soon after their arrival Thomas was informed of the projected branch railroad from Kirkham to Lytham, which would pass through his property for almost its entire length. As was the case when the railroad went through Clifton with Salwick some years previously, he did not like the idea, though was willing to admit its advantage to the village. When it was pointed out that the line would skirt along the side of the estate without serious severance of the farms he withdrew his objections but observed: 'I suggest, however, the terminus should be at such a distance from any building ground for houses as may be consistent with its general convenience as no one would like to be in the immediate neighbourhood of a railroad.'

II

THE railroad reached Lytham in 1846:

> The 16th February initiated a new era in the history and progress of Lytham, for on that day the branch line connecting this popular resort with the Preston and Wyre Railway was formally opened. At an early hour the town evinced manifest signs that the inhabitants were bent on doing full honour to the introduction of their valuable ally; flags and banners floated from the church and the residences of many of the inhabitants and later in the day the streets were thronged with processions and spectators of all grades. The directors and a large party of the neighbouring gentry assembled by invitation at Lytham Hall and after partaking of luncheon proceeded to the newly erected station, where the 'opening train', consisting of an engine, gaily decorated, and fourteen carriages awaited their arrival. The train departed amid a volley of cheers and discharge of cannon and proceeded to Kirkham; the return journey was performed in fifteen minutes.[14]

Thomas and Hetty Clifton were, of course, of the party, acting as hosts, and no doubt the wine cellar door at the Hall had again been unbricked.

The new rail link, making commuting to the towns of industrial Lancashire possible, stimulated the growth of Lytham by the erection of more seaside villas, but another factor encouraged house building. When new development first commenced in the early-1800s, the estate had granted leases for three lives, then forty years and in some cases sixty years. For some time James Fair had been advocating longer leases and now terms of ninety-nine years became the norm.

Fair's zeal for improvement grew with the increased demand for building sites; new streets were planned, sand dunes levelled, the now famous Green was created and the stone hulking or revetting to prevent the incursion of the sea commenced. One improvement, mercifully, did not go forward, and that was the removal of the windmill, now Lytham's most famous landmark. Thomas comments, 'I have some recollection of having stated to you . . . that the Mill and kiln, might and would, have to be moved at no distant time, which you appeared to admit. I am not therefore surprised at objections being made to build on the eastern part of the beach so long as the mill and kiln remain.'

These would be looked upon as industrial buildings in those days and, as such, offensive to the eyes of people building a house in which to reside or spend the summer months far from the grim cotton towns. The drying kiln probably emitted smoke and fumes offensive to the noses of those who came to enjoy the health-giving breezes off the Irish Sea. In fact, the kiln did go, and was replaced by the Lifeboat House, generously built by the squire in 1851.

Again residing at Hyde Park Gardens, the flow of comment and instruction to his agent flowed unabated from Thomas's pen. He agrees there should be a new inn near the railway station for the benefit of visitors, but as he cannot afford to build it himself, hopes that it will not adversely affect business at the new Clifton Arms, built on the front by the estate. He deems 'a public house capable of becoming a greater nuisance in a village than any other building.'

Having expressed this pious sentiment it must have come as a shock to learn that all was not well at the Clifton Arms and that Mr Mills, the tenant – late butler to Lord Stanley who 'lamented much' his loss – has mismanaged the place to such an extent that he was on the verge of bankruptcy.

Once again, Thomas's generous nature shows itself: he agrees that Mills will have to go, but as offering him the job was the cause of his losing his previous situation, he felt that 'we ought not to be the persons to adopt measures which either he or others may deem harsh.' He also instructed Fair that if by any sacrifice of rent owing he could assist the family, 'that I am disposed to do; and I am certain it will give you pleasure to do so. As to any odium attaching to this matter, if by strict impartiality to all his creditors and kindness towards his family – after the very general complaints which have been made of the manner in which he has conducted the house – we may be prepared to meet it.'

Some indication of the nature of Mills' mismanagement was given by a lady whom Thomas met at Leamington and who told him that, while visiting Lytham, she was obliged to leave the hotel as it was impossible to stay longer because of the 'extreme disorder' on Saturday and Sunday nights!

Despite the squire's long absences from Lytham, very little went on in the village that did not come to his attention. The Reverend Robinson, vicar of St. Cuthbert's, was in the habit of robing and disrobing in the presence of the congregation, he had heard, 'not directly, but in confidence, from a letter to Mrs Clifton from Miss Wilson!' This Thomas considered disrespectful to the place and the congregation, and it would be a kindness to let the vicar know how offensive it was:

I cannot ask you to do so, but perhaps you could suggest some means of

> its coming to his ears without my informing him of it by letter. I hope the Wesleyan Chapel may make him a little more cautious how he offends the feelings of his parishioners and I shall be glad to hear they are about to begin it.

One cannot help wondering how James Fair dealt with that one. The Wesleyan chapel was, in fact, completed before the end of the year (1846) and the Reverend Robinson doubtless took care not to offend the sensibilities of his flock in any way for fear of losing them to the opposition.

There is also news of Wykeham, the youngest son, who has obtained a lieutenancy in the Rifle Brigade. His father is pleased to learn that the regiment's destination has been changed from the West Indies to the Cape of Good Hope, 'a most delightful climate and country where he may amuse himself by hunting kaffirs.'

Arthur, who had gone to India two years previously, was now in trouble. During September Thomas received a letter by the overland mail and 'its contents have caused me more annoyance and surprise than I can express and first impression was to allow the bill to be dishonoured.'

He was informed, however, that the disgrace of allowing the bill to be returned might seriously affect Arthur's prospects, possibly preventing his obtaining any other appointment or further promotion in the one to be held. In these circumstances, Fair had to send the London bankers £500 to meet the bill and Thomas wrote to his son informing him that no bill of his would be paid in future, nor would he render him henceforth the slightest assistance, and that he must trust to his own interests and income.

About this period a minor religious war was in progress in Lytham over the manner in which the school was being conducted, and Thomas, as squire and lord of the manor, and having the advowson or gift of the living of the parish church, was the recipient of letters, from, as he puts it, 'the two Rev. Gents'.

As we have already seen, he, though brought up as a Catholic, had become a Protestant in 1831 and the correspondence between him and Fair reveals an antipathy, sometimes almost vicious, to members of the Roman Catholic Church.

The Rev. Fr. Walmsley had withdrawn the R.C. children, as morning and evening prayers had been introduced by the Rev. Robinson, vicar of the parish church, and 'very warm words had passed between them'. For himself, Thomas considered prayers unnecessary in a school 'tho' admitting the necessity of religious instruction as of paramount importance.' Mr Robinson had offered a compromise which Mr Walmsley would not accept and asked the squire if he would let them have a piece of land to build their own school. This, Thomas declined to do as 'I cannot but think someone has instigated Mr Walmsley to take this step, as I hear the beach has been quite black with R.C. priests during Wykeham's stay at Lytham.'

Mr Walmsley apparently refused to be put down, and Thomas considered that his conduct deserved the severest censure of the school trustees, and he hopes 'that they may not be induced to make any concessions to the R.C. party'.

Thomas later expresses his satisfaction at a solicitor's letter addressed to the Rev. Walmsley on the instructions of the Trustees of the Lytham Schools, in which they expressed their opinion of the 'unbecoming expressions and unfounded charges he had thought fit to bring against them'. His final comment on this affair was 'I am glad the school matter has ended peaceably, and am quite of Mr Robinson's opinion, from whom I heard this morning, that R.C. teachers in the village would be a great nuisance'.

His prejudice shows again the following year: 'I hope Mr Kenyon who proposes building in Warton Street is not a Roman Catholic as so many houses as six would give him considerable influence in the village'.

His spleen is once more exhibited in the following as regards Talbot's again standing for Parliament –

> If you could discover that the movement against Talbot's return began with the Roman Catholics, which I strongly suspect myself, I should not hesitate to inform Mr Walmsley that in consequence his salary from me will cease, and that should he continue to occupy his present house and land I shall expect a rent for it such as I should obtain from any other tenant.

He wrote to Fair again two days later:

> Most certainly if we can ascertain that the Roman Catholics have applied to Mr J. Heywood for the Post Office appointment, I shall not one moment hesitate to withdraw my allowance and use of the house and land from their priest whom they may support in future themselves.

His rancour was such that only a fortnight before he died he wrote in his last letter to Fair:

> In any cases for building land, I hope you will use the greatest caution to prevent any house being built for the priest, at least upon the beach.

He died at 49 Belgrave Square on 17th February 1851 aged 63, as a result of his ailments coming to a climax, as described by Hetty:

> Dear Sir,
> It is with great grief that I tell you I have sat up three nights with my beloved husband who is *most* dangerously ill – He brought on inflamation of his lungs by not being able to bear the heat of the fire on

his legs and sitting three days in a cold room - the cold flew into his lungs. It has been a most sudden attack, Sunday night he had a mustard poultice, a blister, was cupped and bled, which I do believe saved his life. He is a *degree* better now but still seriously ill - I will write again after the Doctors have been. Of course he cannot read your letters -

2 o'clock

My dearest Husband sends all sorts of kind messages to you and begs you will do as you like. But *in his present state* he thinks the more kind and generous he is the better.

I copy Dr. Watson's report to Talbot.

Mr Clifton is in some respects a little better this morning than he was yesterday.

Feb. 12 Chas Watson
R. Stocker

The truth is the expectoration has not so much blood in it to day as before, but I am broken hearted to see his sufferings.

I do grieve to hear James does not improve believe me.[15]

H. Clifton 12th Feb.

I know not what I write.[16]

So died Thomas the Tree Planter, four days later, and one cannot help wondering, why, instead of moving about seeking 'changes' of air and allowing himself to be subjected to the 'cold water system', the sulphur baths, the mustard plasters, blistering and cupping, he had done as others were doing in increasing numbers; and sought a cure through regular and more lengthy sojourns in his native Lytham.

Had he read (or perhaps he had read) Whittle's *Marina* published in 1833 he would have learnt the high regard in which Lytham was held as a health resort by people from inland towns - and had he read therein, and put to the test, the following advice of 'Geoffrey Gimcrack' of Leeds, he might have lived much longer:

> Riches are only vain without health. Sea bathing is a luxury, and ought to be considered a treat by him that enjoys it. The people here bathe not at all - whilst those at a distance think it is a blessing. Holmes the barber said he had never bathed in his life, nor could I persuade him to do so. He said that he was sound in body, and if so, why dip in the sea at all?
> . . .

He might have found another comforting passage in the same article:

> I asked a man, how long people lived in this part? He answered, 'that they generally averaged, (unless by hard drinking) upwards of eighty years of age, before they slipped off the sod.'

Chapter Two

The Colonel

ITH the death of his father, John Talbot became tenant for life of the estate and squire of Lytham, and had to shoulder the burden of responsibility this entailed, as well as enjoying the vastly increased income and privileges his inheritance brought. One of the first matters he had to deal with was his mother's future; she was in an excess of grief at the loss of her husband and who had got herself into a wildly emotional state.

> Dear Mr Fair,
>
> It would indeed grieve me to think I was never to see or hear from so kind a friend again. Talbot told me you would write, but you did not!!
>
> Did you receive the desk and *his* snuff box, I never heard you did so. I am leaving this on Monday; can you not come and see me before I go. It would give me much pleasure, but do not go till Talbot has gone to Catmose as I wish to speak to you, can you be here Saturday night or Sunday morning.[17] I must pay all expenses.
>
> If James goes to Nice I can give him very strong letters to the Consul there. Should I go myself you need not doubt my taking care of him.
>
> Farewell my kind friends. Farewell Dear Lytham *for Ever.*
>
> With love to Mrs Fair and your family and my May Flower. I am too miserable to write more I return Monday to the house, my wedding day and the day month I lost him.
>
> Yrs. Very sincere
> H. Clifton.

Thomas had left James Fair his writing desk, a not inappropriate legacy in view of the number of letters to Fair he had penned on it. James was Fair's ailing son who was being sent to France seeking health and May Flower was probably a pony.

Hetty was most resentful of Talbot's handling of matters not specifically mentioned in Thomas's will - such as plate, linen and glass, and proposed making her pay for the items she wished to retain for her own use. 'Talbot has been perfectly *just,* as to a stranger, Frederick is to buy knives and lends me four silver spoons and four silver forks on which we can manage until we can purchase some.' Later she says that they are using black horn-handled knives they bought for the kitchen: 'If I could laugh, this reverse for the present, would make me. I am sorry Talbot is coming up for he has been anything but kind, but very *just* to *himself;* 'Fair words go far!' and it is wonderful how far, believe me.'

Talbot seems to have relented and did not insist on her paying for the things she retained. The brougham and horses were sold and she was hurt that he did not give her the chance to buy. The house, 49 Belgrave Square, was left to her, however, and she sold it later for the price she asked. Nevertheless, she owed money, and for a year or so pleaded poverty until she bought 16 Park Lane where she set up her establishment and lived in considerable comfort. She frequently wrote to James Fair, to whom she appealed for help and advice in all matters and who sent her baskets of game and vegetables. Like Thomas, her late husband, she suffered from various ailments and her doctors, she alleged, said that game and rabbits should be her main diet. Accordingly the baskets from Lytham contained, in season, pheasants, leverets, woodcock – she did not care for partridge – and wildfowl. Dotterel were always in demand and in spring, plover eggs. Rabbits she seems to have adored and presented no problem as the dunes between Lytham and Blackpool were one vast warren.

During the few years when she was hard up, she sometimes wrote to Fair – on black-edged paper – giving an account of herself with her habitual vivacity, nearly always with 'a thousand thanks from the Elderly Lady for all the good things in the last basket.' The last page of the letter, however, was written in a different vein – how poor she was, no one remembered her, the terrible cost of everything in London. The first part of the letter would have a footnote, 'You may tear off the last half of this and show it to Talbot'!

As things improved she bought a carriage and gave dinner parties, sometimes for sixteen people – usually in the shooting season – and once wrote to Fair, 'I cannot understand why I am such a frisky Elderly Lady, but so it is when I am in better health – I should have written before but was so very much exhausted by my functions that I have done nothing but scold and sleep ever since.'

Whilst recovering from one of her illnesses she wrote: 'but I am an Elastic Elderly Lady and soon revive, please God!'

She died in 1863 and is buried in the family vault at Lytham.

As we have already seen, Talbot became Conservative Member of Parliament for North Lancashire in 1844, and as he has now become squire we must look back in order to trace his career more closely.

In 1846 matters of great importance to England, and particularly Lancashire, were being debated in Parliament – the Repeal of the Corn Laws and the Ten Hours Bill.

The Conservatives were divided because their leader, Sir Robert Peel, who had given his electoral pledge to maintain the Corn Laws, now believed they should be repealed and had proposed in Cabinet that the ports should be opened by Order of Council and that a bill for permanent modification of the Corn Laws should be introduced early in 1846.

The reaction of the member for North Lancs., as recorded in a letter to James Fair, is interesting:

> As respects the state of things at present I certainly shall not consult any public feeling but will vote against this new measure of Sir Robert Peel. I think it would stamp my future life, was I at the beginning to turn round and vote with Peel, much as I admire him as a leader. Besides this on my conscience, I think he is going to do *us* a serious injury. One good thing there will be, I believe, the question will be settled as regards bread. I think those who suppose, that on the settlement of this question, agitation is to cease, are quite mistaken as Mr Bright told me the other night (*Bless* him!!!!) – 'We *will* have this and then go on for the rest.' What he means by the rest I don't know, except a republic of Quakers.

That standing for Parliament was a costly business for the individual is apparent from Talbot writing to the Conservative agent, saying that as a contest in the county was probable he was willing to come forward again, providing he might expect assistance from the Party. It was a public cause and should not be left to a private individual to fight it. Ten thousand pounds was more than he felt justified in asking his father to pay for him. He said later that it was not his intention to stand contested elections and having to battle with, 'the apathy of his friends and the animosity of his enemies.'

Talbot and Cecily were living at 5 Wilton Crescent in Belgravia when their son, Thomas Henry, was born on 3rd March 1845. In July 1846 they took up residence at 18 Charles Street, Mayfair, but during the hunting season stayed in Rutland, as they were both keen followers of the hounds. Cecily's father, Colonel Henry Cecil Lowther, was master of the Cottesmore Hunt and his father, Sir William, First Earl of Lonsdale, had bought for him Barleythorpe Hall, near Oakham, a hunting box where the young couple were frequent visitors.[18] By 1850 they were living in Catmose Lodge, Oakham, which belonged to the Hon. Gerard Noel, son of the 3rd Earl of Gainsborough, who had married Cecily's sister, Augusta Mary.

Whilst the house was described as a hunting 'box', it contained three reception rooms, fourteen bed and dressing rooms and five bathrooms. There were two cottages, stabling for eleven horses and forty-two acres of land. Talbot now tried his hand at farming and had thirty-six sheep, three cows and fifteen pigs. He also indulged in a little horse dealing.

> I have bought a very fine brood mare for twenty-five pounds, she had been knocked about a great deal but is young in constitution. She is in condition and has been singed so you must not turn her out until her coat grows, you can feed her on turnips and hay. I think you will say she is a very fine animal, she is for Kilmoyler [a stallion], I send her on Thursday by the morning train so let Bickerstaffe meet her at Preston and ride her over which will save eight shillings. Write and tell me what you think of her, *mind,* really what you do – the mare goes capitally in harness and she is the size to go in a cart as leader, so make use of her if you like, she walks sound.

An even more remarkable animal was offered for the consideration of Fair:

> Henley Greaves has a mare for sale, lame in fore fetlock, thirteen year old, very fine shaped, he asks twenty-five pounds for her. As he rides twenty-two stone at least you must know she is not a bad one to carry him hunting. She could still work on a farm but can't carry that weight. I advise you to buy her for the farm as without good mares you cannot have good stock. I daresay I could buy her to cost you twenty-five pounds at Lytham.

Talbot was up to all the tricks of horse trading, it would appear:

> I saw a very nice Cob, good to ride and drive, Roan forty pounds, but a Windsucker, very slight, I don't think it matters. I once gave £120 for one, and knew it, and sold him for £170 and told the purchaser this Cob is a gelding.

His infant son, Thomas Henry, was also to be mounted.

> Will you, if possible, buy the least little pony for me, a little bigger than a *dog.* Some of your Scotch friends will be able to get one for you, as if I come to Lytham this year I shall want to put my boy on him in a side saddle as he is getting too big to be carried.

His parliamentary duties took him to meetings in Lancashire and occasionally he stayed at Lytham.

> I hope you will see that I am left coals and *Beer* and *Ale* at the Hall as really the greater part goes to Father's servants and not to me.

Talbot seems to have applied himself to the job of being an M.P. with characteristic vigour. He wrote about ninety-five letters by hand to friends who had signed his requisition.

> Lord Stanley told me the form of a letter to write to Lord Derby, it was not to allow the peace of the Co. to be disturbed. I have also written to Lord Burlington. I am so tired I can hardly write. *I firmly believe* Charles

Townley has as much idea of contesting N. Lancs. as you have. Mind and write me everything you hear.

In July 1847 he was concerned lest he be put to the cost of fighting for his seat, and his canvassing did not always meet with unqualified support:

The Rev. G. Hall will not vote for me if there can be found a *respectable* candidate; anti papist. Mr Parke will be on my committee if I will abjure the voting for the Pope . . . Wilson will not vote for me unless I promise to abjure Maynooth.[19] I shall have some gent begging me never to eat the Pope's Eye in a leg of mutton, you'll see.[20]

His electioneering was not without its hazards either: 'Talbot tells me the mob have broken all the windows in the Bull Inn, but whether in his honour or that of his friend Parker he does not seem to know,' writes Thomas laconically to Fair.

Being, in his own words, 'not the popular candidate' and not prepared to stand unless adequate financial support was forthcoming - his own limit being £1,500 - he retired and so ended his career as an M.P., although he continued to support the Conservative Party.

He then got mumps and went on a continental tour with Cecily which included Rome, 'but please do not mention!'

II

UPON coming into his inheritance, Talbot, like his father, commenced a long and detailed correspondence with James Fair on matters relating to Lytham and the estate, as he was frequently away in London, abroad or spending the hunting season at Catmose or Barleythorpe.

In common with the rest of England, when a town or village lay within a great landed estate, the squires of Lytham exercised almost complete control over the life and development of the village until the various municipal enactments of the nineteenth century gradually eroded their power. One of these matters was education, in which Lytham was fortunate in having a free school under the control of trustees who administered a fund which had originally arisen out of an inundation of the sea in 1720 - a collection had been made in aid of the people who had suffered serious damage but,

> The inhabitants were unable to agree upon an equable distribution of the collection specified, and decided, by way of settling the affair, to make a free school, with it and other sums.[21]

In September 1850 the new St. John's Church was consecrated and new schools connected with it were proposed, and, as the site of such schools had to be provided by the estate, the new squire was involved:

> I have made a fight against a Govt. Inspector, but am prepared to yield because if, as you predict, some day Lytham increases, that day will put it out of the power of a family to retain the control of many similar institutions, a fact, which was commenced when Lytham was placed in the hands of Commissioners. However, I have done my best but will give in sooner than the Schools should be stopped.

This reflects the antipathy prevalent in those days to government-appointed inspectors interfering in local affairs which had commenced with the Factory Act of 1833.[22]

To the proposal for establishing a lifeboat station at Lytham he gave wholehearted support:

> You were quite right in supposing I should give the project of obtaining a Life-boat my cordial support and wish we had had one before a loss of life called attention to the subject. I must leave the subscriptions in your hands as I have no idea of how much it costs - but if you attend the meeting I think you will find that an annual sum will be required, also a boat house, and many other little things to which I should also wish to be a benefactor. I trust that a crew will be found at Lytham not more

> backward in their duty than the many brave men who are putting out to help vessels in distress.

And so in 1851 the first of Lytham's epic lifeboats came on station. However, tragedy struck swiftly. On her first exercise she capsized drowning eight of her crew, leaving eight widows and twenty-eight children. Undeterred by this, a gallant crew went out in the same boat within three months of the disaster and effected a rescue on Salthouse Bank.

Talbot was as good as his word, building the new boathouse at his own expense and being thereafter a staunch lifeboat supporter.

Some idea of the real affection Talbot had for James Fair may be gained from the following letter. Fair's son, who was then twenty-one years old had been sent to Nice in the hope that his health might benefit from the climate:

> My Dear Fair,
>
> I assure you my wife and myself were truly sorry to hear your account of your poor boy, but altho' it seems to be hoping against hope, I trust you will not give way prematurely to despair, his life may yet be granted him - I know your feelings of delicacy but I do hope that if you have any idea of going to your son or any desire to do so you will not allow yourself to be deterred by any fears of detriment to your engagement with me. As also I know the expense such a journey would incur, I think considering the many years I have known you and the feelings with which my father regarded you, you will not feel hurt at my offering and insisting on being allowed to be your banker on such an occasion. I know you will not feel any offence at my proposal as the Gifts of Fortune are so unequally distributed and it is not those who deserve them most enjoy them - but I think I shall not have affronted you by my candid proposal and expect you to shew me your friendship by an equally candid acceptance. Give me a line to say you are going or are gone and I trust that He who can do everything may spare you this impending affliction. I strongly advise you to shew this letter to your wife who will be a good counsellor to you and I remain, my dear Fair, with the deepest sympathy.
>
> Yrs. Very truly
>
> Wednesday J. Talbot Clifton.

Soon after writing this kind and moving letter, Talbot and Cecily had their own personal tragedy. She was delivered of a baby girl who died only a few days after; she was their first and only daughter and was christened Althea Beatrice.

During May 1851 they moved to 19 Bruton Street, Berkeley Square,[23] which Talbot had taken for eight weeks. He sent to Lytham two mares and Captain Henry Clifton's charger which his father had given him. The charger was seventeen years old and was being honourably retired, to be kept in moderate conditions, as 'I have promised him a berth till he dies or is shot'. The gallant Captain had sold out of his regiment as it was under orders for the Cape and transferred to the 7th Dragoon Guards; as he himself wrote to Fair, 'I am lucky in getting out of my regiment as it is ordered abroad immediately'. He appears to have been doubly lucky in getting himself at the same time a staff appointment as *aide-de-camp* to the Duke of Cambridge.

During 1851 news of Arthur's death ('the late sailor', who had gone to India as a writer) was received, and that the Accountant General of India held 2,000 rupees which he had left. He died on 12th July 1850 at Jellasore, Bengal, aged twenty-six.

On 19th April 1852 Talbot writes to Fair from 36 Brook Street to which they had moved:

> I have been induced to go to Peterboro' and have engaged myself to stand for that place. I have a fair chance of success. Bribery is unknown there and the number of voters 475 – the probable expense small, say £500, however, it would be ruin to make a canvas now or to give publicity to it on account of Lord Fitzwilliam putting on the screw, so say nothing about it.[24]

In June 1852, Talbot, apparently tired of frequent changes of address in London, purchased a house in Charles Street, Berkeley Square, for £2,500 including fixtures. In view of the state of the property he proposed pulling it down and rebuilding at a basic cost of £3,000 plus the cost of mantelpieces, bells, stores, painting and papering, making a total of £5,500. New furniture would cost, at the outside, £1,500, so that he required the sum of £7,000 and asked Fair to borrow £5,500 immediately, the furniture not being required until the new house was ready.

> I trust I have not done a foolish thing but I go a good deal by Col. Lowther who thinks well of it. It is a capital situation and will be a good house.

What Fair replied to this letter is not known but it certainly released the flood gates of Talbot's wrath and reveals once again the frustrations of owning a large and valuable estate while being restricted to an annual sum by the provisions of the settlement. This, of course, was the object of entailing, so that the property should be preserved and not dissipated by the extravagance of a tenant for life.

From Talbot's reply to Fair's letter it is clear that he was heavily overdrawn and payment had not been received from several expected sources: the tithe lease, railway money and drawback from probate duty paid after his father's death.

> You make use of one expression 'to say nothing of indulgences'; now this expression I cannot allow and do not wish it to be a correct one. I

> am very uneasy at your statement and now fully understand the curse of landed property, it is work, work, work; economise for your life; however, I shall await with considerable anxiety your answer to this, and remember, I wish to know how I stand. However, we have a large stock at Lytham of horses (including mine) and farming stock which can be made available . . . I sincerely wish I had gone and lived abroad as I find myself poorer by far than I was with an *increase of income of £1,500 per annum* and an increased demand on me, of, in proportion, as many thousands . . . as you know I will do anything I can for the property, yet when it comes to a question of *our actual comfort* against the property, while being a life tenant, it may go to the wall.

The reference to disposing of the horses and farm stock at Lytham was a cunning dig at Fair, as Talbot knew full well that he would go to any other extremes to raise the money rather than dispose of his beloved animals on the home farm, his especial interest.

The deal appears to have gone off, as no more is heard of the Charles Street property and, as subsequent events showed, Talbot's financial position was not nearly as desperate as he feared.

One of his anxieties was the Peterborough election campaign, which was proving more expensive than he had anticipated, but he felt that whether he got in or not he would have done his duty in supporting Lord Derby in person and purse. If he was beaten for Peterborough he would be prepared to have another go at North Lancashire if a sufficient sum could be raised by subscription, and was prepared to subscribe himself if another suitable candidate could be found. He was not now a protectionist and comments, 'after Lord Derby comes Bright and Cobden, Sir James Graham and Newcastle, a combination likely to excite alarm in those who may not win in a scramble and I think are to be avoided at some little expense by the Landowners.' [25]

III

IT was in 1852 that the Old County Regiment, or 1st Royal Lancashire Militia (Duke of Lancaster's Own), was ordered by Act of Parliament to recruit its men by volunteering and beat of drum, from the northern districts of the county, including the towns of Manchester and Bolton. John Talbot Clifton, formerly of His Majesty's Life Guards, was appointed Colonel. The regiment had remained disembodied, with no annual training or exercise, for twenty-one years.

During the months of September and October, a new staff of sergeants and N.C.O.s had been appointed and parties were sent to Manchester, Bolton and Ulverston to drum up recruits.

On November 8th, the regiment was called up for twenty-one days' training and exercise at Lancaster, with headquarters at the Kings Arms; nearly all the officers were strangers to each other. At three o'clock in the afternoon all captains with their colour-sergeants went to take over the men assigned to their companies on their arrival by special train from Manchester and Bolton.

> When the train arrived and discharged its contents, the uproar and general appearance of the men gave me some misgivings; it seemed as if the wildest ruffians, the veriest scum from the streets, had been collected as recruits. Very shortly, however, with the assistance of the staff-sergeants, these 500 wild-looking recruits, yelling, shouting and running about in helpless confusion, were got together by their several Captains and were made to fall in and march to Dalton Square. An inspection of the Company proved anything but reassuring, nor was the prospect of commanding such a set of ruffians quite pleasant to contemplate. On the writer, who as senior Captain, had been appointed to the Grenadiers, expressing this opinion to his Colour-Sergeant, Sergeant McCalla, a fine old soldier of His Majesty's 92 Highlanders, he replied, with a quiet smile 'Ye need na be afread, Sir, the're no a canny lot the noo, but I ken afore a week has passed, ye'll find I have licked them into some shape!'[26]

After the officers had dined that night the question arose as to the proper terms in which the Queen's health should be proposed, and after much discussion Colonel Clifton decided it should be 'The Queen, the Duke of Lancaster', which is still the form of words for proposing the Loyal Toast at important functions in Lancashire today.

The rapid progress made in training the men seems to bear out

Sergeant McCalla's prediction that he would 'lick them into some shape', as on November 18th the regiment paraded in Market Square, complete with band playing 'The dead march in Saul', to attend a special service on the day of the funeral of the Duke of Wellington.

On November 28th the men were paid off and sent back to Manchester and Bolton by special train, and Major Williamson remarks in his *History*; 'One of the most disagreeable duties of a Captain of Militia, is that of paying off his Company on the termination of a month's training and exercise. The men usually assemble in the place of payment in a state of some intoxication, many quite unable to sign or mark their names on the acquittance roll!'

In 1853, events were stirring in Europe which led to the Crimean War. The Earl of Sefton, the Lord Lieutenant, received directions from Viscount Palmerston, Secretary of State, to recruit the three Lancashire regiments up to their full strength of 1,200 men each. Accordingly, on May 24th the officers and men assembled at Lancaster for twenty-eight days' training, and it was during this period that Eleanor Cecily, as the Colonel's lady, presented new colours to the regiment. On March 27th, 1854, war was declared and Colonel Clifton lost no time in offering his regiment for foreign service, being in fact, the first offer of a militia regiment to serve abroad during the Crimean War and was ultimately accepted.

Whitehall 9th June 1854

My Lord,

I have the honour to transmit to your Lordship herewith Her Majesty's Warrant, directing your Lordship to draw out and embody the 1st Regiment of Royal Lancashire Militia, in such proportions of the same as Her Majesty may direct, under the hand of one of the principal Secretaries of State, and I am at the same time to signify to your Lordship, Her Majesty's directions that you do draw out and embody 500 men of the said Regiment, and that you do take the necessary steps for carrying the said measure into execution with the least possible delay.

The Queen has been pleased to direct that this Regiment when embodied shall be placed under the orders of the General Commanding-in-Chief.

I have the honour to be,
My Lord,
Your Lordship's most obedient Servt.
Palmerston.

To the Earl of Sefton
Lord Lieutenant of the County of Lancaster (Sig.)
Croxteth Park,
Lancashire.[27]

On receipt of this letter, a general parade of the whole regiment took place on the Giant Axe field, Lancaster, where, the letter having been read to the men, the Colonel selected officers, N.C.O.s and 500 men to form the service companies.

It was while the regiment was quartered at Cambridge Barracks, Portsmouth, awaiting embarkation that an incident occurred which shows that the Lancashire militiamen were not to be tampered with. While on sentry duty at the gate leading from the High Street, Portsmouth, to Portsea, and having been cautioned to let no one pass unchallenged, a militiaman was approached by a number of regulars, who, thinking that he was unaware of his duty, and they being late for tattoo, tried to get past. 'Who goes theere?' came the challenge in broad Lancashire; getting no satisfactory reply he came down to the charge, shouting 'Sergeant of the Guard, look sharp! Here's a lot o' chaps wanting to force guard!', and adding, 'I's got some o' them in sentry box, and gien one or two o' them a bit o' a prod, who tried to disarm me.' [28] 'A bit o' a prod' with the bayonet of those days, would, one imagines be no laughing matter!

Towards the end of July the Royal Wiltshire Regiment of Militia under the command of Colonel Lord Methuen arrived and was quartered at the Clarence Barracks. This resulted in a military riot as there was an antipathy between the two regiments, which had first arisen in 1762 when in camp together at Winchester, and again at Chester in 1781. Major Williamson in his account says how extraordinary it was that the tradition of these past feuds had survived among the men. The two Colonels with their officers managed to supress 'these disgraceful proceedings' and through the influence of the N.C.O.s, the regiments became fast friends, as did their Colonels.[29]

On August 25th, Prince Albert arrived in Portsmouth from Osborne and inspected all the troops in garrison. 'His Royal Highness was also pleased to notice the band of the 1st Royal Lancashire Militia, and expressed his surprise and admiration at its superior performance, remarking to the General that it was one of the best bands he had heard for some time'.

The regimental mascot was not, however, a success: 'a fine, bald-faced stag from the Highlands of Scotland', which marched with the band and was kept in a shed, but was also allowed to roam the Barrack Square. The men taught it all kinds of tricks to obtain food and it soon became a nuisance. One evening, after mess, the officers were alarmed by feminine screams, followed by a loud crash from the staircase adjoining the mess room. Upon rushing out they found part of the balustrade broken down and a woman lying at the foot of the stairs with the stag standing over her, eating the contents of her basket, with his antlers still wedged in the broken bannisters. The woman, an old hawker, had come to sell cakes, fruits and other wares to the servants and the stag, scenting the basket, had followed her from the Barrack Square to the stairs leading to the mess kitchen. The woman, who was screaming 'The Devil! Murder! I'm being kilt!,' had received some serious wounds. After attacking several of the men, one of whom was a hospital case, the stag was dismissed from the service, one might presume with disgrace! He was sent to Lancashire where he was shot some months later at Feniscowles Park after nearly killing a man.

March 3rd 1855 was a proud day for the regiment, as with band playing, colours unfurled, and Colonel Clifton riding at the head with his lady riding beside him, the lads from Lancashire marched through the streets of Portsmouth to embark in the transport *Calcutta* for Corfu. This was the first militia regiment selected by government to serve abroad and they received a great send off from the inhabitants. Just before embarkation, a brooch was presented by the officers, N.C.O.s and men of the regiment to Mrs Clifton, who was most popular.

From Corfu the Colonel wrote to James Fair,

> Here we are waiting to go ashore; as the men were becoming somewhat restive I had a fellow flogged yesterday, pray do not mention it to Mrs Clifton as I should not like it to get into the newspapers. I trust the partridges at Warton are doing well this year!

From Corfu the regiment went to Zante, where they arrived in May 1855, enjoying general good health until, in the middle of September, cholera broke out among the troops and townspeople. In the space of fourteen days, one officer, two non-commissioned officers and 275 privates were dead and fifty-four men invalided. Drafts to replace these losses were sent out from the depot at Lancaster, but by the time the regiment was again up to strength, the war was over.

What a tragic anti-climax to all the training and preparation for war of the men who had volunteered to go to the Crimea; to die a loathsome death against which musket and bayonet were of no avail.

Augustus Wykeham, the Colonel's youngest brother, was also at the Crimea; commissioned 2nd Lieutenant in the Rifle Brigade at the age of sixteen, he served in Africa during the Kaffir and Basuto wars, where he and the Hon. Henry Clifford became close friends. Thomas Baines in his journal, relates how he met the two lieutenants, who were travelling northwards in search of game:

> After partaking of a better breakfast than for some time had fallen to my lot, I continued my journey; and my friends, resolved to let slip no opportunity of making a closer acquaintance with the *feral* of South

> Africa, saddled up for the chase, taking leave of me with their warmest wishes for my success and a comfortable prophecy, moreover, that some of these fine days I should get my throat cut.[30]

After its second campaign in Africa the regiment returned to England, landing in January 1854, and in July of that year embarked for the Crimea. At Malta where the transport *Orinoco* put in for coaling, Clifton, or 'Gusty' as he was known in the regiment, won a wager by swimming from his ship to a French transport vessel whilst towing a dozen of champagne.[31]

Clifton was soon struck down by sickness. Clifford in a letter to his parents says, 'My dear friend Gusty Clifton is on his back with dysentery. My duties and the distance his camp is off me prevents me paying him what little attention I could if together.'[32]

It was during the Battle of Inkerman that Clifford won the Victoria Cross. He was A.D.C. to Major General Sir George Buller, and, being mounted, charged with the 77th Regiment. Observing enemy skirmishers trying to flank some of the 77th, he charged the nearest; his revolver missing fire, he drew his sword nearly decapitating one of the Russians and almost severing the arm of another, thereby saving the life of a soldier. Clifford had a distinguished army career, becoming Major General the Hon. Sir Henry Clifford.

Violet Clifton told how, soon after her marriage to John Talbot the second in 1907, Wykeham was staying at the Hall and one winter's morning, on his coming down to breakfast, she said 'What a cold day, Uncle Wykeham,' and he replied, 'Yes, my dear, but not as cold as it was at Balaclava, by God!'

IV

THE Clifton records enable us to draw aside the curtains of time in order to reveal glimpses of the family's way of life during the period of its greatest affluence, commencing with the victory of Waterloo and ending with the outbreak of the First World War. The Enclosure Acts, better drainage, improved methods of husbandry and injections of capital from wealthy manufacturers all helped to increase the returns from the land until, in the 1870s, England was flooded with produce from the prairies of North America, which meant the ruin of British agriculture for years to come.

The Clifton estate, however, was not wholly dependent on agriculture for its income, as the barren sand land bordering the Ribble estuary was already producing a richer and more easily harvested crop in the form of ground rents from the new houses being built by the wealthy manufacturers from the inland towns. This development increased with the coming of the railway in 1846, which made travel between Lytham and the various centres of industry an easy matter. One wonders, also, if some of these newly rich wished to move their families away from the industrial centres, where the appalling conditions under which the mill workers existed had sparked off the riots of 1842 which started at Stalybridge and spread to all Lancashire, until suppressed by the military.

Due to preoccupation with his political career and his regiment during the Crimean War, John Talbot did not have a great deal of time to devote to his estate until the end of hostilities in 1856. Even then, owing to indifferent health, he spent a lot of time yacht cruising in the Mediterranean. Whilst his agent, James Fair, was an extremely able man and dealt with the multifarious matters that arise in the management of a large landed estate, some decisions arose which, strictly, should only be made by the squire. In his absence many of these matters were dealt with by his wife Cecily, as advised by James Fair, and this led to a considerable amount of correspondence between the two, as she, during the hunting season, was usually staying at Catmose Lodge or Barleythorpe Hall or at the town house during the London season. James's handwriting was appalling and his nephew had to make fair copies of his letters for sending; fortunately, some of the drafts have been preserved, a typical specimen of which follows:

Dear Mrs Clifton,

I received your note yesterday and beg as you request, to enclose the envelope. Whatever irregularities may happen at Oakham P.O., I am afraid we are not exempt at our own Lytham, judging from what too frequently occurs to myself, but I have hitherto foreborne making complaints to the authorities for the dreadful affliction of two of Mrs Crook's daughters who doubtless are a source of great anxiety to her.

I am glad you approve of the Bishop's account being settled, I saw at once from the tone of his note to the Colonel that it could soon turn out a County court affair and in the absence of a contract his own people would readily give such evidence as would obtain a verdict against the Colonel, heavy costs would have been given, to say nothing of the annoyance caused by contesting the case unsuccessfully.[33]

The rabbits go to Mr Leslie tomorrow morning.

Dr. Hammond who attends the old woman Atkinson called here on Wednesday and told me he had prescribed Bark and Port Wine for her. I at once had a bottle of wine sent from Knowles. I heard on Saturday afternoon and again this morning that she was very poorly but I will take care she is not left without proper nourishing support.

Young Shepherd at present sleeps in the Plate Pantry at the Hall as I have really been unable to find an elderly person to do so, but I have every confidence in him and he is armed with an old double barrelled gun which I have requested Cunningham to see kept in good order. I have likewise arranged for Old Dash from the Kennels (a capital watch dog) to make the Hall his head quarters and he has the range of the court yard at night.

I am quite of your opinion that the coming winter is to be a very trying one and every precaution should be taken to prevent both burglaries and poaching. Eleven of the latter fraternity paid a visit to Clifton last week and I should not feel at all surprised to hear of an encounter between a gang of them and our own people but I have arranged with Cunningham that such Hares and Cock Pheasants as the Colonel authorised to be thinned should be killed this week as soon as Ridgeway meeting is over and in the meantime and during the coursing I have given the Keeper extra assistance especially for night watching. Cunningham knows the Hen Pheasants are not to be shot and how many Cocks can be spared and the Hares for many reasons ought to be reduced which in some degree at least will lessen the temptation to the poacher.

You mentioned Mr Wakefield, Miss Wilson, Mr Robinson, with some others having some game and the Colonel told me to send to Mrs Clifton and Colonel Henry. You did not mention Miss Hall or Dr. Hammond and I think a little might go to the neighbouring Clergymen as they may think far more of it than the value of the present they receive.

You astonish me about the dry weather in the Midland Counties. We had again our share of rain on Thursday and Friday but am glad to say escaped the effects of the storm on Saturday which appears to have raged fearfully elsewhere.

I think your roan horse fetched a capital price.

I do hope I shall soon hear a better account of Colonel Lowther than that you were good enough to give me. I am glad you like the linen.

Rent days begin on Monday next and for which I will have my revolvers put in good working order and after Tuesday week I will let you know the result.

I have the honour to be your obedient Servant
James Fair.

The letter gives a clear picture of how Fair and Cecily managed things in the absence of the Colonel. The letter indicates her concern for the sick and the poor, for which she was well known, and from Fair's reference to Oakham Post Office, that she was staying at Catmose Lodge for the hunting season. On such occasions the whole establishment of butler, cook, maids, footmen, grooms, horses and carriages were moved to the hunting box for the season and then on to the London town house. Silver, glass, napery and wines would be packed in hampers and the whole ménage travelled by train to their destination. Game in season was also sent in hampers by train, together with fruit, vegetables and flowers from the walled gardens and greenhouses at Lytham.

In the absence of the establishment the Hall was closed, the furniture covered in dust sheets, the internal wooden shutters to the windows closed, and the securing bars dropped into place. There were, of course, sufficient daily staff left to keep an eye on the place and open up the house on the return of the family, when two cows in milk had to be supplied by the estate. The mention of young Shepherd with his old double-barrelled gun sleeping on the premises with Old Dash, the watchdog, indicates that the house was completely closed down and that fears were entertained that it might be broken into. This, coupled with the mention of poaching gangs at Clifton, and James preparing his revolvers for the rent days, confirms the poverty and unrest of the town workers, many of whom were unemployed due to the cotton famine caused by the American Civil War, 1861-1865. The Ridgeway meeting was the hare coursing event held at Peel, between Lytham and Blackpool, and was the forerunner of the Waterloo Cup now held at Altcar near Liverpool.

The Game Laws then were not quite so savage as they had been prior to 1831, when it was illegal for anyone to buy or sell game, which had resulted in the prices obtained by professional poachers being much increased. It was also illegal for anyone below the status of a squire or a squire's eldest son to kill game, even on the invitation of the owner; this, however, could be evaded by a process known as 'deputation'. By a law of 1816, a man who was caught at night in possession of nets for taking hares or rabbits could be transported for seven years. The protection of game preserves by the use of mantraps and spring guns which could kill and maim was legal until abolished by an Act of 1827.[34]

Upon receiving word that a certain well-known poacher had been taken, the Colonel wrote to Fair: 'Ask Mr Greene, the Inspector at Kirkham for a certificate of his conviction, name in full and whether a pensioner of Army or Navy, and his habitual residence.' This information was to be sent to the authorities with a view to getting his pension stopped: 'I have heard of him for some time and intend to get him well trounced; it is a very bad case, it could only be excused for want, which plea the fellow has not got.' He learned later that the authorities would not stop a pension for a felony.

During January 1861, Fair reported to the Colonel that heavy poaching was occurring at Westby and that seven watchers were out every night: 'the keeper has not had his clothes off for two nights in twelve'.

The Colonel and Cecily were devoted followers of the hunt when in Rutland, riding hard and sometimes taking tosses which they affected to make light of. 'I got a fall this morning hunting', writes the Colonel to James Faïr, 'and a fellow jumped on the top of me and broke my collar bone, which tho' of no great consequence is a great bore at the beginning of the season as it will be a month before I can ride again I suppose'. He writes again in about a fortnight's time, 'I thought you would be glad to find I was much easier and better and hope in three weeks or a month to be in the Pig Skin again.'

Cecily also wrote to James from Catmose Lodge, 'I had rather a disagreeable fall hunting yesterday, but I hope in a few days to be all right. I pitched on my head, which made me rather faint at the time, I have strained all the muscles of my neck and shoulder, besides sundry bruises on my face; it was a great bore, as the Hounds were having a good run and I was obliged to come home.'

Shortly before these episodes the Colonel had written, 'Hunting every day, very conducive to health!'

Shooting also held a prominent place in the family's sporting activities and, although Lytham was not one of the classic shoots, quite respectable bags were taken and many notable personages were guests at the Hall during the season.

Thomas Joseph - the Treeplanter - was, in his own words, 'no sportsman', and makes little mention of shooting in his letters, although game formed a large part of their diet in season. Hares (usually leverets), rabbits, dotterel and sometimes partridge were caught by the keepers for the pot, though partridge, pheasant and woodcock were usually only shot by the gentry. No mention of wild fowl is made in correspondence or game books, despite the fact that the area abounded in wild duck and geese.

As the countryside was somewhat bare of natural cover, the estate, and indeed most of the Fylde, has man-made tree plantations which were intended to hold game, act as windbreaks for livestock and relieve an otherwise barren landscape.

Before St. Anne's-on-the-Sea was built, the area between Lytham and Blackpool consisted of sand dunes and starr grass extending about a quarter of a mile inland from high water mark and had become a vast rabbit warren. Partridge were also numerous and in 1856 eleven thousand rabbits and nearly a thousand partridge were taken! The rabbits were mainly netted by the keepers and sent to market. Hares were very prolific over the rest of the estate and in the same year over two thousand were shot. As already mentioned, hare coursing attracted large numbers of spectators until the meeting was transferred to Altcar.

It was after the Crimean War that military and political friends of the Colonel, as well as relationships created by marriage, produced shooting parties including many well-known names. Lord Ranelagh – for whom the Colonel, as a young man, had acted as second in the affair with Count Paul Esterhazy – made one of the shooting party on several occasions in 1857-58. On October 12th, 1859 the guns were H.R.H. The Duke of Cambridge, Lord Methuen, Hon. Percy Barrington, Col. B. B. Wood, Mr G. C. Bentinck,[35] Mr Randolptious de Trafford, Col. Fitzroy Campbell, Col. Henry Clifton and Col. J. T. Clifton.

Further idea of the abundance of hares is given by the game book entry for three days in December 1882, when Lord Stair, Lord Carnegie, Col. Stanley, Mr Bromley Davenport, Mr James Lowther, Mr Wykeham Clifton and Mr Quintin Agnew shot 846 hares, and during November the following year, Lord Elgin, Lord Edward Cavendish, the Rt. Hon. Col. Stanley, Mr James Lowther and Mr Agnew shot 1,087 hares, also in three days.

Such slaughter would not appeal to most modern shots, many of whom will not raise their gun to a hare, but the damage done to the tenants' crops by such numbers necessitated their reduction. In the early 1900s however, the hare population was ravaged by a venereal disease and the whole stock had to be destroyed and replaced with fresh blood from Scotland.

The Colonel kept a keen eye on the political scene and in April 1860 comments, 'I hear the Reform Bill is not likely to pass owing to its being about to be much mutilated. I hope it will not pass, but if it does it will be a retributive justice on the radical cotton spinners as it will swamp even their influences!'

In another letter to Fair he says –

> In considering the case of a future county election I do not see how I can even afford to stand for it, as supposing it cost £5,000 I could get £1,000 subscribed, and I see my way to no more, if so much, the balance would be more than I could afford. Preston is different and the cost can be counted in hundreds instead of thousands. I am persuaded that if gentlemen in my position do not exert themselves the representation will fall into very low hands and tho' all elections are expensive yet we must accept them as a part of our position – if you can make any person go to Oxford to vote against Gladstone, do, he is a rascal and has stated he intends to put all the taxation on the land. Lord Derby says he will not again accept office, I am very sorry for it.

He then wrote from 38 Portman Square, their town house, saying that he had been very unwell and after having a chill had 'a little congestion of the brain' which was so unpleasant that he had gone to town to see his doctor. The condition was responding to 'cupping and calomel', and he hoped to return and resume his hunting in about ten days. He did return, and Fair received another note: 'Sending on Monday per train a black Russian puppy retriever, six months old, for Cookson in the sand hills to break in, name is 'Moses' and he is to be vaccinated for small pox, anywhere he cannot scratch, as it is a certain preventive for the distemper.' A later letter says, 'don't bother as he has already had distemper!'

The Colonel's condition, however, seems to have given his wife considerable concern, and she writes to Fair, 'for tho' he certainly is far from well, yet his illness shows a tendency to apathy, not irritability, and we endeavour to rouse and make him think of things as much as possible . . . the Colonel is rather tenacious at not being considered *quite well* and therefore it wd. be a great misfortune if he took it into his head that I was interfering in any way that I am not accustomed to.'

On Heyhouses Lane, between Lytham and St. Anne's-on-the-Sea, the Trawlboat Inn used to flourish and in 1821, according to Whittle in his *Marina,* one of the attractions for visitors to Lytham was 'You may trip to the Heyhouses and get bad ale.' One afternoon Cecily was driving past with James Fair and, observing a large number of the farm tenants enjoying a somewhat noisy carousel – despite the bad ale – said, 'Mr Fair, have that house closed immediately.' And closed it was, shedding the hearty conviviality of a house of good cheer for the sober respectability of a farm dwelling!

During the London season a weekly shuttle service went on between Lytham and 38 Portman Square by means of two hampers, one large and one small. When a dinner party was pending, the large hamper was usually dispatched containing, as available in approp-riate season, pheasants, partridge, leverets, rabbits, dotterel, plover eggs, four or five couple of fowls and occasionally half a lamb. Plover eggs were collected by the gamekeeper who visited marked nests daily to ensure the eggs were fresh-laid. They were hard boiled, rubbed over with olive oil and then wrapped in cotton wool ready for sending. Cecily gave precise instructions as to packing grapes: 'they should be lightly covered with silver paper, then the *smooth* side of cotton wool put round them, the outer or soft side of the cotton being next to the basket or box in which they are packed.'

The butterman in London was charging one shilling and eight pence per pound for the family, and one shilling and four pence for the servants, so Fair was instructed to send butter from Lytham at fifteen shillings the stone.

On 31st December 1862, Cecily took up residence in 2 Grosvenor Square, which the Colonel had purchased as the lease of 38 Portman Square had run out. Cecily wrote, 'considering the handsome house that it is, and the situation being the best in London, I do not think, tho' the sum sounds large that it is at all too much.' Unfortunately, she does not mention what the sum was, but the house was resold five years later to Sir William Hutt for £22,000.

The Colonel was a member of the Royal Yacht Squadron and had his own graving dock at Lytham. His last two yachts were *RYS Derwent,* a large two-masted schooner and *RYS Taurus,* a three-masted screw schooner.

The Manor of Lytham was unusual in that its southerly boundary extended to the low-water mark of ordinary tides or the centre of the main channel of the River Ribble, whereas usually the shore between high- and low-water marks is vested in the Crown. With the ownership went the rights of piscary, anchorage and wreck, and the estate had its own custom house for the collection of tolls. Vessels would anchor on the beach and discharge their cargoes into lighters, which floated up to Preston on the tide, as the river was then only navigable by light-drafted craft. Early in the nineteenth century the shipowners of Preston – who keenly resented paying toll – decided to challenge the squire's right, and a captain who had anchored his ship on the beach refused payment. That night at low water the squire's bailiff arrived with workmen, horses and wains and, cutting the cables, loaded both anchors into the wains and took them up to Lytham Hall! This sparked off a great lawsuit – which the squire won – and a few years afterwards he built the first Lytham Dock, which was leased to the Ribble Navigation Company in 1841, and continued to be used for shipping until the new dock at Preston was built and the Ribble dredged to permit shipping to use the new port in the 1890s.

The Ribble estuary has always been notorious for its shifting sands and fast-running tides and many a ship has come to grief there. When returning from the Mediterranean – his favourite cruising ground – the Colonel would write from Cowes requesting Fair to instruct a Captain Whalley to meet the yacht at Kingstown, and from there pilot her into Lytham.

Writing to Fair in 1860, he said 'Glad to hear the Life-boat has again been of use; it is a noble institution. I regret to see how few subscribers there are in Lytham, some of the money the Parsons collect would be better bestowed on saving life!'

Fair kept him well posted as to affairs in Lytham: the building of the baths, housing development, the Lytham Dock, tree planting (always going on) and the new railroad from Lytham to Blackpool. The latter project necessitated taking down the main gates to the Hall, which stood near the centre of the village, and re-erecting them on the north side of the line which severed the original main entrance drive. In writing from Naples in January 1863 he comments 'and mind and get the drive to the new Lodge finished for me by the time I return and don't get an ugly old woman for Peggy's successor as she will make the horses shy in passing the gate!'

V

IT was in 1859 that the Volunteer movement commenced in Britain, owing to uncertainty as to the intentions of Napoleon III in Europe, and Lytham had its Rifle Corps, composed of locals who drilled and manoeuvred under the command of one Captain Lennox. Bazaars were held and subscriptions raised to provide suitable uniform clothing.

The Dowager, Mrs Hetty Clifton, wrote from 16 Park Lane:

> I shall have much pleasure, dear Mr Fair, in being one of the Patronesses for the Bazaar for your gallant Volunteers. When Mrs Clifton has paid what she means to give I will add my *mite; less* than hers.

Captain Lennox, however, had to decamp hurriedly from Lytham as it had been revealed that he had swindled several leading locals and a number of tradespeople and shopkeepers. His two yachts had been seized and executions taken out against him. There was no suggestion that he had misappropriated Rifle Corps funds, but he resigned his command, which pleased Fair as no interference by Colonel Clifton was necessary.

Whilst battling with the manifold problems of the estate and the growing town, Fair kept an ever-increasing correspondence with Cecily and other members of the family, all of whom had their own particular queries and problems for James to sort out.

Thomas Henry, now forty-one years of age, a Lieutenant Colonel and unmarried, lived in the Albany but looked after Hetty, his mother, living in Park Lane. He was still *aide-de-camp* to the Duke of Cambridge and a Deputy Ranger of Richmond Park. He requested that a sow in pig should be sent to him at the Albany, which arrived within three days, and whilst eagerly awaiting a successful farrowing he was suddenly overcome with anxiety as to how the piglets were to be safely penned! Fair may have quietly enjoyed the thought that this was one problem the Colonel would have to sort out for himself.

He also requested that the keeper be instructed to send some live hares to Richmond Park as had been done previously. The Lytham hares were famous for their quality and were in considerable demand by other estates for freshening up the local strain. They were caught up and sent to the Earl of Lonsdale, Lord Methuen and other landowners, as well as to the Duke of Cambridge.

Thomas Henry was promoted Major General and in 1877 married Annie, Lady Cosmo Russell, widow of Lord Cosmo George Russell, ninth son of the 6th Duke of Bedford. They lived at Robin Hood Farm, Kingston Vale, Surrey, where he died in 1900. His ideal in domestic arrangements was 'good stables and a house attached to them!'

Charles Frederick, the third son of Thomas and Hetty, born in 1822, had gained a BA at Oxford but little is heard of him until in 1853 when he marries Lady Edith Maud, eldest daughter of the 2nd Marquis of Loudoun and Hastings. In August 1856 they are living at Dallars House, Kilmarnock, which had been lent to them by Lady Bute, Lady Edith's aunt, and which was near Loudoun Castle. As usual with the younger members of the family, Frederick was hard up. When he married he had been endowed with a terrace of newly erected houses in Lytham called Hastings Place, in honour of his bride, which were apparently rather slow in letting and for the next year or so he plagued James Fair with schemes for cashing in on them. He had raised a mortgage on them for a thousand pounds, but considered the rate of interest exorbitant and wanted to raise a loan at a lower rate and pay off the mortgage.

In explaining to Fair how he thought this could be managed, by money due to his wife and rents due to him, he mentioned that he had in hand about twenty-three pounds, and finished his letter saying:

> I am in want of a lad or young man to act under a butler. I want one about seventeen or eighteen, but well grown and likely in a year or two to become a good footman. I would as soon have one that has never been in service. Should you know of anyone at all shapeable and willing will you let me know, of course the wages would not be great at present, but he would learn his business.

Even in those days it was important to get one's priorities right.

During January 1857 he asks for his quarter's allowance in advance, as Lady Edith has been very ill and he has been obliged to have a doctor from Edinburgh to assist the local man and the poor lady is now wrapped up in flannel and cotton wool. She had recently had another child - they had four sons and two daughters - and Frederick comments rather sadly:

> As you know, my family increases, but my income remains the same, which causes some difficulty in making the two ends meet, thus you must excuse my pertinacity in writing about my houses.

In October 1857 they moved to Mid-Ascoy House near Rothesay, Bute and Frederick writes to Fair with another scheme whereby he wishes to borrow £3,000 in order to buy some land:

> We find living in the country without occupation very dull work, indeed impossible to continue, so either we must live in Town, which would be very expensive, or else find some means of amusing ourselves in the country. To do this we must have a little land of our own. By borrowing a little money on the houses and the rest on the land itself we should be able to buy some; it would be as cheap a way of housing ourselves as any, and even if I were so desperate as to farm a little, I do not think I could lose if we consumed the produce ourselves and my household do seem to eat a great deal. Do not mention this plan to any one yet; of course the first step is to borrow a little money, so perhaps you wd. try if you can succeed in doing so. I would like very well to sell my annuity of £300 a year if I knew how to do it, or what it was likely to fetch as then the produce of it might be invested in land and settled for those who will survive me. It really would be a great thing to borrow a little money, so I hope you will do what you can.

This was penned on 31st July, 1858 and on the 8th August he writes to Fair again, announcing 'a great thing' that neither he nor Lady Edith appear to have realised was about to happen. Let him speak for himself:

> I wrote to Colonel Clifton some days ago and begged him to tell you of Lady Edith's accession of wealth, of course we are much pleased. We always had expected to inherit something considerable from Sir Charles but not as much as we do.[36] The deed settling the land is dated /44, so that it is no wonder that he was particular abt. Lady Edith's marriage, the will is dated /54 a year after our marriage and I am gratified at this, as it shews that he was pleased with us and our goings on. In case of Lady Edith[37] succeeding her brother the land passes to Lady Bertha, but there is doubt whether this is legal, the legacy and succession duty will be heavy, not under £20,000 I fear, and we find that since the deed of settlement Sir Charles had purchased some 12,000 or 15,000 worth of land which we shall probably have to buy back as it passes to his heir at Law Jn. Abney, of course the money I requested you to borrow on my houses will not be required for the purposes I then spoke of. Still if you could get it me at four per cent (I mean the £3,000) I should like it, if not I will not borrow any, as I grudge the expense of deeds but will pay off Miss Wilson in six months or less – We proceed to 6 Cavendish Square tomorrow.

Under the conditions of the settlement made by Sir Charles in 1844, Charles Frederick was authorised to assume the surname and arms of Abney Hastings, which he did in 1859, and on the death of her brother the 4th Marquis in 1868, Lady Edith became Countess of Loudoun.

Despite Lady Edith's stroke of good fortune in 1858, Frederick was still feeling the pinch in 1864 and bombarding Fair with letters about selling his houses; 'I want all the money I can get to buy myself a place of my own. For any interest or occupation or benefit I get from

Lady Edith's estates, she might as well be as poor as when first I married her, and as I like all the occupations arising from the possession of land I am anxious to get some of my own. Hence my reason for pressing for money.'

Upon Lady Edith becoming Countess, however, money must have become less of a problem and they certainly moved in the highest circles. Their eldest son, Charles Edward Hastings Abney Hastings, who became the 11th Earl on the death of his mother in 1874, married the Hon. Alice Mary Elizabeth Fitzalan Howard, and their second daughter, Lady Flora, married Henry, 15th Duke of Norfolk. On 4th May 1880, Frederick was created Baron Donnington of Donnington Park, Leicester, and died on 24th July 1895.

On 11th December, 1855, Captain Augustus Wykeham Clifton, then aged twenty-six and newly back from the Crimea, married Lady Bertha Lelgarde, sister of Lady Edith. As when Lady Edith became Countess of Loudoun on the death of her brother, the 4th Marquis, Lady Bertha became the twenty-third holder of the Barony Grey de Ruthyn. The barony fell into abeyance on the death of the Marquis but was terminated in Lady Bertha's favour by Act of Parliament in December 1885. This very ancient title goes back to 1324 and when the son of Wykeham and Lady Bertha succeeded his mother, who died in December 1887, he became Rawdon George Grey Clifton, Baron Grey de Ruthyn, hereditary bearer of the gold spur at the coronation of the Sovereign.[38]

There is little reference to Wykeham Clifton in the records and he very seldom wrote to James Fair. He was not particularly well off; he seems to have been an amicable, easy-going sort of man. In 1871 he took up residence at Warton Hall (a small mansion near Lytham) that had been renovated for him by the estate. He became a popular and well-loved figure in Lytham, attended St. John's Church and enjoyed a drink and a chat with the locals.

If, on Sundays, the sermon seemed to be growing tedious and Wykeham's thoughts were beginning to forsake worship for visions of lunch and a comforting glass, he would open his purse and lay down, with some deliberation, five separate shillings on the pew shelf in full view of the vicar. He would then snap open his gold hunter and after one minute had passed, remove one shilling, another minute, another shilling; usually the vicar's discourse ended before Wykeham's contribution to the collection had dropped to three pieces of silver!

VI

AS Christmas approaches, the winter of 1861 is hardening in with severe frost and snow and Cecily agrees that Fair should put on a dinner for the poor fishermen and workpeople in the Colonel's employ.

During December the vicar of St. Cuthbert's writes in great agitation to Fair, telling him that his eldest daughter has agreed to marry a local widower of whom he does not approve – 'There is no prospect before Agnes if she is headstrong and unguided by our wishes, but poverty and misery, and how any Widower with four children can be so cruel and selfish as to kidnap a child from her home is to me marvellous'. As the vicar has been advised to leave the district on health grounds, he asks if the Colonel would agree to him exchanging his living.

In the absence of the Colonel, the matter is of course referred to the lady of the manor who is truly sorry for the minister – in her opinion Agnes was always a headstrong girl, but must have been very anxious to leave home if willing to bind herself to the widower for the rest of her life, and as regards the exchange of living, 'it is difficult for me to say anything. I do not like the notion of it at all, as I really think St. Cuthbert's Church ought to be distinctly in the Colonel's power, as it is more in conjunction with the family and Hall, than the other end of the Parish and, of course, it makes a great difference to us, who, is in residence there – The Clergy are not what they used to be, I mean the same class of men, and if we happened to get a person there, like some I could mention, it wd. be a great annoyance and I do not see how we could depend on Mr Robinson's selection, as you are aware his acquaintances must necessarily be limited. I think it would be almost better to suggest that he took leave for a year, not much harm cd. be done in that time and perhaps matters might be more comfortably arranged.'

James Fair's character assessment of the amorous widower was that of a 'sanctified humbug!'

Hard times had come to Lytham, as in most of Lancashire, and Fair was very pleased to report that he had eighty of ninety hands all belonging to the property working on the extension of roads and the levelling down of sand dunes to create new building sites. Those so employed were from elderly men down to strong lads, and Fair seriously believed that half of them would have otherwise been thrown 'on the parish'. 'This rather puts upon the office at present but I know in the end it will be profitable and a good return for the expenditure will ensue.

How right he was, as the future proved.

Things were so bad that Lord Derby called a meeting in Manchester in aid of the Lancashire districts and in the Colonel's absence abroad, Fair was asked by Cecily to attend.

> I enclose the circular sent to the Colonel, you see how the subscriptions are not a matter of choice but in a manner compulsory (thanks to the *Times* which always toadies the Manufacturers) and I would be very sorry that in a crisis like the present when all the Lancashire Land owners are coming forward to assist, that the Colonel should be backward in doing so – You see Ld. Derby being now Chairman of the Meeting, some letter of apology should be sent, and also I suppose, a further subscription must be sent.

Later she writes,

> I would like the Colonel's subscription to be on equal terms with other gentlemen of his position in the County.

Fair, on her instructions, was sending supplies of clothing for the poor of neighbouring Kirkham, badly hit by the slump.

Another worry for Fair, and sometimes a matter of acute anxiety, were the sea defences of the estate, whose low-lying lands were often threatened by savage gales from the Irish Sea. The tides in the Ribble estuary have a rise of up to thirty feet on springs and even medium tides when whipped up by south-west gales could overtop the embankments, sometimes causing their collapse and serious flooding of the farm lands. In January 1863, for example, violent gales lashed the coast and the estate suffered severe damage. Lytham lighthouse, situated on the sand dunes, crashed to the ground, undermined by the elements.

Thomas Henry, son and heir and only child of the Colonel and Cecily, was sixteen in 1861 and on leaving Eton his tutor and housemaster, Russel Day, wrote informing them, rather sadly, that he did not pursue his Greek and Latin studies *con amore,* his health was not robust and 'a scholar he will not be'.

What seems to be his first letter to James Fair has not the graceful flowing prose of his grandfather, Thomas Joseph:

> My Dear Mr Fair,
>
> Mama has asked me to write to you and tell you we are going away Monday to the Isle of Wight, therefore if you have anything to write to Mama will you direct it to the Gloucester Hotel, Cowes. Mama says she is quite satisfied with the Plan you sent and we will explain it to Papa when he comes, Mama had a letter from Papa and he does not expect to be at Cowes before the 12th or 14th. Mama says she is delighted that Sir

T. Hesketh got such a large majority. We are looking forward to the Plover eggs as you said the keepers were finding them.

Having no more to say,
I remain yours
Harry Clifton.

He was, however, to cut the first sod for the new railway from Lytham to Blackpool and was to sail from Cowes to Lytham for the occasion in papa's yacht as a special treat. At school he had joined the Eton Volunteers, there being 300 boys in his corps, and he was 'much pleased at having been made a corporal'.[39]

In November 1861, Cecily is again staying at Catmose Lodge, the Colonel is on a Mediterranean cruise and Master Harry has been sent to Paris with his tutor – 'Mr Clifton [Harry] don't write in spirits, but I hope he will cheer up when he begins to know a little French'. Her father, Colonel Lowther, is in town and has been suffering from an eye affliction for some time – 'My father's eye has only just commenced to show any active sign of improvement, the D[octo]rs. are trying to give him more strength by ordering him to take Brandy and water and Port Wine, so that I hope he will soon now be much better'. Soon after, however, she writes that he has received a setback as his horse, slipping, threw back its head breaking his spectacles!

In January 1862, Cecily hears from Henry's tutor in Paris and writes to Fair that

all is not going on quite satisfactorily there in the matter of Learning. I consider it expedient that I should just run over to Paris and see how matters really are . . . If any one asks about me, you need only say I am gone to Paris *to see* Harry, as there are no complaints made of his conduct (in fact the Tutor says he is very steady), only he is so idle and I never spare myself trouble for his benefit now that I am so wholly responsible.

She writes from Paris, 'found Harry looking well and grown a little, he does not like Paris at all and required a little talking to, to make him more diligent, I hope, however, my visit will benefit both him and the tutor.'

The arrival of mama must have been something of a shock to both Harry and the tutor, and despite her restrained comments it is pretty certain that she administered a salutary lecture to them both.

In accordance with the military tradition of the family, Thomas Henry was commissioned Lieutenant in his father's regiment, the 1st Royal Lancashire – The Duke of Lancaster's Own – at the tender age of seventeen, on September 25th 1862, being promoted Captain in April 1868.[40] Having attained his majority, and as was customary with a settled estate, he now joined with his father in various transactions and gradually became involved with its administration.

In 1867 he married Madeline Diana, daughter of Sir Andrew

Agnew, 8th Baronet of Lochnaw, Wigtown, who had married Lady Louisa Noel, daughter of Charles, First Earl of Gainsborough. Thomas Henry's aunt, Augusta Mary Lowther, had married Gerard James Noel, the second son of the Earl. Violet Clifton states that Thomas Henry 'grew up endowed with a brilliant mind, and cursed with a scarlet temper. He had never felt himself cherished at home'.[41] His mental brilliance seems a little surprising in view of Russel Day's report from Eton and his apparent reluctance to learn; it is, however, understandable that his mother's anxiety for his success, and, as she said, 'being so wholly responsible for him' - due to her husband's failing health and long absences abroad - caused her to be stern and seemingly lacking in affection.

There was one thing Thomas Henry was not slow to learn, and that was how to spend money. Upon marriage he received £625 a quarter, but apparently found this quite inadequate and began showering Thomas Fair - James's eldest son, who had now joined the business - with tradesmen's bills, who had to write to him pointing out that he, Fair, was quite unable to pay them without express written authority. As time went on and the bills remained unpaid, threatening letters began to arrive, and so, like father like son, history repeated itself.

Again, following in father's footsteps, his name is put up for Member of Parliament for North Lancashire and Fair writes anxiously to the Colonel at Algiers hoping that he is not annoyed and expressing hopes that the seat will not be contested. The Colonel approved - probably recalling his own entry into politics and his father's dismay at the possibility of heavy expenses being incurred.

He was, however, elected unopposed in March 1874, and as it was considered essential that he should reside in the county, Ashton Hall, Preston, was taken on lease and there he set up his own establishment. Owing to his parliamentary activities, to which he seems to have applied himself diligently, it was considered that he should also have a town house, and in 1877, No. 5 Richmond Terrace was purchased from Quintin Hogg for £10,000.[42]

The house was built in 1822, and a report made in 1879 gives an enlightening description of its sanitary condition:

> I was not present when the drain was opened but the men report that a very bad smell indeed was emitted. It would seem that the rats having worked their way out of the drain - being made of brick - have made runs in all directions through the entire basement, working their way into the various apartments, consequently, a smell was being continually conveyed from the drain into the house via the rat runs . . . As the old drain contains at present about six inches of soil you may imagine the effluvia that arises from it.

Thomas Henry had never been robust and for the two years before his death in April 1880 had been chronically ill, and his condition could hardly have been helped by the 'effluvia' arising from the drainage system.

As Thomas Henry died before his father, the Colonel, he never became squire and consequently there was not a great deal of correspondence between him and James and Thomas Fair. Because of this we do not get so clear a picture of his personality as of other members of the family.

In 1875, Thomas Henry's six-and-a-half-year old son, John Talbot, laid the foundation stone of St. Anne's-on-the-Sea, and Thomas Fair had an anxious time arranging the ceremony so as to ensure that the date was convenient to everyone concerned. Unfortunately, this appeared to eliminate all dates except All Fool's Day, but to his great relief he managed to arrange it instead for 31st March.

Thomas had to shoulder heavy burdens and responsibilities. Farming was fast deteriorating due to vast imports of cheap corn from the prairies of North America; trade was bad in Lancashire and little building was taking place. In June 1878 he writes to the Colonel in Rome:

> The weather and everything else is rather out of joint in Lancashire and I have been on duty a great many nights for the last month at Clifton Hall and Lea in consequence of the Cotton Riots – So far I am glad to say all is safe at Clifton and I don't think there is any danger, tho' the Military are still there.[43]

It is necessary here to digress, as James Fair died in 1871 and so ended a truly outstanding career as land agent. The most remarkable tribute paid to him was by Lady Cecily who, at her own cost, erected St. Anne's Church to his memory. There can be few land agents who have ever been so commemorated. It was by royal warrant in April 1872 that Eleanor Cecily and her sister Augusta Mary were granted the precedence of Earl's daughters when their brother Henry became 3rd Earl of Lonsdale, and both assumed the title of Lady.

Thomas Fair was born in 1836 and joined his father in the management of the Lytham estates in 1862. He had previously managed their Preston office where a general land agency and surveying practice was conducted. He gradually took over full control as his father's health deteriorated, though the old man took an active interest in all matters up to his death. It was, accordingly, Thomas Fair who now had to deal with the management of the estate and the affairs of the family, including those of Thomas Henry, the heir apparent.

Thomas had inherited his father's zeal for improvement and development, for long they had cherished the idea of a new town amidst the vast tract of sand dunes between Lytham and Blackpool, and the construction of the railway between the two towns made the project even more attractive. On September 4th, 1874, Thomas wrote to the Colonel:

> You will be glad to hear that I have let eighty acres of land at St. Annes for building upon, which I think is a pretty good start and will help to open up the place. The rent for the first two years is £400 a year, third and fourth years £600 a year, and afterwards £800 so that this will pay the interest on the cost of the new Roads and when a few Houses get up I hope we may soon let more land.

The above almost casual reference to the letting of the land was probably the first intimation the Colonel received of the commencement of the town of St. Annes-on-the-Sea, so named after the Parish Church of St. Anne recently built by Lady Cecily. Ultimately, the St. Annes-on-the-Sea Land and Building Company took up some 600 acres and built the pier; but that is another story that has been told elsewhere.[44]

Thomas Henry died young, but he made sure that the name of Clifton should not become extinct, as he had seven children by Madeline in ten years: Madeline Edith (1867), John Talbot (1868), Cuthbert (1870), Constance Gertrude Cecily (1871), Harry Arthur (1874), Frances Victoria (1876) and Charles Carol (1877).

Once again, after his death, the problem of houses arose. Richmond Terrace was too large and expensive and had to be sold. Madeline wished to live at Lytham, but this was vetoed in no uncertain manner by Lady Cecily. Lady Louisa Agnew, mother of Madeline, wrote, rather unwisely, to Lady Cecily asking if she could do something about a house: it was hard being left with seven children and no home, 'and she does so want to live at Lytham. Could she have the Hall, as she hates the idea of living in London.' Most unfortunately she ended by saying: 'She loves Lytham and you don't care for it; never say I have said a word, let it all come from you, it will be so kind and I am sure dear Harry would have loved it.'

It certainly did 'all come' from Lady Cecily, but it was Lady Louisa who got it!

She replied that she had heard from Madeline that she had *decided* to live at Lytham and Lady Cecily does not agree as she thinks it ill advised that Toby (John Talbot junior), as heir apparent, should be brought up in the town. Madeline should consider her own position and that of the girls, as associating with the townspeople would lower her position. As long as Talbot (the Colonel) lives *she,* Lady Cecily, will live at Lytham. Lady Louisa, like many others, was under the wrong impression that she did not like Lytham. In fact, she had very deep interests, 'altho' she does not live in the Hall very much, as it is a large dull house for one alone'. When Harry was alive it was different. She makes a point of never giving advice unless asked to do so, in which case, Madeline should take a small house in London and visit Lytham during the holidays, and in conclusion: 'I wish you to understand that Lytham Hall cannot be given up to Madeline during mine or Talbot's life time.'

So spake the lady of the manor; had she forgotten, one wonders, how, when she married the Colonel, he as a Member of Parliament had sought to live in the Hall as his father was so frequently absent, and how outraged *he* had been at the suggestion?

Lady Cecily's reign however, ended with the death of the Colonel at Hammam Birkha, Algiers, on 16th April 1882. He had again sailed to the Mediterranean in his yacht *Taurus* accompanied by his doctor, C. H. Stanley Stevens. He died of pulmonary catarrh, and his embalmed body was sailed back to Fleetwood in the yacht. He died a Roman Catholic, having embraced the faith of his forefathers in 1874 during one of his frequent visits to Rome. There is a letter from a Fanny Lecroix written in Aix-les-Bains saying that when he came back to Paris from Rome he returned Protestant but again became Roman Catholic before he died. She said Lady Cecily was unaware of these changes.

Thomas Fair must have known, as in writing to Dr. Stevens he says, 'Of course the Service will be a Catholic one.' He was, nevertheless, buried in the family vault in St. Cuthbert's Parish Church.

In the yacht was a number of religious books and it seems that he must have had many struggles with his conscience and whilst at sea seeking bodily health was also seeking spiritual guidance in his religious beliefs. He was, presumably, brought up a Catholic until twelve years of age, when his father turned Protestant in 1831.

Talbot must always have had in mind his father's almost rabid dislike of the Catholics and his own apparent indifference was manifested during his parliamentary campaigns, and in his correspondence with the Fairs.

His last instructions to the trustees under his will were carried out:

> my funeral to be conducted in a plain and unostentatious manner and that my body may be borne to the grave by such twelve labouring men employed on my Estate as they shall select and I bequeath to each such bearer one pound and a suit of mourning.

Thomas Henry having predeceased his father by two years produced problems of administration as John Talbot, his son and heir apparent, was only fourteen years of age when the Colonel died. Under Thomas Henry's will, Madeline, his wife was executrix and guardian of the children.

The Colonel had made a new will in 1867 after Thomas came of age, but had appointed no trustees. The last family settlement had been made on Thomas Henry's marriage and provided in great measure for the management of the estate, and under such settlement, Major Hornby of Dalton Hall, Burton, Westmorland and Lawrence Rawstorne of Hutton Hall, Preston were named trustees.

Madeline had to be provided with £2,000 a year, and a smaller town house in Hill Street, London was purchased for her. In order to finance these arrangements and pay off the Colonel's debts, further economies had to be made. The yacht was sold and, as Fair wrote to her Ladyship, 'every shilling is required to pay off the Banks and other liabilities.'

Chapter Three

John Talbot

CCORDING to Violet Clifton's *Book of Talbot,* he suckled his mother so fiercely that she had a wound on her breast. 'That', said Nurse Patch from Devonshire, 'was the start of the discord between them.' Like his father and grandfather, John Talbot went to Eton and then to Cambridge (his grandfather went to Oxford). Owing to the early death of his father and the long absences of his grandfather abroad, he probably did not receive sufficient male guidance and control at home and resented the efforts of his mother and stern grandmama, Lady Cecily, to discipline him. His childhood was not happy and he had run away at the age of seven, being absent for several days until found in Preston. As he grew up he developed into a character more fitting to an Elizabethan than one born in the nineteenth century. He was proud, adventurous, and often arrogant, but had a deep appreciation of beauty, books and music.

When not at school or university he spent much time at Lytham, where he probably first developed his love of nature and became proficient in the handling of horse and gun.

The first muttering of things to come contained in the records are in a letter from Thomas Fair to Talbot's tutor:

> I am very sorry to hear that you have had so much trouble with Talbot, but as time goes on I sincerely hope that he will show more appreciation and value the good advice and assistance which I am sure you will give him. You can only do your best to influence him and we must hope that as he gets older he will see that it is all for his own advantage and good.

This was written in 1885 when Talbot was seventeen years of age and only just beginning to try his wings.

In January 1887, he sailed for Australia and New Zealand with a Mr Pollock, his medical attendant and companion, as his health required that he should have a sea voyage. This was to take four months for the round trip, and Fair had carefully estimated the cost at £550, which included the return ticket, Pollock's salary, hotel and travelling expenses and £13 15s 0d for wine. Talbot was to have £20 for pocket money, to which he strongly demurred, so, with his mother's consent, it was increased to £25. This was to be doled out by Pollock a few pounds at a time, 'for he seems to have no idea of taking care of money', Fair wrote to Madeline, and continued, 'One bill of Talbot's for over £10 is nearly all for riding whips, dog collars and such things, and as they are put down instead of being paid for, he has no idea of how fast money goes.'

The next letter referring to the travellers is written by Fair to A. Noel Agnew, Talbot's uncle:[45]

> I hope you will excuse me troubling you. You will remember my telling you when Talbot and Mr Pollock left that their return passage was paid and that I paid Mr Pollock £300 including £25 for Talbot's own pocket money. I am sorry to say he has drawn on me the enclosed Bill for £76 thro' a Lieut. Colonel Clark; of course I felt bound to take the Bill up or Talbot would have been disgraced. I need not say that he had no right to draw on me – I cannot think that Mr Pollock was aware of it, tho' I cannot see how Talbot could have command of so much cash and Mr Pollock not notice it – Talbot must have been 'put up to it!'

Fair was also concerned that Talbot, having found out how to draw bills, might do it again and was further dismayed upon receiving a telegram through Reuter asking for £200.

Agnew apparently knew all about the matter, as Fair writes to him again:

> It did not occur to me that Talbot had drawn on me to pay a gambling debt . . . the Manchester and County Bank has a branch and sub-manager in Lytham and I felt that to dishonour the Bill would bring disgrace and dishonour upon Talbot – I was assuming that he had received value of some kind for it. If however it was to pay a mere gambling debt I must admit that I have made a mistake.

Fair's reaction seems surprising after reading his views on extravagance and the dangers of drawing bills. One would have thought he would be appalled to hear that Talbot at the age of nineteen was playing for comparatively large amounts.

In due course a letter arrived from Mr Pollock, from which it appeared that Talbot had been the 'dupe of some designing rascal', as Fair put it, and that perhaps, 'his inexperience and want of knowledge of the world might to some extent condone his folly.'

In the autumn of 1887 Talbot again embarked on a cruise, as it was considered he should be at sea as much as possible; his companion was Mr Montague Wood. It was proposed to visit Australia, New

Zealand, China and India and be abroad eight or twelve months at his mother's express desire and seemingly not solely for health reasons! Once again, meticulous arrangements were made for letters of credit, banker's drafts and suitable banks in the countries they were to visit and Thomas Fair confided that Mr Wood would be 'considerate and kind enough to exercise every due regard to economy.'

They were at sea for eighty days and the schooner in which they sailed was nearly overcome by heavy gales. The first we hear of the voyagers is in a letter from Fair to Lady Cecily:

> I have just had a telegram from Mr Wood and must go and see Mrs Clifton – I fear he is finding Talbot more than he can manage and intends to shorten the tour.

Instead of eight months Talbot is back in England in less than four and, now in his twentieth year, is really getting the bit between his teeth. Since January he has got through £2,500 – nearly four times his allowance – and is telegraphing Fair for more money. Fair writes to mama:

> The great danger to be avoided is his going to money lenders in London as once in their hands we cannot but fear the consequences.

He writes to Talbot reminding him that until he is twenty-one Fair cannot pay him more than his allowance without his mother's consent, and that he is putting Fair in a very awkward position. He also tells him that it is better to write than to telegraph about money matters. 'You see the telegraph clerks here are lads belonging to the place and it exposes everything to them.'

Much of the expenditure had taken place on the last tour and Mr Montague Wood who had been asked to 'be kind enough to exercise every due regard to economy,' wrote to Mrs Clifton on his return to England:

> I am afraid you have not felt altogether disposed to be gratified at the length of the bills, but anything like rigid economy was quite out of the question.

An explanation which, in the circumstances, might have been better expressed.

During April 1888, Talbot arrives at Fulwood Barracks, Preston, for militia training and during May was in camp at St. Annes. Fair took the opportunity of asking him to dinner at his own house and administered a fatherly lecture on economy, to which Talbot was an attentive and polite listener. Next day he was off to the Chester races and lost yet more money, and Fair departed to Bath for a short holiday having 'never felt more thankful at the prospect of a little rest!'

Whilst in camp with the militia there had been 'some unpleasantness' between the younger officers and Talbot who resented their chaffing him. The Colonel said that in his opinion he had no chance of passing exams for the army but added that the senior officers liked him.

On 30th January 1889, Madeline, Talbot's mother and widow of Thomas Henry, married Sir James Hamlyn Williams Williams Drummond Bart, of Hawthornden, Midlothian, and she and her family took up residence at Edwinsford, Llandilo, Sir James's Welsh seat. She retained her connection with Lytham as executrix and guardian of the children under the will of her late husband and a frequent correspondence took place between herself and Thomas Fair. She was nine years and four months older than Sir James and they had one son born in 1891.

It was in 1889 that Talbot came of age amid celebrations that went on for a week. A wooden pavilion 162 feet by 74 feet was erected in the grounds and the guests numbered eight hundred. There was a roasted ox, as well as a magnificent buffet provided by the Grand Hotel, Liverpool. There were fireworks and a torchlight procession, the young squire being hauled by the tenants through the streets of Lytham in an open carriage. Realising that all the county would be present, and to allow their carriages unimpeded access and turning space, a section of the ancient wall along the Monks' Walk was taken down and later rebuilt.

Now that Talbot was squire, his reckless spending increased to an extent that almost drove Thomas Fair out of his mind. His concern was to hold the estate together, a task made almost impossible by the heavy outgoings produced by family payments, mortgage interest, repairs to buildings, money laid out for the development of the estate to produce new ground rents, and the maintenance and expenses of three establishments. The depression in farming had become so serious that in October 1885 Fair had received a signed petition from the Westby farm tenants asking for an immediate reduction in rent of twenty-five per cent. Things were so bad that landowners were discontinuing the excessive protection of ground game, while on the adjoining manor of Weeton, Lord Derby had given all the game and shootings to his tenants. This was something unprecedented and with which Fair did not agree. He was, however, anxious that the coursing of hares on the estate by the Ridgeway Club should stop, as this would mean that their preservation for sport would cease and their numbers could be reduced to minimise the damage done to growing crops. Fair also wished to finish the coursing, as he considered the amount of gambling it produced on the field and in the town was a bad thing for the community. When this became known, he received a deputation from the Lytham tradesmen and hotel and inn keepers, who looked to the large crowds attending the coursing for increased business, asking that the events should not be discontinued. Building was slow and the increase of the rent roll from new developments was not commensurate with the decrease of farm rents.

Talbot, however, continued his prodigality and the inability of the trustees of the settlement - made on his father's marriage - to control his spending, was due to Thomas Henry predeceasing the Colonel, and the latter dying before the young John Talbot attained his majority. His mother as executrix and guardian under her husband's will, when faced with his debts while still a minor, would sanction their payment in order to avoid Talbot being disgraced and dishonoured in the eyes of society.

Fair and Lady Drummond might have suffered even more anxiety had they known that Talbot was having an affair with Lillie Langtry, the 'Jersey Lily', who, though sixteen years older than Talbot, wrote him a number of love letters. These came to light after the television series about her life which appeared in 1978, and were produced by Mr J. B. Clarke of Hardhorn, near Blackpool, whose grandfather had paid three pence for three sacks of old papers at a farm auction sale in Yorkshire some forty years previously.

The letters are undated but, as they are written from 18 Pont Street, which she bought during 1890, and the St. James's Theatre, where she was then appearing in *As You Like It,* it seems that they first met during that year. Talbot sailed for America in May 1890, so the amour was of short duration; nevertheless, she seems to have done her best to add his scalp to her collection, thinking that he was a young man of great wealth - an impression created, no doubt, by his reckless spending.

The first *billet-doux* skilfully baits the trap.

18 Pont Street
S.W.

Dear Mr Clifton,

The parasol is found! Thank you *very* much for the chocolates; they are my special weakness. Will you come to supper this evening if you are doing nothing better?

Yours truly,
Lillie Langtry.

Subsequent notes indicate that Talbot was not prepared to surrender tamely, and angry scenes took place. Claude Lowther, Talbot's cousin, and Robert Peel were ardent admirers of Lillie at this time and it is likely that they introduced Talbot. His cousin, Hugh, 5th Earl of Lonsdale, had also sought to win Lillie's affections, which resulted in the fight between him and Sir George Chetwynd in Hyde

Park which both scandalised and delighted Victorian society in 1885.

Robert Peel accompanied Talbot to America and before sailing Lillie sent him a letter to hand to Talbot.

Seven o'clock

My darling Talbot,

I *was* so sorry to say good bye and to feel that we had wasted the last three days in quarreling. Why won't you let me come with you. Will you be glad to see me if I come out to America? I feel that I must see you again soon. I was so pitiful to see the poor coach left behind – I wept all the way back and feel so blue – Do be a good boy and don't drink too many brandies and sodas, you will kill yourself if you do – and write to me from Queenstown to say you care for me, my own darling, and telegraph the address that will find you in America – I suppose you will go to the Brevoort House in New York. God bless you, my darling boy.

Love you – L.

Their correspondence did not finish with his departure for America and the tone of her letters makes one wonder if she genuinely loved him or was just reluctant to let him off the hook.

18 Pont Street
S.W.

Darling Talbot,

I was delighted to hear from you today from Queenstown, altho' your letter wasn't half affectionate enough. Marie Tempest came to the play last night. She looks miserable, I think we both feel so. We agreed you are a pair of hard hearted wretches to go and leave us. What have you done with beautiful Champagne? I wonder if I shall see him careering about. Oudia sends her fondest love, she is very well and never leaves me, she consoles me a little. Did you get the letter I wrote you at Queenstown? *Au revoir,* soon I hope.

Yours ever
L.

Champagne was a horse which was sent to Lytham and Thomas Fair, writing to Talbot, says 'Vet named South has crabbed the horse damnably and says not worth £30.' Fair's valuation was £400. Ouida was a dog which, without doubt, Talbot had given her, and as he had more regard for dogs than he had for most humans, indicated that he held Lillie in very high esteem!

18 Pont Street
S.W.

Darling Talbot,

We have all been reading the harrowing accounts of your being robbed. Was it the bracelet I gave you that you confided to him. I am very seedy, the result of recklnessness at Walton but I hope to be better soon.

I shall probably close the theatre about the end of June and then sail for America where I hope I may see you. Have you met Fred Gedhard? Do write and tell me how you like ranching. I feel sick of London and shall be so delighted to get away – Ouida sends her best love, she never leaves me, I hope you won't think her spoilt when you see her again. I have tried to make her obedient and good as you wish her to be.

I hope you haven't quite forgotten me – dear – I think of *you* rather too much.

Yours ever,
L.

Lillie had broken with Fred Gedhard – her most ardent American boyfriend – before Talbot came on the scene, but, we are told, was still hotly pursued by Lord Dudley and the Marquis de Vrémont and had no need to complain of being lonely in Talbot's absence.

When she closed the St. James's Theatre she rented the Prince's Theatre in Oxford Street where she staged *Anthony and Cleopatra,* an elaborate production that almost bankrupted her.

During April 1891, Lillie was smitten with pleurisy and almost died. Talbot had returned from Wyoming where he had lived as a cowboy for six months and was now cruising the Mediterranean in his yacht *Soprano;* he cabled Lillie upon hearing of her illness.

June 29th

Darling Talbot,

I was so glad to get your cable and have just answered it. Wasn't it bad luck by getting pleurisy just as I was getting all right. I never suffered such pain as I did in my lungs, they thought I was going to die for two days and left me under chloroform. I am of course very weak from lying in bed so long but am otherwise on the high road to recovery. No, I *don't* expect I shall get to America till the autumn. Among the wild reports that were circulated was one that I wasn't ill at all but didn't want to play and that I was waiting for the Marchesa to be got ready in order to join *you.*

Didn't I tell you the heat was awful – wait till July and August – then you will scorch. Little Ouida never leaves me. She lies on my bed day and night and I really love her better and better. She *is* a darling, I take great care of her. Bourchier has taken the theatre off my hands for a month and is playing to *nothing* – but he is quite happy. Can't you see him managing, losing his temper with all the stage hands and then making it up with half a crown – I've no news but I'll write again later.

Yours Ever,
L.

Also with the Langtry letters are a few from Talbot's sisters, one of whom – the signature is indecipherable due to water damage – wrote: 'My friend does not know you, but he has been friends with me for years . . . told me there is a report in London that Mrs Langtry, finding her acting not a success, is pretending illness, has thrown up her engagement, and is going to follow you out to America to induce you to marry her.'

As Lillie's association with the notorious George Alexander Baird 'The Squire' began in 1892, she must by then have given up Talbot, but it is interesting that the negotiations for purchase of Talbot's yacht were carried out through Theodore Lumley, who was also instructed by Talbot to arrange with Thomas Fair for the loan of £5,000 to Robert Peel. Lumley was the name of Baird's lawyers and Walter Lumley was the principal executor of his estate.[46]

Before the death of Baird in America in March 1893, Lillie had tried to shake him off as she was becoming tired of his boorish behaviour. Having joined Robert Peel in a visit to Paris, she was taking tea with him in her hotel suite when in burst Baird who, being drunk, appears to have gone berserk, beating up Peel and throwing him out of the room. He then attacked Lillie, savagely striking her in the face, giving her two black eyes, a damaged nose and bruised mouth. Not content with this, he smashed up the contents of the room, leaving the apartment in a shambles. After sojourns - in jail for Baird and in hospital for Lillie - they made it up and she received a peace offering of the 750 ton yacht *White Lady* and a cheque for £50,000 for running expenses.[47]

When Talbot sailed from Liverpool for New York in 1890, he left instructions that 'the yacht' was to follow when ready. This was the screw schooner *Soprano* of 176.93 registered tons which he had bought for £17,000 and spent a further £9,000 in fitting her out and uniforms for the crew. The vessel was 138.5 feet overall and had a beam of twenty-five feet; she would have a crew of about fifteen and her running costs, even in those days, would be high. It is not impossible that, knowing Lillie's love of the sea, Talbot purchased *Soprano* to impress her, but there is no evidence that she ever sailed in her. In writing to Talbot's mother, now Lady Drummond, Thomas Fair says of the American trip and yacht, 'I am very glad that Talbot is leaving London and I do hope that this terrible expenditure will be stopped, or it can have but one end - I feel most anxious as to the future and my present position is most perplexing.'

II

DOUGLAS Sutherland in his biography of Hugh Lowther, 5th Earl of Lonsdale, *The Yellow Earl,* describes Hugh's adventures in Wyoming - before he became Earl - when he was invited to go for a few months' big game hunting, by Moreton Frewen who, with his brother, had started the Seventy-six Ranch on the banks of the North Powder River. Lowther, then aged twenty-two, like many other Britishers, became imbued by the tales of fortunes to be made from cattle and laid out all his available means in the purchase of stock to be reared for market on the Frewen ranch. Due to disastrous losses during a winter of freak severity and subsequent falls in the price of beef, he lost every penny. This was during 1879-80, and it was in May 1890 that Talbot Clifton, also aged twenty-two, went to Wyoming. Hugh loved telling his stories of the West - excepting how he lost his money - and it is not unlikely that young Talbot, listening to his cousin's tales of Indians, outlaws, buffalo and grizzly bears, decided that he must go out and see for himself.

Lady Cecily, Talbot's grandmama and Hugh's aunt, may also have asked him to encourage Talbot to go, so as to get him away from London. He remained in Wyoming for six months, living the life of a cowboy - herding cattle, improving his horsemanship, becoming proficient in the use of the lariat - and returned to England in November, with his stock saddle and other trophies of the Golden West.

During the next two years Talbot cruised the Mediterranean in *Soprano,* visiting many of the places his grandfather had put into: Algiers, Malta, Palermo, Alexandria and on to Constantinople. Like his grandfather, he always sailed with a doctor on board and was joined by friends and relations from time to time. When he became bored he would proceed overland to Paris and then back to Lytham for the shooting, *Soprano* being sailed back to Fleetwood by her captain, so as to be handy for the young squire whenever he felt disposed to put to sea again.

This way of life was, of course, extremely expensive, and when in October 1892 he decided to go to St. Petersburg and instructed Fair to pay another £1,500 into Coutts' Bank for onward transmission to the Imperial Bank there, Fair once again tried to put the brake on. He wrote to Talbot informing him that the yacht had cost him £7,248 since the 1st July and that with the large sums paid to him in Paris, he is now living at the rate of £29,000 a year, almost the entire rental of the estate, 'without one shilling for interest, family payments or ordinary expenses. Pray do not think that I wish to "grumble" or to spoil your pleasure, but such a rate of expenditure means absolute ruin to yourself and everybody else connected with your property.' Talbot agreed that the yacht should be sold and that the shooting could be let, and proceeded blithely on his way - Bergen, Trondheim, Archangel and St. Petersburg, and managed to get through a further £4,300. How he spent so much and what he did on this trip is made clearer by Violet Clifton writing about his second visit to Russia and Siberia in 1901 and saying that he and his friend, Prince Serge Belosselsky had, 'Nine years before, in 1892, through Bergen, and through Archangel, Talbot had come - sowing tares and cockles. Weeds maybe; but how gay had been the cockles! Rushing wanton days had swept the friends along together.'[48]

In the meantime the yacht was undergoing repair, of which she was so in need that she had lost her classification at Lloyds, and Fair, wishing to get the best possible price for her, had put the work in hand, 'as the proceeds will be very useful.'

What then must have been his chagrin and fury when he heard from the yacht master, Captain Deason, in January 1893, that Talbot had instructed him to again sail to the Mediterranean as he wished to go to a warm climate. It is reasonable to assume that Fair must have heartily wished that his principal *would* go to a place with a *very much* warmer climate!

Once again, however, he penned one of his homilies on the immediate need of restraint, lest the most dire consequences ensue.

> Pray bear with me while I put matters before you, which it is my duty to do, tho' it is unpleasant to you, and also painful to me to be looked upon, I fear as a 'grumbler' - You will I know believe that it is not from grumblings sake, and give me credit for better things, for I assure you it is for your own future position - You will know from the newspapers what a trying year it has been to Farmers everywhere, and how difficult it is for them to pay their Rents and how necessary it is in the present day when you have (as you happily have) a good set of tenants to do all that you can to keep them on their farms. This cannot be done without a certain expenditure of money - You cannot spend it both on the Yacht and on your property without getting into trouble with your Bankers.

Apparently not taking the slightest notice of Fair's warnings and forebodings Talbot is at Cannes before the end of February with the yacht and Lord and Lady Grey de Ruthyn on board. A good time is apparently being had by all and Thomas Fair has received from St. Petersburg a belated gift of 1,000 Russian cigarettes and writes to Talbot thanking him for this apparent peace offering and for 'remembering his little weakness.'

Any mollifying effect the cigarettes may have had on Thomas was quickly dispelled by Talbot querying the sale of some land at Great Marton which was not part of the entailed estate and which was necessary in consequence of Talbot's extravagance.

> I have given a life long service to your family and am thankful to feel that I have hitherto enjoyed their confidence and friendship - If I have lost your confidence I beg that you will at once tell me so, for I confess to feeling much hurt that you should, without a line of explanation, cancel business arrangements which I have made as your Agent.

His feelings could not have been improved by Talbot having bought, meanwhile, a steam launch and searchlight for the yacht which had to be shipped from England.

Whilst sojourning at Nice, Talbot received a number of documents to sign, including deeds for the sites of churches at St. Annes and one for the new golf links and Fair, in his letter comments, 'The Links I think will be almost as attractive to St. Annes as Places of Worship, but both you may rely upon it will do good.' Priorities in St. Annes have perhaps changed since Thomas wrote the above.

Having apparently had a surfeit of life on the Riviera, Talbot felt in need of another holiday and went to Rhode Island during April and did not arrive back in England until early July.

Talbot at last agreed that *Soprano* should be sold; she was to be sailed from Fleetwood to Southampton which was reckoned to be a better market for her. His reckless spending has increased the mortgage debt by £100,000 and he has been induced by Lord Thurlow to sign a bill for £50,000, with no provision made to meet it. Miss Cecily Clifton, Talbot's sister, had married Lord Thurlow's son and heir, James Bruce Cumming Bruce during 1893.

As Talbot was leaving for North America in January, Fair wrote his last appeal to him on December 13th, 1893:

> I am much disappointed not to have heard from you in reply to my letter of the 4th inst. before you left Lytham.
>
> Will you be so good as to inform me when you propose to return here?
>
> Matters are coming to such a serious crisis that I cannot answer for the consequences unless you do return shortly to confer with your Solicitors and myself as to what is to be done to meet the additional heavy liabilities falling due next month.
>
> No arrangements can be made to provide the money in your absence and unless it is provided I fear that you will very shortly see the Bailiffs in possession of Lytham Hall.

III

TALBOT sailed for America on 29th January 1894, and we must assume that satisfactory arrangements were made to ward off a visitation by representatives of the law to Lytham Hall, as feared by Thomas Fair.

In the meantime, while Talbot is at sea, a convenient moment presents itself to look back and see how another member of the family has been faring.

Cuthbert, the second son of Thomas Henry and next in line to John Talbot, was born on 16th March 1870, and we hear little of him until 1888 when he was receiving an allowance of £260 a year and is intended for the army. He did his militia training but did not join the regular army; in fact, he had a marked aversion to work of any kind which, coupled with expensive tastes, a meagre allowance and rather dubious friends, could only lead to his running into debt - which he very soon did.

In February 1890, Thomas Fair, in writing to Andrew Agnew says he is 'staggered' to receive an account for payment from a Mr Comfort - Fair does not say what for - but comments that Comfort deserves to lose his money and proposes letting the matter stand over until Cuthbert came of age, when payments could be made from the accumulation of interest on his portion, and this would be applied first to *'legitimate* debts only'.

Fair wrote to Cuthbert at Whites' Club, explaining that he could not anticipate any part of his portion and his mother, Lady Drummond, had absolute power of appointment over it.[49] His mother, being sole arbiter over his funds from the estate, seems to have embittered him against her and he thereafter nursed a strong feeling of resentment.

Getting no satisfaction from Fair, Cuthbert tries to borrow from his sister Madeline, and she - now of age - asks Fair for the accumulated interest on her portion. Fair does not approve of this and consults with Agnew as to whether they should advise Lady Drummond to agree that Cuthbert's debts be discharged as far as the interest on his portion would go, as

> if Cuthbert really is alive to his past folly and will make up his mind to settle down to work it may be of consequence to his own future that his mind should be set at rest about his debts.

In the event, he was baled out to the tune of £500 and Mr Comfort received his money through the agency of the estate solicitors, as it was not considered wise to allow Cuthbert to handle it.

In just a year's time he was in debt again and Fair was authorised by Lady Drummond to send him £50 to pay his household bills and tells him:

> It is scarcely right in you to blame your mother for your present difficulties. You will remember that a year ago she empowered me to pay all your bills on the promise that you would make your allowance suffice in future if it was paid to you direct.

Fair continued his letter to give Cuthbert a moral lecture on the dangers of getting into debt, similar to those he wrote to Talbot, and with as little effect.

In less than a month Fair hears from Robert Peel that Cuthbert owes him money and receives a claim for £200 from another party for dishonoured cheques. This is followed by the news that he has lost heavily at play, and in writing to Quintin Agnew – another brother of Lady Drummond – Fair says:

> I don't know who Mr Cohen is but I cannot understand anyone playing to such an amount with a young man under age, and in the event of Cuthbert being made bankrupt, which I fear is highly probable, I doubt very much whether one shilling of Mr Cohen's claim would be allowed in Court. Cuthbert has only £200 or £300 left and there are tradesmen's claims for as many thousands.

To everyone's relief Cuthbert goes to Calcutta with the intention of seeking his fortune with the firm of Duncan MacNiel and Company with which Henry Agnew is connected, but by February 1892 he has had enough of India and wants to come home. His mother passes Cuthbert's telegram to Fair and instructs him to wire Henry Agnew requesting him to pay Cuthbert's passage for a sea trip to Burma and back, and Fair adds that it would not be safe for him to return to London unless he was prepared to face considerable trouble and risk.

He did not go on the cruise and is back in England in May, to Lady Drummond's great disappointment. His grandmother, Lady Cecily, considers that he should be left to take the consequences of his folly and Fair says he should join the army.

By June, writs are coming in and the estate solicitors and Fair advise that he should go bankrupt as he now owes over £4,000 in unpaid accounts. He is still a commissioned officer in the militia and has been reported to the Paymaster General, 'if not to the Duke of Cambridge', for issuing dishonoured cheques.

Talbot said he wished to save his brother from bankruptcy and was prepared to intercede with Lady Drummond to pay the debts from

Cuthbert's portion, but this would leave him destitute and Talbot himself declined to pay anything. Fair points out that if Cuthbert's portion is expended, Talbot will have to provide an income for him and strongly advises Talbot:

> to let Cuthbert feel the inconvenience of his own extravagant folly before anything is done to help him.

Fair also counsels Lady Drummond in the same manner:

> Cuthbert's debts are so large and he appears so callous and indifferent about them that I fear it will only encourage him in a selfish, extravagant and discreditable life if they are again paid for him. I will not trouble you again on this painful and distressing matter if I can avoid it, but will leave everything in Messrs. Wilson and Deacon's hands.[50]

And so Cuthbert was thrown to the wolves.

He was indeed made to swallow the bitter dregs left by his extravagance; he had no option but to resign his commission in the militia and Messrs. Wilson and Deacon advised Fair that Cuthbert had forfeited his portion and that he could not make him any payments. His mother, however, sent him £50 as he was going abroad and Lady Cecily took up a bill for £500 which he had given, which intercession possibly saved him from arrest and prison.

Cuthbert, however, was no grovellor, and any hopes Fair may have entertained that he would humbly bow his head and become a respectable member of society were soon dispelled.

In March 1893, Cuthbert went abroad with a Mr Banks of Winstanley, ostensibly as his private secretary, and Fair comments, with foreboding of things to come, 'I fear the emoluments of the office are not great, nor is he the most desirable companion for Cuthbert to be with.'

Fair's instincts, as usual, were right, and in less than a month news of bouncing cheques, issued by both parties, comes from Monte Carlo and other places on the Riviera.

This unfortunate partnership did not last long, however, as Cuthbert left his employer – apparently for non-payment of salary (at a rate of £300 a year) – and Fair comments, 'indeed I do not think he has as many pence to pay him with!'

It is now proposed to pay Cuthbert £5 per month on condition he keeps away from London, but Talbot instructs Fair that he is to inform Cuthbert, that he, Talbot, does not wish him to stay at Lytham Hall. Fair justifiably feels that Talbot himself should have informed his brother of this uncharitable gesture.

Heads are now put together to consider what is to be done with the black sheep – Wykeham thinks he might get a job with one of the large African companies; Lady Cecily suggests the South African

Police; and Fair has heard that the Canadian Mounted Police is 'a very fine force'.

The need of getting Cuthbert out of England had become urgent.

May 5th '93

Dear Cuthbert,

I am very sorry to have to send you the enclosed letter from Monte Carlo, but for your own safety it is right that you should know about it at once.

Have you made any arrangements about going abroad?

Believe me,
Yours faithfully,
Thos. Fair

Cuthbert Clifton Esq.,
at The Burlington Hotel,
London.

James Fair, the son of Thomas, is now taking an active part in the management of the estate, and as they are much of an age and more or less brought up together as boys, Cuthbert writes to him in preference to Thomas, knowing he can confide in him to an extent not possible with the father.

Cuthbert is now in lodgings in London, and managing to keep one jump ahead of the irate Monte Carlo recipients of the bouncing cheques by frequent changes of address. His guns and watch and chain are in pawn at twenty-two-and-a-half per cent interest, but he goes to the theatre and is attended on by his valet. This was George Bennet, who wrote to James Fair in desperation saying he was destitute, Cuthbert owing him over £300 for arrears of pay and money he had borrowed. Cuthbert's baggage had been detained by his landlord at 28 Half Moon Street for non-payment of rent, and in order to obtain release Bennet had pawned Cuthbert's cuff links. Bennet was so hard up that his own mackintosh was in pawn and he had been locked out of his lodgings. This was confirmed to Fair by Cuthbert's landlord, who said the latter also owed a friend of his £10, for a box at Covent Garden.

Far from being grateful to his mother, Lady Drummond, for continually helping him out of trouble, Cuthbert bitterly resented the control she exercised over his portion, which after all, it was her duty to do. In a letter to James Fair his rancour pours out,

> I am sick of all this wrangle and no longer wish to have anything to do with the woman who unfortunately for me is my mother . . . I dare say I shall be able to struggle through this world without her pretended help. I can at any rate beg, borrow or steal, probably the latter, and if I am locked up, I shall not spare her in my defence.

Poor James was also the recipient of Lady Drummond's wrath:

I won't pay another penny for Cuthbert, he has behaved so ungratefully and never says thank you for anything . . . I am sure you must be as sick of Cuthbert's affairs as I am.

Her Ladyship is clearly very cross with Cuthbert, but as usual she later relents and he goes to Australia where she finances the purchase of a sheep station. From a letter he wrote to James Fair it is clear that he had had some practical experience before the purchase of the station.

Dear Jim,

Many thanks for your letter. I am on my way to Roma where I shall stay till I hear about the money. I am going to inspect the grazing farm as soon as I can. I hear on very good authority that it is a real good thing. I am absolutely done up by the heat. I have been away droving for three weeks and will be glad to get to a house again. I am looking forward to a bath under a roof. I am writing this letter in a log hut.

I am so glad to hear that your wife and the child are doing well. How awful being a family man, I pity you. My fingers are quite stiff so I can't write any more so Goodbye and love to all.

Yours sincly,

Dec 14/95 Cuthbert Clifton

The Springfield station was situated in the Warrego District of Queensland and seems to have lain somewhere between Roma and Charleville, some 700 miles west of Brisbane. It must have been an extensive spread, as it was carrying 7,500 sheep, fifty-four cattle and twenty-seven horses. The place was acquired early in 1896 but by July things were going wrong.

Cuthbert had been selling off the breeding stock of sheep, put a man called Kirk in as manager, then drew all the money out of the bank and went on holiday. When news of this reached Lytham, instructions were cabled to the solicitors in Roma who entered into possession on Lady Drummond's behalf.

By January 1987 Cuthbert is sending frantic cablegrams to Thomas Fair for money, saying that he is ill, but Thomas is by now so disillusioned that he wonders, 'is he really ill or determined to have money.'

By September Cuthbert is in danger of arrest and Fair suspects that Frances, his youngest sister, is sending him money as she is drawing heavily on her portion.

Sir Thomas Fowell Buxton was Governor of Australia and had married Lady Victoria Noel, the aunt of Lady Drummond. It was from her that Cuthbert next sought assistance, and Lady Buxton apparently showed him considerable kindness. His Excellency, however, wrote to Thomas Fair from Government House, Adelaide, with further details of Cuthbert's misdemeanours and indebtedness, which necessitated more financial help from home.

Nothing more is heard of Cuthbert until he writes from Petty's Hotel, Sydney, saying that he is in a very bad way and wishes he could get out of 'this God forsaken country.' Seven months later he returns to England completely broke, but his mother takes him in at Edwinsford.

Events were moving fast towards the outbreak of the South African War, and Cuthbert became imbued with patriotism and war fever. On 1st January, 1900 he wrote to James Fair from 67 Jermyn Street:

> I am trying to go out to South Africa in the yeomanry. I have tried to join the Lancashire Hussars but I have just heard from Col. Hopwood who says that the 1st Company is already formed but he has put my name down in case there is another company raised. I have just telegraphed again to Lonsdale asking him to give me a commission in his yeomanry. Is your brother-in-law Pilkington going? About my debts, it is very good of you volunteering to come up, I should like to see you, of course, but I think it would be a mistake for me to see the creditors, far better allow them to imagine I am in S. A. and a chance of being shot, as much better terms could then be made. However I should like to have a talk with you about it.

Cuthbert seems to have reconsidered James Fair's offer to come to London, as he again writes to him on the 4th January:

> Thanks for your letter. I should be awfully glad if you could come up to London and dash round the creditors with me. I have been too busy trying to arrange something about S. A.. Have any of Talbot's tenants volunteered, I think they ought to in the Lancs Hussars; a big county like Lancs ought to be able to raise two troops, they must be an awful unsporting lot if they don't; I have arranged that Albert Osborne goes out with the galloping hospital, I think it will suit him, but he doesn't look at all keen.[51] When do you expect Talbot back?
>
> Goodbye Jim,
> Yours sincly,
> Cuthbert Clifton.

He did get to Cape Town, but by 9th April news arrived at Edwinsford that he is seriously ill, and on the 20th he cables; 'Fair, Lytham, England, Coming home; cable money; Cuthbert.' - and his mother writes, 'How trying Cuthbert is. Kindly send him money for a second-class ticket, as you know I have no money at present.'

So Cuthbert did not take part in the war he was so keen about. He returned to Edwinsford where he died on the 14th October, 1900, aged thirty years.

He must have been typical of many a younger son of those days who was unable to live on a small fixed annual income - brought up to enjoy the good things of life but without the means to do so -

unable to find a wealthy bride or settle down in trade or business - unwilling or unfitted to join the navy or army.

Canada, Australia, New Zealand and other colonies had the 'remittance men', as they were known, receiving their remittances from England on condition that they remained where they were and did not come home to sponge on and embarrass the more fortunate members of the family.

Despite all his misdeeds, he must have been a colourful and doubtless charming person, and one cannot help feeling - Poor Cuthbert!

IV

TALBOT arrived in New York on 5th February, 1894, after a sea crossing during which he played poker and 'did devillish well' Unfortunately for him, however, there were 'no pretty girls' and the 'biggest set of bounders going!'

For five days he enjoyed himself with Wyndham Quinn, an old friend of his, going to the opera and attending a 'splendid ball at Sherry's, cotillions magnificent, a girl there worth fifteen million dollars, useful supper, charming.'

Arriving in Montreal he entrained and crossed Canada, spending one night in Vancouver: 'Splendid hotel, went to music hall, twenty bottles, three in the morning singing "we won't come home till morning".' The next day he crosses to Victoria, Vancouver Island and again has 'capital sport' in a music hall. In the morning he receives a *billet doux* and feels nervous that 'she might come on to Frisco.' He does not say who!

Embarking at Victoria in the 'City of Pueblo' with an 'awful looking crowd on board' he arrived in San Fransico on February 27th and lost no time in joining up with the sporting set. Sir Thomas Hesketh of Rufford Hall, Lancashire, had married Florence, daughter of William Sharon, United States Senator for Nevada, and Sharon, their son, introduced Talbot to the Burlingame Club.

Talbot's first concern was to provide himself with suitable riding and driving horseflesh, to which he added a small string of racehorses, amounting to fifteen animals in all. For equipage he had a four in hand coach with rugs, trappings and harness complete, a four wheeled Studebaker buggy and had sent out from England his two wheeled buggy or gig and his dog cart.

Two of his favourite companions and advisors were Daniel 'White Hat' McCarty and his son, Joseph D., who were horse dealers and trainers, and, as subsequently transpired, usually got the better of him on horse deals.

For the next three months, he played polo, rode in steeplechases and drove his coach, the first man to do so for pleasure in San Fransisco. This way of life beginning to pall, and feeling in need of something more adventurous, during May he went to Durango in Mexico, from where he proposed hunting the Sierra mountains in seach of bear and deer.

Purchasing ten mules and a horse, provisions for four months, and accompanied by his valet Betts, and a boy Santiago, he started at 6.30 a.m. on the 20th May.

The expedition was not a success; spending the first night at a placienda, made sleepless by fleas and bugs which he remarked 'do great credit to the country', he found that the mules had bolted during the night. Having rounded up the stubborn creatures and proceeded, an abcess on the left side of his chest began to fester and steadily grew worse, until after four days he was in such pain that he had to lie up at a ranch belonging to a Mexican called Mario.

A maya was sent to the nearest town for ointment, and Betts and Santiago were sent out to shoot deer. Talbot lay in his room, bandaged, reading Shakespeare, learning Spanish and sketching.

After four days his chest was worse, despite the ointment the maya had arrived back with, and Talbot notes in his diary, 'I can't move, damn it, chest worse than ever, wish it would get right into my heart and kill me!'

Mario came into the room, which they shared, and said his servant had killed a deer, whereupon in apparent celebration he picked up Talbot's whisky bottle and drained the contents! Next day Mario won Talbot's forgiveness by bringing him milk, but fell from grace again by being sick all over the room: 'Dirty hog, I should like to kick him!'

He left Mario's ranch on June 5th, 'stingy blackguard, made me pay for horses and mules, hid behind house while he sent a maya to collect, did not say goodbye to him.'

Too ill to go further, Talbot had to stop after five hours' travel and sent Jesus, a maya – who seems to have joined the party – for a doctor. He could not sleep, and we learn that a man arrived who had been bitten in the head by a snake 'all swollen, looks ill'. Talbot studies Spanish and learns Anthony's speech from his Shakespeare to pass the time, Jesus returns, but no doctor.

By June 11th he decides he must abandon his expedition and return to Darango. Arriving back at Mario's ranch he spends the night, then starts again in the early morning, 'very cold and miserable, no feeling of merriment in my composition, couldn't even stand a ballet.'

After a final hard twelve hours' ride he arrives at Durango, drinks 'a pint of filthy champagne' a doctor sees him, and then rests. His legs refuse to carry him and he is in bed for a week, looked after by a German doctor, who he considers is 'beer and sauerkraut all over.'

Getting up to hear the band he saw 'two rather pretty fillys, I don't think I managed to attract them as much as they attracted me', he notes, from which we must assume he was at last getting better.

When on his travels, Talbot meticulously kept a journal, making daily entries no matter his own physical state – and he was sometimes desperately ill - and no matter the climatic conditions under which he wrote. His mode of self expression and pithy comment reveal his wit and power of observation.

V

WITHIN a fortnight of his return to San Francisco he seems to have been fully restored to health and he entered once more into the sporting and social whirl of the Burlingame Club. He had purchased a horse named Guadeloupe, who had been gelded but was still unmanage-able and notorious, as he had already killed one man and also had two broken collar bones to his credit; even McCarty said 'he's a cannibal, but he's a winner.'

Talbot decided to ride him at the races in Monterey, and took part in the first gentleman's steeplechase held in California. He was thrown but remounted and came third. He rode him a second time and was leading, but was again thrown at the water jump, and though stunned suffered no injury. Finally, some time later, he was thrown for the third time in a hurdle race and was treated by an estate agent who practised part-time doctoring and surgery, and who set his shoulder blade but failed to notice that his collar bone was broken. After weeks of pain another doctor was called in who, with agony for Talbot, completed the job.

Before he left San Francisco, he was approached by a man who wished to buy Gaudeloupe, 'I'd prefer not to sell him', said Talbot, 'I'd rather shoot him, he's not fit for anyone to ride.' The man pressed him; Talbot put the price high to stave him off. 'A horse that takes the bit in his teeth and bolts deliberately through temper (and not through fear) is useless to a man. Nothing will stop Guadeloupe when he gets frenzied, and he will kill himself one day.' Still the man insisted, and Talbot, getting angry at his obstinacy, let him have the horse. Within a week Guadeloupe had killed his new owner.[52] From the foregoing it seems that Guadeloupe could have been a 'rig' – a horse that had been badly castrated, which can result in frustration for the animal and consequent savage temper.

Talbot's horsemanship and fearlessness greatly impressed the San Franciscans and the sight of him driving his four in hand coach, or drag, through the streets was something they had never seen before. Stage coaches and wagons, yes, but not a private turn-out for pleasure. He hit the headlines by driving a high spirited horse which he had bought in Southern California, harnessed to a buggy and accompanied by his crony, White-Hat McCarty.

The horse had not been driven in a city before and bolted upon meeting a street-car with its bell ringing. McCarty had taken the reins first and only succeeded in stopping the horse by driving it into a board fence.

McCarty commented that night:

> It was the wildest trip of my wild life. That horse has not had a strap on him for five months. He has never been in the city in his life and is a strong animal with a 2.23 record. I thought 'Lord' was joking when he proposed to take him out, but Clifton is dead game and is afraid of nothing. I never saw a horse in all my life go at the speed we made along the Avenue. One of my arms has been paralysed since, and I do not expect to be able to use it for several days. But what commands my admiration was Clifton insisting on driving the horse after it had once bolted and was completely frightened. Not another man I know would have dared to do such a thing, but Clifton is not an ordinary man. It was fortunate that we were able to drive into that fence as the animal was thoroughly unmanageable by that time. I am sure when we struck that fence the horse jumped sixteen feet into the air. And Clifton just laughed![53]

By the end of July, Talbot had become restless. He went to Monterey and after two days, 'Sick of this place . . . played bowls in the afternoon, bored to death in the evening'. On August 2nd 'Sat about all the morning, went for a drive in the afternoon by myself and sketched a little'.

Finally on August 3rd, 'In the evening to see a water party which might be represented like Venice, but like Hell in this quarter of the globe, female got us drunk as a f***t after, what am I coming to'.

During the autumn of 1894 Talbot returned to Montreal and it was here that he became a Roman Catholic. In *The Book of Talbot,* Violet Clifton says, 'It may be that the low aims and the self-seeking of the men about him drove him sheer and sudden to the God self-sacrificed. It was like finding an orchid on a dung heap. That is what he said of a Mass heard in a low part of the city. He was at variance with himself; he was cast down by hollow-hearted women'.

Many years after, she told the writer of this chronicle that he did it to spite his Scottish mother.

VI

EARLY in 1895 Talbot was back in San Francisco 'whooping it up' with his American buddies. The days were again spent in polo, steeplechasing and driving his four-in-hand.

During a dinner party given by a friend, Dick Tobin, Talbot came to the defence of White Hat McCarty, who was absent. Sitting opposite was a formidable character by the name of Jack Chinn, whose face was pock-marked with powder burns from an abortive attempt by someone to kill him. He was reputed to be highly dangerous and habitually carried a gun which he was prone to use if provoked. In the midst of the meal, Talbot was heard to say to him in a loud, clear voice, 'You are a liar!' Chinn, apparently, was so astonished that he did nothing. Tobin, in writing to a friend, said, 'I think the fact that Clifton was not killed was due to two things; I think Chinn, himself, was impressed by Clifton's extraordinary courage and that he knew he was unarmed.'

Once again tiring of the social life during July, Talbot, accompanied by Betts and his dog, Bob, sailed from San Francisco for Alaska and after an uncomfortable voyage in the small, overcrowded steamer *Quebec,* arrived at Juneau. Here he met a man called Maas who gave him written directions as to how to go down the Yukon River. Maas also accompanied Talbot for a day's fishing and shooting and, getting out of a boat, 'shot a bit off his foot with his rifle.' Talbot's laconic comment in his diary continues 'Very careless, I hear he is always doing something like that.'

Gold was the lure that drew men to this wild, inhospitable land, and gold dust was still the currency used in Juneau. Talbot, however, seems to have gone there to satisfy his own curiosity as to the terrain, the people, the wild creatures and plant life. The stories of his travels all reveal his keen interest in natural history and different ways of human existence in the wild.

There is no mention of him prospecting, although he followed the routes taken by the gold seekers and endured their hardships and privations purely, apparently, to satisfy his love of adventure.

In order to reach Lake Lindeman he and Betts with sixteen Indian bearers ascended the notorious Chilcoot Pass, packing twelve hundred pounds of stores. This was before the pass became famous during the Klondyke gold rush. Reaching the lake, they camped and for eighteen days were busy building a boat in which to travel on to

Forty Mile Town. They were helped by two miners bound for the same destination and felled trees which were whip-sawed into planks to build the cumbrous craft.

When completed, they rowed across lakes, were swept by the current down rivers and dragged the boat overland at portages past rapids.

Coming to the White Horse Rapids, which were considered unnavigable, Talbot, who was by this time tired of lugging boat and stores over the rocks, decided to go through the gorge. One of the miners and a stranger volunteered to go with Talbot and before they cast off he pulled Bob the dog out of the boat saying, 'Go back old manny, it's too risky for you.' Bob was led away by Betts and accompanied the others who preferred to negotiate the rapids on foot.

For another six days they journeyed on, by lake and river, encountering more rapids, until they arrived at Forty Mile Town, seven hundred and fifty miles from where they had launched their craft into Lake Lindeman. Here, Talbot waited for a steamer that was to take him on the last part of his journey. For nine days he lived in a log shack and joined in the life of the small community. The Mounted Police had recently arrived in the area and were building a barracks. To fill in time Talbot started a newspaper. 'We are working at it. We are all disappointed because we cannot find any scandal. Twenty-five copies are to be issued at five dollars each. It is not too dear as the papers will all be written by hand.'

He attended the opening of the new saloon and danced a waltz with an Indian girl. Another dance lasted until eleven o'clock the next morning and he watched a poker game that lasted thirty-six hours. The place was full of dogs, as they were used as beasts of burden. They were fed only at night and fought for food, occasionally eating each other. Bob had to be carried by his master or he would have been torn to pieces.

Owing to a collision between two steamers, the *Wier* and the *Artic,* stores were running low. This included whisky, and hootch was drunk instead; made of molasses and spirit distilled from berries, even old leather was thrown into the cauldrons; the whole was fermented and drunk hot.

Tired of waiting for the steamer, Talbot went hunting with men of the Tinne tribe. He shot a bear, and only one moose, since he was fascinated by the animals and wished to have a head to send back to England.

On the last day he fell in with two miners who were wearily making their way to Forty Mile. They had been to 'the pups' of the Klondyke River and were certain that the area was rich; all the same they wished to sell their claims. The wife of one of the men was dying and he had to travel down the Yukon by the next steamer.

Talbot believed the men were sincere and offered to buy their claims. As he could only afford to speculate a third of the price they asked, he promised to cable his assent or refusal from London, where he hoped to raise the remainder. Hurrying back, he tried vainly to interest businessmen and friends, but 'Who has ever heard of the Klondyke?' they laughed.

Next year the Klondyke was discovered to the world.[54]

In October 1895, Talbot returned to San Francisco, where he spent a further seven months before returning to England in May. That his departure from San Francisco did not pass unnoticed is apparent from a news item appearing in one of the local papers:

Going back to England
Talbot Clifton remembers his friends
Generous presents to the McCarty's
A farewell stag party

Lord Talbot Clifton will leave for New York this morning on his way to England. The Noble Lord gave a stag high jinks at his richly-furnished apartments on Grand Avenue last night at which were present guests of honour, White Hat McCarty and his son Joe. Lord Clifton took his separation from his bosom companions much to heart and the parting scene was said to be affecting in the extreme.

He urged White Hat to accompany him to old England, offering to pay all expenses and to return with the horseman in four months. McCarty, however, was obdurate. He almost melted to tears when Lord Talbot in a voice trembling with emotion presented him with a check for £1,500, the beautiful furnishings of his apartment, including paintings and bric-a-brac.

To Joe McCarty, Lord Clifton gave all his horses, tally hos, carriages, phaetons and drags, in fact all of the vehicles and animals of which he was possessed in California.

The health of the guests was drunk in bumpers of sparkling champagne.

The stag party was kept up nearly all night.

VII

LADY Cecily had been ailing before Talbot sailed for America in January 1894, and on 25th November she died, aged seventy-two. The previous year she had been in communication with Thomas Fair regarding her will and the disposal of some of her possessions. In acknowledging her instructions, Fair says, 'I hope Lytham may always belong to a Clifton whatever becomes of the rest of the property.'

During Talbot's absence, Lytham Hall and the shooting had been let for two years to Henry Tate, son of the founder of the famous sugar refining firm and of the Tate Gallery in London. In writing to Talbot, Thomas Fair somewhat naively trusted that 'you enjoyed your rambles in Alaska', before telling him of the continuing agricultural depression and that the mortgage debt on the estate had increased to £187,000 and 'imploring' him to check his expenditure. This was followed by a letter from James Fair informing him that in accordance with his instructions his lawyers in San Francisco had commenced the sale of his horses, carriages and other possessions, but White Hat McCarty and son had claimed everything as theirs. James enclosed the news cutting describing the farewell stag party, which he felt must have given good grounds for the claim. When Thomas Fair read the cutting and came to the part where McCarty 'almost melted into tears' upon receiving from Talbot the cheque, contents of the apartment, the horses and equipages, he also may have been near to tears!

By dint of much pressure, McCarty allowed the contents of 'Maison Riche' - Talbot's San Francisco apartment - and the coach and trappings to be sold, but would not part with the horses except 'Rosalba', a thoroughbred for which Talbot paid McCarty $2,500 and was sold for $200!

Undismayed by Fair's warnings and the proceedings in California, Talbot leased the deer forest Rhidorroch, near Ullapool, and set up his establishment there to enjoy the shooting and stalking. He agreed that Lytham Hall and the shooting should be let to the McGees, brewers of Bolton.

It is hardly surprising that by now Thomas Fair's cup was full and that he felt he could take no more of Talbot's irresponsible behaviour. The following letter was enclosed with a covering letter from Wykeham Clifton to James Fair;

Norfolk House,
St. James's Square, S. W.
March 9th, 1895

My Dear Uncle Wykeham,

I am very sorry I am not in want of an Agent, Mostyn's son has practically taken his father's place now for some years and there is therefore no necessity. Apart from this it is true that I also always look out for a Catholic for many reasons, not the least of which is that Catholics depend so much on their own body for opportunities of employment.

But I am very sorry indeed I cannot be of use to Mr Fair, and not only do I know how great a boon it would be to anyone to have the great benefit of his services but to me personally it would be most agreeable and pleasant.

I am truly sorry I can be of no use. Thank you very much for letting me know of what ought to be to many so happy an opportunity.

Yours affectionately,
Norfolk.

Warton Hall,
Lytham

My Dear Jim,

I am very sorry to say that the report of the Arundel Agent leaving is unfounded. However, I send you the Duke's letter as it cannot but please you to see how completely, he, the best man I have ever known, shares in the esteem in which your Father is held by those who know him.

I don't want the letter back.

Very truly yours,
Wykeham Clifton.

It was during 1896 that a matter of the utmost importance to Lytham arose. A few years previously, Preston Corporation had opened a new dock and extended the channel training walls towards Lytham. Despite having stated that the extensions permitted by powers granted in 1883 were final, the Corporation was now seeking to construct five more training walls directly in front of Lytham. Thomas Fair wrote to J. W. Lowther Esq., M.P.[55] for Mid-Cumberland, and nephew of Lady Eleanor Cecily Clifton, saying that in his opinion, and that of three other well-known civil engineers of great experience, that such works, 'will ruin our foreshore'. He asked Lowther if he could use his influence to secure a strong chairman of the committee which would be considering the Bill before Parliament.

The Bill, however, went through and the new walls were built. Alas for Lytham, how true Thomas Fair's prophetic words were. Where children once played on the golden sand, there is now mud, rapidly becoming a marsh.

Lytham and St. Annes had now become urban districts, and Fair mentions with satisfaction, in January 1895, 'I am glad to say that the elections to the new District Council under the Act of last year were very satisfactory. We have now got a very good Board in Lytham, with Dr. Fisher as Chairman and every one of the old Commissioners who were unfriendly to the Estate got kicked out.'

By the end of October 1896, Talbot, whilst having had good fun with the black game at Rhidorroch, was again becoming restless, and informed James Fair that he was going south as, 'I greatly need a change of air' - and early in the new year he was again possessed by the wanderlust. Lytham Hall was let for five years and it was decided that Rhidorroch should also be let for a year while Talbot journeyed to the Barren Lands, north of Chesterfield Inlet, off Hudson's Bay, in the hopes of finding further trace of Franklin and of capturing and bringing alive to England some of the musk ox that inhabit that region.

VIII

TALBOT sailed from Liverpool on 27th February 1897. He had with him his brother Arthur and his man Betts. Bob, his faithful spaniel, had to be left behind, as he was too old for the journey. In his diary, Talbot made frequent reference to the dog, often finishing the account of a day's events with 'Love to Bob', or 'I wish Bob were here'. Such was the affection between them that after Talbot's departure, Bob ran fifty miles from Elgin to Rhidorroch looking for him. He was taken back to Elgin and died there before Talbot's return.

Arthur was then aged twenty-three and had previously entered the Royal Naval College at Greenwich. He served in *H.M.S. Howe* in the Channel Squadron and in *H.M.S. Cruiser* on a Mediterranean cruise, but like his namesake, and great-uncle Arthur, he did not like the navy, and wished to go to India. He inherited money under the will of his grandmother, Lady Cecily, but, instead of going abroad, seems to have taken a keen interest in agriculture.

Winnipeg was the starting place for the expedition, and it was here, with the help and advice of officials of the Hudson Bay Company, that the necessary stores and equipment were assembled. The first part of the journey was undertaken by horse-drawn sleigh as far as the company's post at Berens River which they reached on the 24th March. During the journey they encountered deep fissures in the frozen lakes they traversed, and over which the horses were jumped, to 'the mortal terror of the drivers.' Stopping at various camps, they were introduced to the food of the wilderness – three beefsteaks for breakfast; moose and caribou for supper. At Berens River, Talbot collected his personal dog team – Barry, Bismarck, Pointer and Paddy.

Norway House, seventy-five miles away, was the next objective, but during the day the going became heavy because the snow had started to thaw and turn into slush, which wet everything during the day, although it froze again at night.

Camping amongst a few pleasant trees one evening, Talbot was horrified on returning from a short stroll to find that his Indian escorts had cut all the trees down for firewood. Having a bad knee and indigestion, he 'showed them his displeasure.' Next day the Indians wanted to camp early, but Talbot drove them on until 6.15 p.m. The Indians were sulky and showed their displeasure by cutting only damp wood for the fire!

Pushing on in worsening conditions, Talbot had trouble in handling his dogs - apparently all males - as whenever they came near a rock or tree, one was sure to make a bolt for it which on one occasion almost resulted in the sleigh, dogs and Talbot disappearing through a hole in the now melting ice. After a final twenty-six hours' hard travelling they arrived at Norway House, the dogs' feet leaving a trail of blood in the snow.

After resting for two days, during which moccasins were made for the dogs, they travel on 180 miles to Oxford House, which they reach in four and a half days. Again it was a rough journey, sleighs and stores having to be carried at some places, men and dogs each having their burdens.

For six weeks they waited at Oxford House for the Heyes River to open up so that they could continue by boat and canoe to York Factory at the mouth of the river on Hudson Bay. Talbot read the *Pilgrim's Progress* from the post's library and always had to hand his Shakespeare, long passages from which he committed to memory. He was also learning Cree.

At night they played poker with Campbell, the company's agent, and a neighbour called Simpson, except on Sundays when they attended church, conducted by a Methodist preacher, who had an Indian interpreter for the benefit of the Cree congregation. Likewise, shooting on Sunday was frowned upon by the pious Scots.

As spring advanced, wild geese and duck were arriving in abundance but, being difficult to get near, Talbot had a hide made down river away from the post and here he would repair at 5 a.m. setting his decoys and waiting for the birds. Breakfast and lunch were served at the hide by Betts, which, in the circumstances, presents to the mind a delightful scene in the wilderness, 'Lunch is served, Sir!'

Sometimes Talbot went far afield searching for wild fowl, camping at night and sleeping in the open. 'Had dried moose, bacon, strawberry jam, bread, cross buns, prunes and tea for supper - who does not envy me? To hear the calls of swan, geese, duck and snipe and the prospect of better dreams by sleeping on top of them.' On this occasion, Barry, one of the dog team, went with him, as his feet were better, and Talbot had got 'some capital duffle boots for him.'

For the rest of May Talbot lived by himself, having pitched his tent some distance from the post. Here he was looked after by an Indian named Jim, who turned out to be a 'highly capable French cook, drinks only tea, no water, as he is a teetotaller!' 'The weather is terrible and the day is the Sabbath. Have not touched a gun all day; is it sanctity or the weather?'

Betts would arrive by canoe from the post with provisions and Talbot visited the post for his 'weekly tub', and to join in the poker games.

The Sunday following the above, Talbot remarks 'Well, I am not going to starve, so I have shot, Sabbath or no Sabbath.' Betts arrived with supplies - rice, dried apples and tea - cooked dinner and stayed overnight. The next day the two of them made duck pemican - 'skin duck, cut in little pieces, boil a little, boil potatoes, put in mashed with duck, add plenty pepper and salt, when cold fry with a little bacon and is most excellent - boiling takes fishy taste out of duck.' He also remarks, 'It is delightful to be by one's self. Arthur does not seem to care for camp life. I wish I had Bob here.'

On one of his hunting trips he discovered 'a real pretty Indian female aged about seventeen; she blushed, I had to tear myself away.'

At last the river was considered to be sufficiently open to commence the journey to York Factory. All necessary provisions and equipment had been assembled and a suitable boat obtained. Talbot and Campbell did not part on the best of terms. Earlier, Talbot had noted in his diary, 'I fancy Campbell and Simpson don't like my play, they are novices at the game; why does Campbell play if he can't afford it? I play to pass the time and make money, I suppose his is the same object.' In the matter of preparing the final account for the stay at Oxford House, Campbell was 'hard to get to the scratch'; he owed Talbot $138.75 lost at poker, who notes with satisfaction 'my card winnings brings the whole affair to $150, cheap for two months including trip to York [Factory].'

For the next eight days they rowed, were swept along with the current, shot the small rapids and portaged past the unnavigable rapids. Once they became stuck, with the water roaring round them and the 'noble Red Men bellowing like oxen.' Feeling ill and in terrible temper, Talbot one day stripped and dived into the icy lake they were traversing, 'trying a hydropathic cure which I think succeeded.' He had lost his sketch book and blamed poor Betts for 'losing everything these days.' On the 6th June they reached 'The Rock' and it was 'nothing but simple rowing for 125 miles to reach Hudson Bay and York Factory.'

Talbot was delighted with York Factory and opened the bottle of medicinal brandy in celebration. There was an excellent library and the clocks kept time, unlike those in Oxford House.

There was a great quantity of ice in the bay and he decided to go hunting for black bear with two Indians - Charles, who speaks 'Scotch' and John Thomas, 'a pure unsophisticated Indian with no knowledge of any language except his own and probably he leaves the 'H's out of that!' They were away for six days and the hunt was not a success. Travelling by canoe along the coast to the Nelson River, John Thomas proved to be an arrant coward of cold water, jumping with fear at each curling wave. The next was 'a most accursed day'. Talbot and Charles argued about sailing the canoe and Charles became rude and rebellious. Talbot sprained his shoulder and missed an easy shot at the geese; all the rice was spoiled, and John Thomas yelled with fear when the canoe was caught in a squall.

Ice still blocked the way to Churchill, so they had to wait for the south wind to clear the bay. Arthur departed to the Nelson River in his canoe to try his luck at hunting, and Talbot passed the time reading, playing his flute and sketching. During the day the weather was becoming hot and sultry, the mosquitos - the blood-sucking scourge of the summer months - were appearing, and tempers were getting frayed. Thunderstorms were sudden and violent; Dr Milner, the agent, became sulky and morose. Talbot taught him piquet - but the Doctor won as Talbot's luck was 'infernal', which made *him* - sulky and morose! 'I shall take very good care not to be on the same terms of intimacy with him as I was before; he is a man I heartily despise, I wrote rather a good skit on him today.'

On Sunday he attended chapel and listened to a Cree preacher, filled with zeal, 'morally scalping his Indian congregation.'

It was not until July that the ice in Hudson Bay receded sufficiently to allow the expedition to proceed by boat to Churchill. The Company's *Black Prince* and *La Perouse* were launched and manned by Indians, whose reluctance to sail at night, combined with head winds and pack ice, conspired to make the 150-mile journey take six days.

It was at Churchill that Talbot said goodbye to his brother Arthur and Betts, his valet, who both returned to England. Arthur was six years younger than Talbot and they found that travelling together was impossible owing to incompatibility of temperament. Betts got the sack, as he 'was getting lazy and not conducting himself like a servant.' This is hardly surprising - living in such an environment, a completely untamed wilderness with a savage climate and inhabited by trappers, Indians, Eskimo and traders, sharing equally the dangers and privations with his fellow travellers - was bound to affect the relationship between master and man. He had endured much with Talbot in the Sierra Mountains and had been lost in the forest twice during the journey from Winnipeg to York Factory. Few gentlemen's gentlemen would have put up with all this, combined with Talbot's uncertain temper. He wrote to James Fair, however, that Betts was to have a handsome golden handshake and all assistance to be given in securing him another position.

For eight days Talbot busied himself buying more provisions, equipment and trade goods from Captain Howes, the company's agent. These he would require for barter with the Eskimo - or Huskys as they were more commonly known – with whom he would be living for the rest of the journey and the hunting of the musk ox. Protective clothing against the savage winter months to come was also necessary, deerskin mitts lined with white fox, moccasins of the same, mukluks (Eskimo boots) and parkas (the native overall smock made of skin). He was given a rabbit skin blanket which proved to be one of his greatest comforts.

On the eve of departure Talbot was feeling ill and feverish and was in serious mood. 'It is a curious feeling being on the brink of civilisation and plunging into the unknown for Heaven knows how long, no flour and wood to be got and in a land of complete savages, many might think it strange, but to me there is an awe in it combined with a mysticism which is bound to weigh heavily on the mind however much the great change is in accordance with ones wishes.'

He sailed in the *Black Prince* on July 20th in company with thirty Huskys, their wives, children, bedding and utensils. The smell was overpowering and he was revolted when he first saw them gorging raw salmon and venison. Cooked fish gave them bellyache and the time was to come when he himself would not despise eating raw fish and flesh.

Talbot had a tiny deck cabin to himself and passed the time sleeping wrapped in his rabbit skin blanket reading the Bible and the *Strand* and *Century* magazines. Eight days later they arrived at Hell's Gates, where the vessel put in to trade with the Eskimos for furs. It was here that Talbot engaged a redoubtable hunter named Atonguela. Before consenting to accompany Talbot, however, he had to obtain his wife's agreement – 'an amicable woman who did not care two straws – so he comes.'

A fine whaleboat was purchased complete with mast, sails, pump, everything for a double-barreled muzzle loader, fifteen pounds of powder, ten pounds of shot and ball.

Then, George Oman, a half breed who had come as interpreter, refused to go further and wanted to return to Churchill. Talbot had not been wasting his time, however, and having picked up a few words of the Eskimo tongue, decided to proceed. 'This is rash even for me, going by myself into a bitterly cold country with no interpreter.'

Atonguela went down with influenza, which he had caught from the crew of *Black Prince.* That night Talbot 'physicked him' with about twenty grains quinine and two tablets of phenacetin all at once. Next day they embarked in the whale boat. Atonguela was 'as ill as a man could be' and Talbot covered him up with three of his own blankets. Two days later they arrived at Chesterfield Inlet where Atonguela's tribe was encamped, and he, somewhat recovered, addressed them at length. The outcome appeared to be satisfactory, so Talbot pitched his tent and treated three of the men to Eno's fruit salt, 'which they considered big medicine'!

As they had to wait for snow and hard frost to make the musk ox territory fit for travel by dog sleigh, they remained in camp for the rest of August. They were also delayed by influenza, which broke out among the tribe, and a number of them died. Talbot did what he could, dosing them with rhubarb pills and playing the flute(!); when he played softly they grew sad and wept. By 20th August, there were six dead in the camp and Talbot was deeply distressed. 'My advent among them seems to be most calamitous.' To add to his worries and discomfort he contracted eczema and ringworm and had lost the solace of his darkest hours – his beloved Shakespeare.

Being now completely on his own with the Eskimos, he applied himself diligently to learning their language, and compiled his own dictionary of words and expressions.

Cookery was a great problem as driftwood was the only fuel available for open fires and was almost non-existent. He had a coal oil stove, but the fuel had to be carefully husbanded as long, cold months were ahead. To cook his salmon he wrapped strips of fish in moss the then set fire to it – 'Excellent!'

He was getting on well with the natives. 'The ladies think I am "The thing", and if I speak to them are highly pleased, my pronunciation is quite "bon ton" – had a bath in fresh water, very cold, when I came out many females were standing and sitting round my clothes and I had to walk placidly up and take possession, they seem to regard nature "in toto" natural without clothes.' He then had a half-mile run and came back so hungry that he ate a ten-pound salmon 'My physical strength has developed enormously like my appetite.' The ladies were so impressed with him that he was offered a wife, but felt that 'he really must decline!'

On the second day of September they left 'Dead Man's Point', as Talbot named the last camp, and after twenty days moving about, hunting and fishing, established a new camp on the north side of Chesterfield Inlet from which to travel the Barren Lands in search of the musk ox. The weather was hardening into the Arctic winter, with hard frosts and blizzards of snow, and Talbot was feeling the cold badly. He was feeling ill, had a bad foot, a swollen hand, a cut tongue and the stopping had come out of a tooth. The pain became so bad he asked Atonguela to draw it with a pair of tooth nippers. 'He manipulated the instrument as he might have done with a two-handed sword and after several futile attempts broke the tooth off. My first thought was that of rage but the pain was so intense it brought me to my senses and aware that I only now possessed half a jaw to eat with, so must now be careful to apply that portion of my jaw which is whole to the tough Captain's biscuits which were the cause of all this misfortune; made some mince!'

He became so cast down that he called Atonguela to him and said he would start back for Churchill immediately, but Atonguela refused to go, saying that the boat would be caught in the ice: 'Which I think is a lie, told him to be hanged and would get someone else; but no opportunity of finding someone else, so am in a deuce of a fix.'

Resigning himself to the situation, he moved into a large igloo Atonguela had built, as his tent was too cold to live in. He hoped he would not be 'too violently attacked by bugs' and was looked after by Cuckoo, a koone,[56] who helped him to bring in supplies from his cache, including soap – 'I don't know why, I don't wash.'

The igloo was large and they all turned in to sleep stark naked, and as the air warmed up, water dripped from the roof. When they gutted and cut up deer inside the stench became almost intolerable.

When the weather permitted, the men, accompanied by Talbot, hunted for deer, of which the natives' main diet consisted, and they ate vast quantities of the flesh raw. Fat was especially prized and one day Talbot shot a magnificent stag with three fingers of fat on the haunches. He still suffered intensely from the cold and his aristocratic hooked nose was particularly prone to freezing. When this happened, one of the Huskys would warm it with his hand. His own hands also suffered, especially when hunting and carrying a rifle, the trigger mechanism of which also sometimes froze. When he came in from hunting the koones would warm his hands in their own, and, on one occasion, having gone out for a few minutes without his gloves and come back suffering frightful pain – 'a koone warmed my hands by putting them next her skin under her fur chemise, they all seem to be at boiling heat!'

The days dragged on, as the ice had to be four feet thick before the Husky would enter the musk ox country. When wind and snow made hunting impossible they had to remain in the igloo; the koones were always busy stitching fur clothing and making mitts and fur boots. In order to thaw out the boots and make them supple and wearable, the koones' chewed them, and to dry out Talbot's socks, they hung them round their necks next to the skin. The koones were making additional clothing for the musk ox hunt, and Cuckoo brought him a pair of gloves and boots, for which he paid her with packets of needles 'Her mother, a wretched old woman, cursed me afterwards, why, no one knows. I think it is because I do not return Cuckoo's affection; curious people'. His outfit for the musk ox hunt was 'two fur coats, two pairs boots, two pairs fur stockings, two pairs gloves'.

To relieve the monotony of waiting, Talbot organised leap-frog and jumping competitions for the boys, got the koones singing, played with an eighteen-month-old baby, and one night 'watching koone catching bugs off another koone and eating 'em. The women will never be celebrated for their modesty.' He also remarks – 'to hurry up a Husky would be like trying the same on with a Lytham cab horse'. One evening he showed the Huskys pictures in the *Century* Magazine and when he came to a pretty face, down went their heads to rub noses with the picture. He also delighted the koones by trying on his new fur pants in front of them.

At last, on 16th November, they started for the musk ox country; Atonguela and his brother with Acoulah, Monah, Ahwateir, Kinohena and Talbot, a large sleigh pulled by eight dogs and a smaller one pulled by four. For the next nine days they travelled, camping at night in snow houses they built for shelter against the piercing winds. Seal oil was used for the very limited amount of cooking Atonguela permitted as the oil had to be sparingly used and enough meat was cooked at one time to last several days. They hunted as they went and if they did not kill enough the dogs went hungry, sometimes for several days. To begin with Talbot was in high spirits – 'capital fun, makes up for all the hardships I have gone through so far, no weak man could stand it, though I had a wretched night. Dogs look like barrels from eating deer flesh – to catch and carry to England five musk ox, Ah!'

As they progressed the country became more hilly, and on the twelfth day he recorded the altitude as 1,200 feet above sea level. They were now in the musk ox country and were anxiously spying for their quarry. Talbot was suffering from the cold and his temper was again becoming frayed. On 27th November he lost his temper completely and cursed the Huskeys for not stopping the dogs fighting. This was considered a heinous offence by the Eskimos' and he had to make amends by giving them tea all round. The next day his hands and nose were frozen and he spent the day in camp suffering much from the cold.

November 30th: 'So ends my twenty-eighth year, we are in a land of desolation, if we do not find musk ox starvation will be the only fare for our dogs and probably for ourselves, there are not deer enough in this part of the country as two a day are required for the dogs and one for ourselves. It has been an uneventful year and things have passed very smoothly for me. Goodbye twenty-eight.'

The next day, not having sighted musk ox, Atonguela took Talbot on one side but within sight and hearing of the rest of the hunting party. Producing pieces of bone, tobacco, a match and fur, which he asked Talbot to hold exposed to the wind and repeat the words, 'Oh, Mother Earth I give you this, give me something and that musk ox.'

'Whether I have turned heathen or not, don't know, no refusing, their dark, frowning faces brightened up', he noted in his diary, and, 'one hour before sunset saw two musk ox in a valley surrounded by high hills, and made camp by a little lake and tomorrow, shoot. Exciting birthday, twenty-nine.'

In the morning they set off – running, as the dogs were then mute and would not alarm their quarry as they approached. By noon, Talbot was dead beat and lagging three quarters of a mile behind the others. Then he heard two of the dogs and, spurting up a hill, found they had brought a bull musk ox to bay. He took his rifle from Atonguela; a dog cowering at his feet caused the bull to charge straight at him; he fired and missed, the dog bolted, and for a moment Talbot and the bull looked at each other, then it turned and he killed it with his second shot. That night he was so exhausted that he spat blood, but made his diary entry for the day, finishing with a thought for his dog in Scotland, 'How is my dear Bob?'

Having secured the head as his trophy and tangible evidence of the success of his venture, the carcass was cut up and the dogs, who had not been fed for three days, given four pounds each of the flesh. It was so tough that the men could hardly stomach it and all had hiccoughs afterwards!

Despite the protests of the Eskimos, who wished to continue the hunt, Talbot had had enough and insisted on returning. They agreed only when he promised each man a rifle and ammunition, far superior to their smooth-bore muzzle-loading guns. They were three hundred miles north of the base camp at Chesterfield Inlet and it was nineteen days before they got back. By the eleventh day they were all starving. 'Eat my last piece of biscuit, boiled tea over again for third time. I feel hungry, with neuralgia and a sore throat, no one could go through a rougher time, bitter cold and scarcity of food and thoughts for the miserable dogs outside. Tetra's teeth chattered today [one of the dogs]. No tea, tobacco, biscuits or food of any sort left. It is worse than Hell.'

A deer was killed the next day and all had food, the dogs for the first time in ten days; then they reached caches where meat and fat had been stored on the outward journey.

> December 19, 1897
> All things good or bad must have an end. Arrived igloo evening, there all the koones fastened round my belt little pieces of deer skin which shows I am a full fledged hunter. A fearful mental strain as to the dogs and great hardships, on arriving have a violent fever. And there was much feasting.'

Despite it being mid-winter, Talbot was anxious to get back to civilisation and determined to travel overland the 350 miles to Churchill, as Hudson Bay was frozen over and unnavigable.

The only known representation of the pre-1754 Lytham Hall. Taken from a fragment of a plan/map of Lytham dating from around 1610, it shows the Jacobean house (probably in part the early-16th-century manor house of the priory) with St. Cuthbert's Church which was rebuilt in the 18th century and the old windmill that stood by the Hall; it also shows some of the cottages in the village. North is on the left side of the map. (L.R.O. DDCl 1056, by kind permission of Mr J. C. Hilton.)

One of a series of estate plans drawn up in 1812, showing Lytham village, hall and park. The main road to Blackpool runs across the park and then past the hall itself. (L.R.O. DDCl 522. Reproduced by kind permission of Mr J. C. Hilton.)

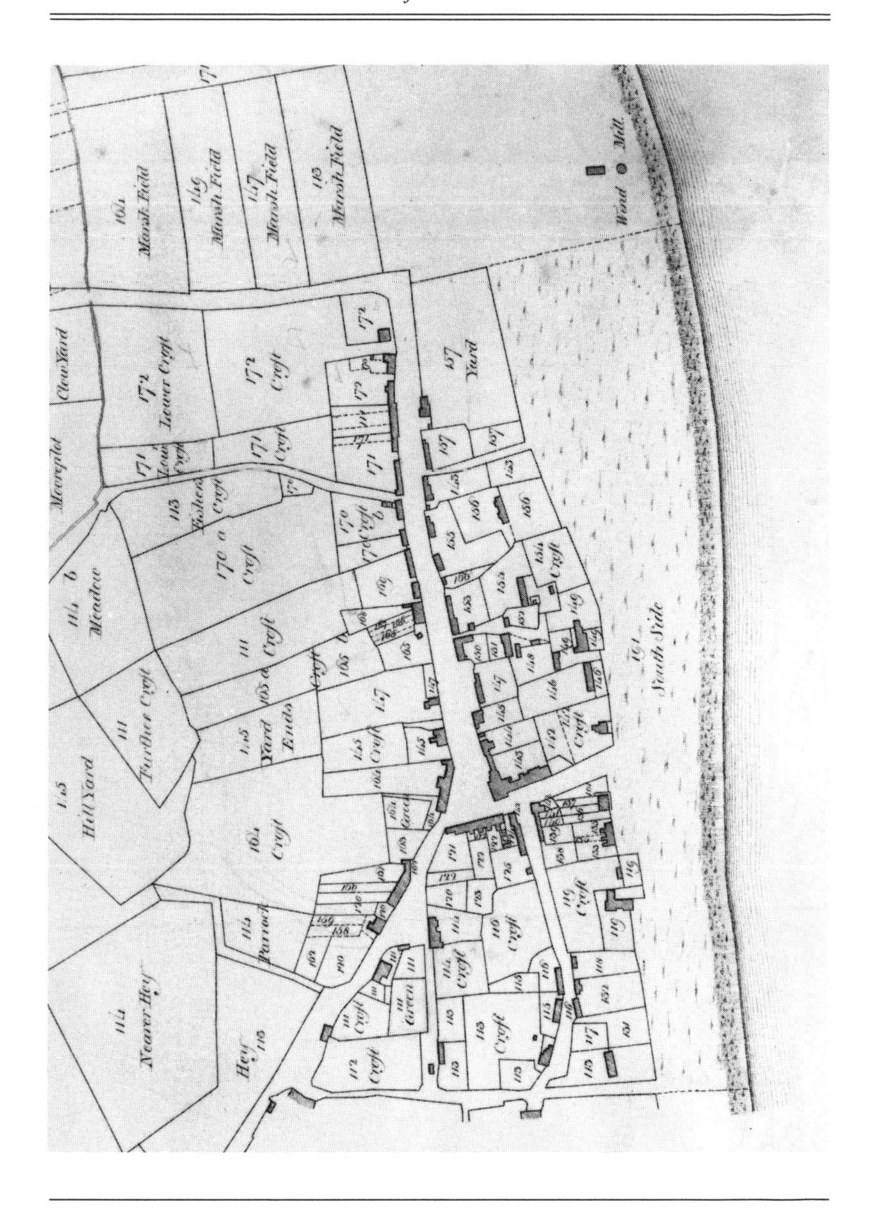

Detail of the 1812 estate plan, showing a single street (now Clifton Street), with crofts behind. On the south side are sand dunes (where Lytham Green is now). Note the windmill, the Marsh Fields (the Town Marsh used as grazing land) and the road running north-west to the Hall and on to Blackpool; this road was closed off when the railway was built in 1863. (L.R.O. DDCl 522. Reproduced by permission of Mr J. C. Hilton.)

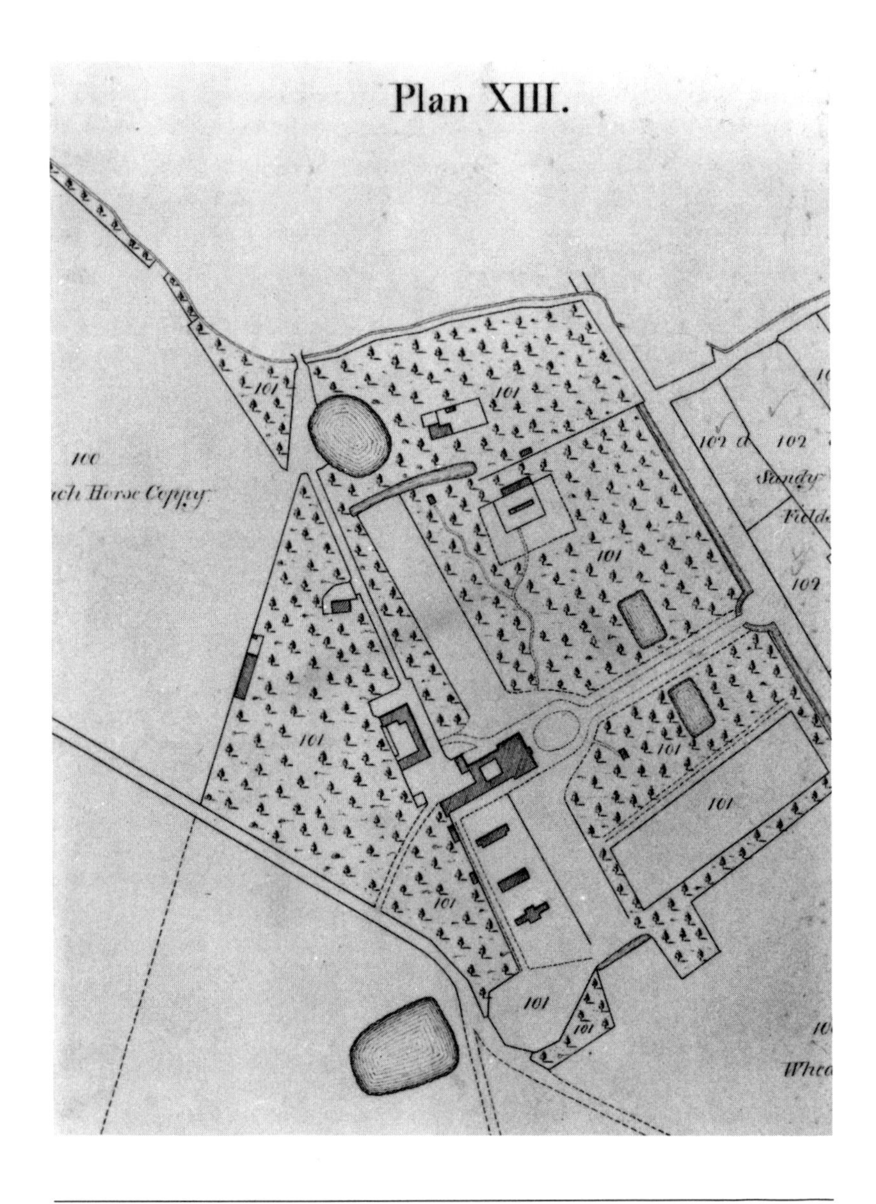

A further detail of the 1812 estate survey, showing the 18th-century Hall (by Carr of York), with late-18th-century ornamental gardens (altered in the late-19th century). The buildings at the rear of the hall are the 16th/17th-century hall which was retained for a time as servants' quarters, offices etc. (L.R.O. DDCl 522. Reproduced by permission of Mr J. C. Hilton.)

James Fair, the highly influential agent to the Clifton estate, whose enthusiasm and determination were major factors in the successful development of Lytham as a watering place. It could even be said that the town's essential character owes more to Fair than to any other single person. Three generations of Fairs were agents to the estate; James's son, Thomas, was involved in the letting of the first lease for the new town of St. Anne's-on-the-Sea to the St. Anne's Land and Building Company.

Augustus Wykeham Clifton, the family's representative in the Crimean War. He married Lady Bertha Hastings. When he was at Clifton, he attended the parish church where, if the sermon went on longer than he would ideally have liked, he used to take five shilling pieces from his pocket and line them up in full view of the minister in front of him, evidently as his offering for the church. At regular intervals, however, as the service dragged on, the coins would disappear back into the pocket, providing the minister with a powerful incentive to draw to a close.

Lytham Hall, by the famous Carr of York, dating from the 1750s. This view is particularly important for it shows the relief sculpture in the pediment at the top of the front façade; this fell out during the Second World War and was never replaced. About a third of the way up the building can be seen the string course which Lillian fell off when trying to get into the locked room where her husband was. She was seriously injured by the fall.

A lovely photograph of John Talbot and one of his coaches. He was a great whip, and used to drive to Blackpool in great style. He was also the first person to drive a coach and four through the streets of San Francisco. Note how well the horses are standing.

John Talbot's yacht Soprano. *It is quite possible that Talbot bought the yacht to impress Lillie Langtry, although there is no evidence that she ever sailed in her. It was a huge drain on resources, however, as it was sailed between Fleetwood and the Mediterranean to be 'on call' for her master. Talbot was a keen yachtsman and was the first Commodore of the Lytham Yacht Club.*

With the Sheik of Bahrain outside Kildalton Castle on the Scottish island of Islay. Talbot and the Sheik met in Bahrain and struck up quite a close friendship.

John Talbot in Siberia, a photograph that he signed in 1907. While he was in Siberia he was shot at and nearly knifed to death, and discovered a new species of wild sheep, modestly naming it 'ovis Cliftonii'.

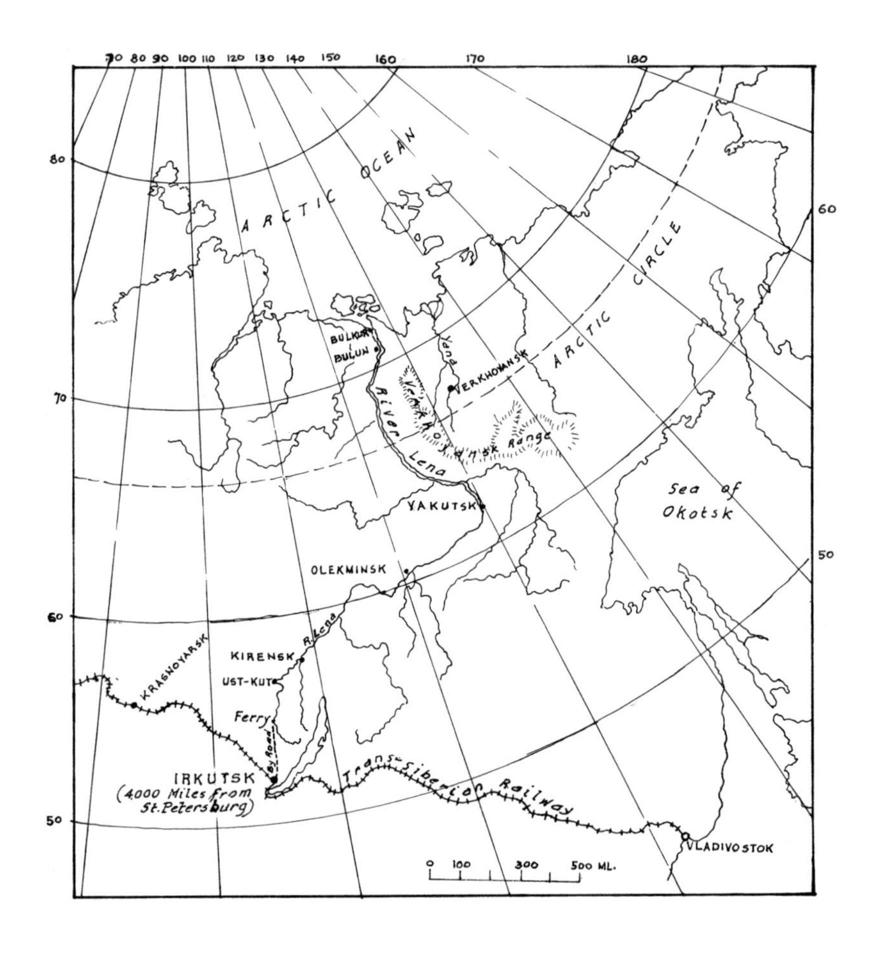

A map of John Talbot's Siberian wanderings. He was the first Englishman to reach Bulun at the mouth of the River Lena, suffering considerable hardship and danger on the way. His services were engaged to kill a savage bear that was terrorising one of the villages.

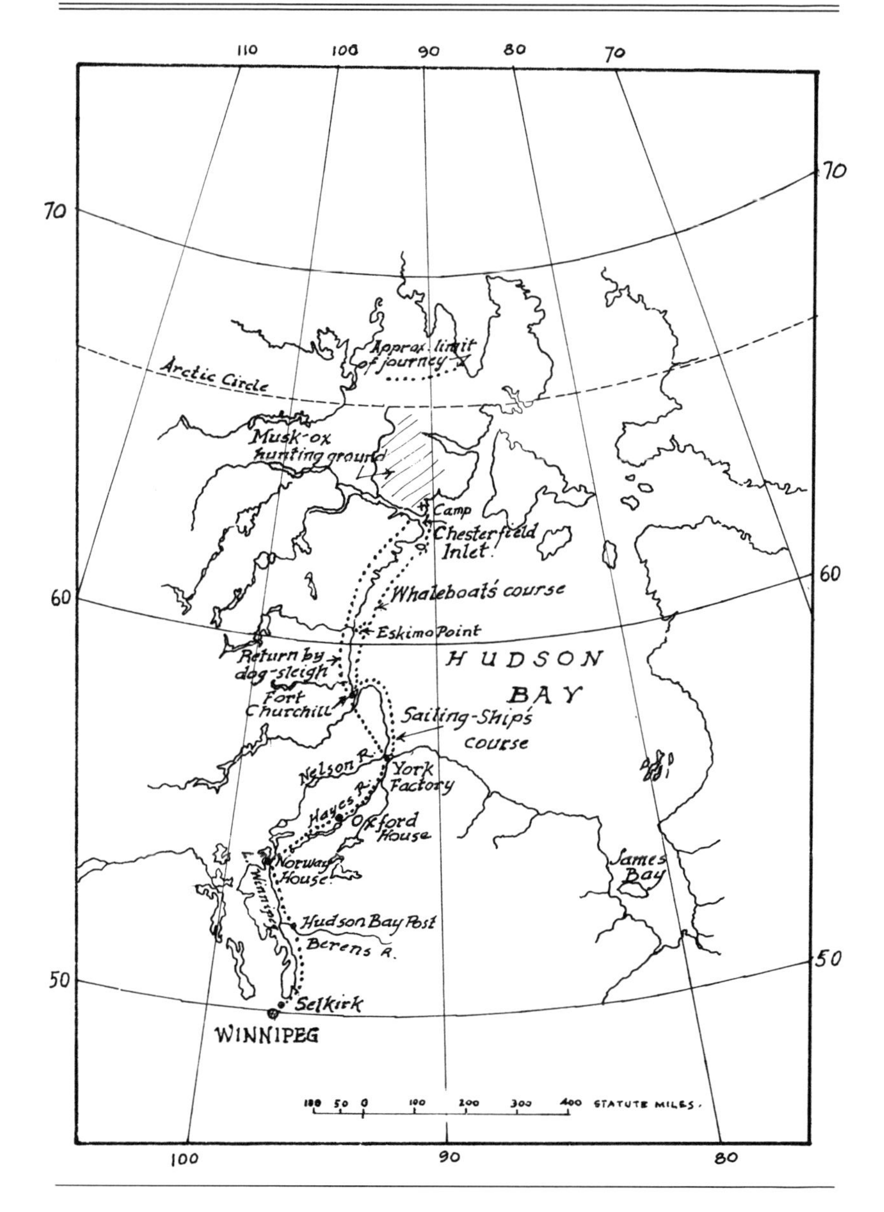

That was nothing, however, to Talbot's exploits in Canada, where he lived alone for ten months with the Eskimo without an interpreter (he even compiled his own little phrasebook and dictionary). He was nearly killed and very nearly starved to death, having to eat raw reindeer for periods. He made the journey to see if he could find any trace of the ill-fated Franklin expedition, and also to hunt musk ox in the north.

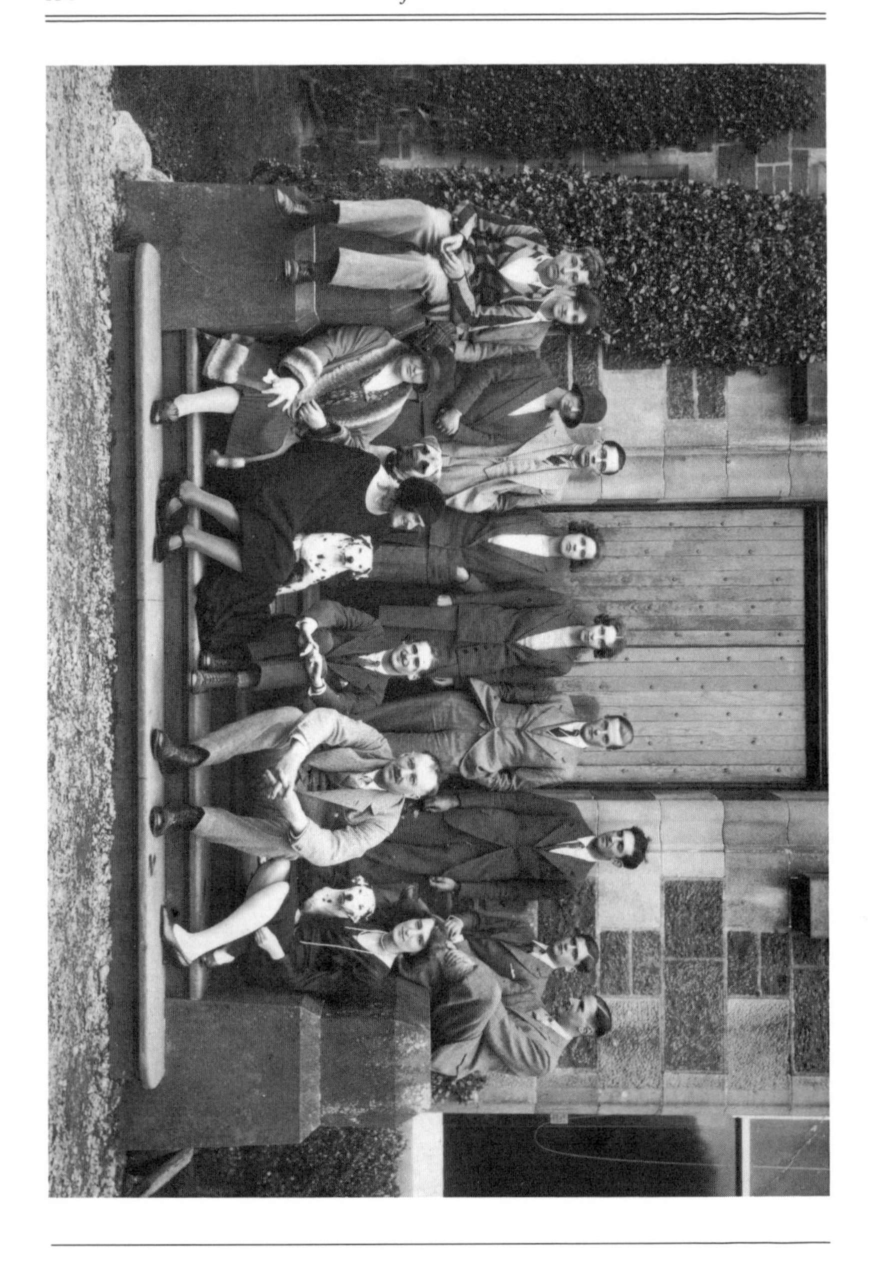

Relatively happy times at Kildalton. A family group, with Violet (second from left, front row) and Harry (third from right at back). Harry's perverse household economies made life difficult at the family home while he spent money like water on racehorses, gambling and collectables.

The striking figure of Violet (right) as she poses for the photographer at the time of her presentation to Court.

Violet in later life outside the main entrance to Lytham Hall. After Talbot's death and when Harry's financial stringency began to bite, she took voluntary refuge in the Convent of the Poor Clares at Arundel to try and save money, although, as we see here, she did come back to Lytham. (Photograph courtesy of the Evening Gazette.*)*

Sir Cuthbert Clifton, who was knighted by James I at Lathom and who purchased Lytham and Little Marton in 1606.

This enigmatic portrait purports to be of Sir Thomas Clifton Bart, but in fact is probably Sir William Clifton who made a pilgrimage to the Holy Land in 1676-7. This would account for the oriental robes and the depiction of Jerusalem in the background.

Thomas Clifton (1727-83), who built the present Lytham Hall

Thomas Clifton's third wife, Lady Jane Bertie, daughter of the Earl of Abingdon.

John Clifton (1764-1832). He devoted much of his time to estate management and to the improvement of his racing stables. He won the St Leger twice and bought Pitzhanger Manor (now Ealing Library) from Sir John Soane and moved to live there.

Thomas Joseph Clifton, known as Thomas the Tree Planter because he insisted that trees should be planted on the lands of his tenants, even going as far as to put clauses in leases to that effect. Although he was often absent from Lytham, he took a very keen interest in his estates and asked for the minutest details from his agent, Thomas Fair.

Hetty Campbell the daughter of Pellegrine Treves, who married Thomas Joseph, the Tree Planter, and with whom she travelled widely from spa to spa in England and on the Continent.

Sir Pellegrine Treves, Post Master General of Calcutta, father of Hetty and friend of the Prince of Wales.

Colonel John Talbot (1819-1882). He and his wife Lady Eleanor hunted with the Cottesmere Hunt, of which her father was master. They cruised the Mediterranean in Taurus *and the Colonel was a member of the Royal Yacht Squadron. John was commissioned in the 2nd Life Guards and was a Colonel of the Lancashire Militia.*

The Colonel's wife, Lady Eleanor Cecily (1822-1894), sister of the 3rd Earl of Lowther. She was well known for her charity and acts of goodness to the poor of Lytham and certainly was one of the best loved of the Cliftons locally. Among other things she built St. Anne's parish church, but closed down the Travel Boat Inn after discovering revelling tenants drinking and cavorting in the middle of the day!

Augustus Wykeham Clifton, Captain of the Rifle Brigade, who married Bertha Lelgrade, 23rd Baroness Grey de Ruthyn.

John Talbot Clifton (1868-1928)

A 1925 family portrait of the Cliftons. Left to right: John Talbot, looking rather stern considering that that very day he had been granted the honorary freedom of Lytham St. Annes; Easter Daffodil; Lady Violet; Michael Clifton; and Henry de Vere Clifton (Harry), heir to the estates.

(Photograph courtesy of the Evening Gazette.*)*

Harry, shortly before the war. Harry really wanted to be an intellectual and scholar and rather resented his father's efforts to prepare him to succeed as squire. His great passions were racehorsing and spending money, both of which he did on a lavish scale.
(Photograph courtesy of the Evening Gazette.*)*

In 1939 Harry (with William Whinnerah next right) 'inaugurated' the new town of St. Christopher. Amid great press publicity, he laid this foundation stone. Unfortunately, he had laid it right on top of a water main and this stone, the only part of the town ever to see light of day, was unceremoniously pulled down by the Water Board.
(Photograph courtesy of the Evening Gazette.*)*

Lillian, Harry's wife, posing for a photograph with her Wolseley. (Photograph courtesy of the Evening Gazette.*)*

Harry Clifton during his last visit to Lytham Hall. He had inherited the huge family estate in 1928, but when he died left just £30,000 in his will.

Atonguela was willing to go but there was some delay in persuading others to make up the necessary numbers for the journey.

Once again, inactivity and delay was getting on his nerves.

> These people have disgusted me quite. Atonguela koone leads by forty lengths. I have given her tea, flour, tobacco, everything in fact, yet she wants more. Atonguela is much the same, they will not give away anything except in return for something. Atonguela is actually trading the baccy I gave him for boots etc. - damn them all . . . to leave these people and their dirt and filthy ways will be worth all the suffering I have gone through. Gods on tin wheels they think themselves, but they know not what a wheel is. My English is getting dirtily mixed up with their wretched Husky expressions and am beginning to feel like the Britons before the Romans, without an iota of self contempt, dressed up in deerskins, unwashed etc.'

Christmas Eve, and he was still furious with Cuckoo koone and told her husband to keep her in order, then he gave some beads she had been looking forward to, to another koone - 'bitter tears in consequence - I was awful mad!'

A little later Atonguela came into the igloo and after sending everyone out, closed the door (by putting a large piece of ice across the entrance!) He turned to Talbot happily: 'peaceably we talked about the journey, start in six sleeps, Cuckoo koone is coming, which I think very amusing, I have a fair knowledge why she is, I wanted gloves and have been swamped with them in consequence all day. Very bad neuralgia but am picking up a little from my starvation fare, the dogs seem all the better for two weeks without food. Am smoking my last pound tin of baccy. All is peaceful tonight, Xmas Eve. Stocking up.'

> 25th December.
>
> Fine Xmas breakfast, deer flesh with a big lump of fat, on opening the tin wherein the plum pudding had been kept for nearly six months I cut two fingers badly. An hour after I warmed it up, gave Atonguela and his koone some and with a beautifully boiled deer's tongue and plum pudding had an excellent Xmas dinner, later on had marrow and boiled deer flesh with plenty of fat so altogether I cannot complain at my Xmas fare. I hung my stocking up but Santa Claus found this region too cold I suppose, for the stocking was bare.
>
> Will I get my musk ox head to England in safety, five sleeps more and we start. Sixty days ought to find us in Winnipeg.

The journey to Churchill took forty-six days and not twenty as Talbot had hoped; mainly due to Atonguela losing the way and ignoring Talbot's own dead reckoning by compass. Again they almost starved, but Talbot was amused to find that Atonguela was in love with Cuckoo and 'mashing her hard', which probably accounted for his koone's evil temper before they left.

Fort Churchill was reached on February 13th: 'Mr and Mrs Howes were more than kind, as weary and worn out after six weeks and a half hard travelling in the coldest time of the year, in one of the coldest countries in the world, I found a great rest.

My life among the Eskimo ends here forever.'

IX

Norway House,
Friday 25th March 1898.

Dear Jim,
All your letters to hand, most of them I received at Churchill on arriving there Feb' 14, 98, having lived with the Esquimaux on Chesterfield Inlet and travelled 300 miles north of there to shoot musk ox of which I got one magnificent specimen and am bringing it south as fast as my dogs will go. The explorations were very successful during my sojourn in the N., having discovered mountains, lakes and rivers which were hitherto unknown, merely rumoured by mention to white men. I am now 550 miles from Churchill and have only 300 more to Winnipeg by dogs, then will hurry on to England. I was rather surprised at your appearing anxious for answers to your letters as I remember telling you before starting you might be some time without hearing from me as I was going to an almost unknown country and it is an awful damper on one's spirits to find reproaches for not writing (foolish very), look at the map, find Chesterfield Inlet; on the 30th day of Dec. '97 started for Churchill with ten pounds of flour, three pounds of tea, nine dogs (Huskys), three Esquimaux and self, arrived Churchill 14 Feb. '98'; two years ago the natives had died from hunger along that route, but we found deer in plenty, it was a wonderful journey helped by the most unprecedented good luck. I was seven months alone with the Esquimaux. My guide (Half breed) left me at a place called (Hell's gates) in the summer, telling me that the (Husky) Eskimo could only look after one man. I found out afterwards it was a damn trumped up lie, he went back to Churchill with my canoe and for seven months I have been absolutely alone with the natives. My strength has completely gone and can hardly eat my teeth are so bad. My heartiest congratulations on your being presented with a son, may he be successful and lucky. Love to my dear old Bob. My best regards to Mrs B, hoping she is quite well.

I remain,
Yrs. truly,
J. Talbot Clifton.

P.S. So Betts has determined to settle down, quite right about the £200 but kindly ask him to find me a really good servant as they are very few and far between. I shall want someone to meet me at Liverpool, will cable what ship. Do not let Rhidorroch, I said last year I would be back for the shooting. Got a slight attack of influenza on arrival here yesterday. Am carrying all the mails from Churchill, York, Oxford and here to Winnipeg.

After his return to England, Talbot went to Rhidorroch, the deer forest near Ullapool that he had leased from the Sutherland Estate, where he continued his stalking, with Highland stags as his quarry, instead of caribou and musk ox.

Edward Hoad was Talbot's butler at Rhidorroch Lodge and upon him rested the responsibility for the smooth running of the establishment and the comfort of his master and guests. Hoad was an Englishman unused to the ways of the Highlanders and suffered many frustrations and difficulties in consequence. As he had no one in Scotland to whom he could turn for advice and assistance – Talbot expecting all domestic problems to be resolved without reference to him – Hoad wrote to James Fair, and his letters reveal some of the day-to-day calamities that beset him!

His first letter is dated July 1898:

> Sir,
>
> I beg leave to say Mr Clifton wishes the solid silver sent here as per list enclosed, I tried all I could for him not to have it but Mr Clifton says he is going to have a lot of visitors here including Lord Lonsdale, there is nothing to use for the Servants' Hall and there was no stores of any kind when I got here, the cook and kitchen maid come on Thursday . . . there are two gentlemen here and there are only two spare beds now, there is no fruit in the garden, the peas and potatoes are not near ready, every one seems to do as they like, but I will do the very best to try and keep things right Sir . . .

Three days later he writes 'begging leave to say' that he was quite disheartened about the state of everything – the linen was nothing but rags, excepting a few tablecloths, and there were very few glasses and china. He sent for a dozen each of cups and glasses for the Servants' Hall and lamp chimneys, but it rained very much and the horse shied and half of them were broken. There were three horses and a pony but one was lame and the bus was to be sent to Lytham and the two traps were disabled.[57] The cook he thought was a very nice person and she had complained of the poorness of the milk and cream and Sutherland – the head keeper – said it was new milk, the butter was one shilling and four pence a pound and not worth eating. He was also distressed to see that Sutherland had got on the right side of Mr Clifton and they sometimes had their meals together.

> Mr Clifton had a bullock here to shoot yesterday, there are some sheep on the place for use as well, I asked for rabbits but have only had a few small ones, and no fish caught. I cannot get Mr Clifton to talk about things. I am trying my best Sir to get things a little straight.

He writes again on the 8th August expressing concern about the sleeping arrangements:

the two permanent maids sleep in a room outside near the stable and the coachman Howard and the piper sleep together in the next room, and the new coachman sleeps at present in the new tin house but will I expect have to move somewhere else, and the Helper sleeps over the coachhouse, the Footman in the pantry, I have a small room and the Cook and Kitchen Maid have two small beds in another room, that leaves four beds besides Mr Clifton's Sir. Mr Clifton talked of putting beds in the gun room for some of the servants, I will certainly see that Mr Clifton is not imposed upon. The Piper Roderick I find expects me to pay him. He was engaged by Mr Sutherland to play during dinner and fill up his time about the house. His wages twenty-two shillings per week and food and beer. He is very little use to me Sir as Sutherland sets him to anything *he* wants doing, he only sets the servants' meal and gets the coal in.

Every week Fair received by post Hoad's catalogue of woe – the footman is not to be depended on and the piper had been put to minding the pheasants and did not help him. Each day he has to give three under-keepers their flasks of whisky and they return and want more;

there is no satisfying them, then the water bailiff says he ought to have his whisky as well. I must ask Mr Clifton what quantity they are to have, Sir, then they hang about here and want more to eat and beer, I am quite tired of their ways Sir. I am so sorry they will not let things go straight, all these Scotch people do their utmost to put the others about Sir.

Poor Hoad was also being harassed by Talbot who wanted more silver plate, ink stands and candelabra sending from Lytham and they already have more than can be looked after. The cows also gave him cause for concern:

they do not give a lot of milk and no convenience for them and they say they ought to be served, I do not understand about them at all Sir.

Three small deer in the garden also had to have their daily milk ration. However, there were now potatoes from the garden and a few broad beans. At Hoad's request a basket cart had been repaired at Ullapool to convey supplies to the house, but;

It started for the first time Saturday evening to do the messages and the wheel came off owing to the man not replacing the pin and now the axle is broken. Things do not improve.

The piper got the sack but was replaced by a very old man who was lame and suffered from rheumatism, who flatly refused to clean knives or boots or undertake any other task but piping!

Finally he wrote in October:

I beg to say Sir that you need not be surprised if I leave Mr Clifton any day as he is treating me very badly lately, since he has not been drinking whisky I cannot do anything right, I am quite certain I have done my best to please him and studied him in every way.

Perhaps the last straw was the arrival of three of Talbot's Husky dogs from Canada; Agilus, Arois and one other, his favourites. The dogs ended their days in honourable retirement in Scotland, as Talbot considered Arois, the leader, the saviour of his life by his courage and endeavour for over two thousand miles of travel.

X

BEFORE the end of 1898 Talbot was in Africa and, because the diary covering this episode in his life is missing, the following account is taken from the *Book of Talbot.* Violet Clifton states that she wrote it in blank verse because the story comes from torn pages and 'barely remembered talk'.

Starting from Beira he trekked for a while with Rhodes.

At Beira he hunted, and sometime
He trekked in a wagon with Rhodes.
The two men, each square to the world,
Bore a fellow liking for one another;
And that because of a loathing common to each,
And that because life is so very quotidian,
That even friendships are founded on little foolish things.
So when the first night the bullock wagon was stayed,
Each was thankful to find the other,
Like to himself,
Away from the caravan
Pissed under the stars.'

With thirty-six carriers he travelled towards Blantyre, through swamps and heavy rain, 'Made niggers [sic] go through morass and finally got through in safety. No one drowned.'

It would never have done for him to have had a quiet time. Once, while waiting by a drinking hole, he felt a breath on his neck and, looking round, came face to face with a lioness stalking him! Then he was charged by a buffalo, which he came upon suddenly in tall grass; he fired and wounded it, then tracked it in trepidation lest it lay in wait to charge again. On another occasion, up the River Pungwe, he was hunting buffalo with a Portuguese, who, coveting Talbot's rifles, refused to pass one to him as a bull buffalo was about to charge. Fortunately, a faithful Swahili speared the animal. What happened to the Portuguese is not recorded!

When meat of impala or eland was plenty, Talbot walked in front and put the boys behind him, because of the meaty stink of their sweaty bodies. But when they had eaten corn and fruit, then they went carrying their burdens before him.

His impatience and love of 'pushing on', as he had done with the Eskimos, again evidenced itself: 'walking from six in the morning, breakfast at ten and covering twenty-five miles a day'. By now he had seventy boys as bearers, who apparently did not appreciate all this haste, as one night they refused to fetch water from the river, so, having apprehended the ringleader, 'baptized his tail and made fetch water, also blood'.

> I have decided to go to Bakari near to Uganda. All my seventy boys refuse to go that way so I have got another headman and hope in two or three days to get off. Fever sores very painful.[58] The Germans tell me the way to Bakari is dangerous (Trash).

The seventy boys of the safari were mustered. 'Tell them', Talbot said to the headman, 'that if any of them steal chickens, or rape the women in any village that we pass through, I myself will give them fifty strokes of the chicate.' They proceeded through untravelled country, exchanging gifts with the chiefs as tokens of friendship.

One chief refused to offer the customary goat to Talbot, which aroused his suspicions that the chief intended to attack and kill him and his carriers, in order to possess himself of the rifles and trade goods.

> So I shinned up a tree and hung a bottle over the place where I knew the chief and his men would squat to parley. We talked, the upshot was not to my satisfaction. He wished me, at once, to go on with my journey and leave behind my goods and all my native porters. I refused his impatient demands, then I reached for my elephant gun and when the moment demanded action I shot at the bottle. It smashed into fragments – down among the natives.

This exhibition of marksmanship apparently put the wind up the natives. Luckily the chief cut his foot on the broken glass, and how he hastened to send Talbot the customary goat! The chief also asked for ointment to heal his foot and Talbot sent him a little every day until he got safely through his country.

And then – an intriguing entry in the month of October – 'I went to the house of the Greek and by force took the Arab half-caste – putting the fear of God into several Arabs. I had to carry the girl four miles through much sand, wrist and arm aching. So I say goodbye to the great inland Lake Tanganyika'. As there is no other reference, the reader must use his or her imagination as to what high adventure this entry relates!

Then there is reference to an incident, which, if true, does not redound to Talbot's credit.

> Talbot was terrible in justice and in anger;
> And that indeed was needful.
> Once to quell a revolt,
> He gave the offending boys
> Into the hands of the loyal
> To work their own way upon those

Who would not abide by their word,
And who endangered the others,
By bringing division amongst them.
But he never again did that,
For the Homatic justice
Meted out by the riverside was so very awful.
It lasted from dawn, till the night
Encircled them; and the roaring of lions
Shook the darkness;
Only there was the fate of the rebels made better by death.

His prowess as a hunter kept the majority of the boys loyal, because they feasted well on meat. His personal servant, Makahuli, had stolen bread on a Wednesday, so for several weeks after he suffered the 'kiboko' on Wednesdays. When he protested, saying 'I am good now, I do not steal', his master informed him, 'you must be whipped to keep you good!'

Not surprisingly, his followers named him 'Simba' – the Lion.

Despite the weekly stimulant of the kiboko, Makahuli so worshipped Talbot that when he sailed for England early in 1900 he begged to be taken with him. Talbot refused for Makahuli's own good, but the negro was so persistent that he swam out, two miles, to the ship as she weighed anchor, but still Talbot refused.

One last verbatim quote from *The Book of Talbot:* 'If ever I write of your travels, what shall I say about those years in Africa?' Talbot had answered: 'Say that I treated my boys with kindness and with the kiboko. People who knew my Africa will know that I understood!'

XI

DURING Talbot's African expedition, events were taking place in the south of the continent that culminated in the declaration of war by the Boers in April, 1899. We have already seen Cuthbert's reactions - his anxiety to join the army, his arrival in Cape Town and almost immediate breakdown of health, causing his return and death at Edwinsford in 1900.

Other members of the family were not slow to become involved. The Hon. James Cumming Bruce, husband of Cecily, sister to Talbot, was killed at Magersfontein on 11th December, 1899. A captain in the Black Watch, he fell in the hail of bullets that greeted the Highlanders in the ill-directed attack.

Arthur, on his return from Churchill on Hudson Bay, had considered buying a 300-acre farm on the Scottish borders, but this seems to have fallen through and we next hear of him in November 1988 in Bethune's Mounted Infantry in Natal.

Caryl, the youngest brother, had made the army his career and having been commissioned in the Royal Scots Fusiliers attached to the 6th Brigade 3rd Army Division, was also in Natal during November.

Lady Drummond, writing to James Fair on November 22nd 1899, says, 'I will send on the letters, though poor dears, they won't be much good just now, they are both gone to the front, the first look at the papers is *dreadful.'*

On February 8th, 1900, Caryl wrote to his sister, Edith Noel, during the fighting for Zwaart Kop. A Boer six-inch gun was lobbing ninety-pound shells into their position for the third day and they are taking cover - a shell has just burst ten feet away from him and one of his corporals has had his greatcoat ripped off his back by a splinter but is unhurt.' Caryl, however, is enjoying the scenery, 'This is a most lovely place and the doves are cooing and building their nest, just as if nothing was going on. The birds and butterflies are beautiful.' His uncle, Major Quentin Agnew, was on the other side of the hill and Arthur's regiment was covering the river between Colenso and Zwaart Kop. There was a general retirement on and they were all very down-hearted, the men itching to fire on the Boers - who were very close - but had to be restrained as they did not want to attract the attention of the enemy's quick-firing guns.

The Royal Scots seem to have been the rearguard and covered the withdrawal of the British guns under cover of darkness. By February 14th, however, they were on the attack as Caryl describes in his letter:

Middlebourg Laager. Feb. 19

Just a line to tell you about the last few days. We started Wednesday 14th and took Hussar Hill, so called because a Hussar patrol was surprised and cut up there. We cleared the Boers out of the bush and then brought our heavy guns up. Lyttelton with his brigade commenced a large turning movement to our right - taking part of a large range of hills covered with timber scrub. Whilst this was going on our brigade gradually moved forward day after day until yesterday when we swung round to our left and captured three large hills and a Boer laager and have got round the enemy's flank. We are now waiting for our big guns to come up before we try to cross the river. We have had about twenty casualties in our lot. Quentin is fit and well and has looted a Boer horse. We are all very tired and dirty as we are up every morning at three with only a couple of ships' biscuits from three p.m. till night. None of us have had our clothes off or a wash of any kind for six days. Bed consists of a greatcoat and a waterproof sheet. General Buller has just passed. Everyone is delighted with our success yesterday, as the Boers considered this position impregnable.

21st. Two brigades are across the river now. We cross early tomorrow. I expect we shall have a big fight.

Caryl's expectations were correct. These were the preliminaries to the relief of Ladysmith on 28th February. Buller, instead of following up the advantage gained by the right-handed movement commenced by Lyttelton and his brigade, drew in the right and began to advance by his left. This resulted in much heavy fighting and unnecessary casualties, as described by Sir Winston Churchill, who witnessed the operations. In *My Early Life* he says: 'The purblind viciousness of the manoeuvres was apparent to many.'

Just a year after the above events, Arthur writes to James Fair from Slik Spruit. He was now Adjutant to BMI and Staff Officer to Colonel Monroe; they are 'de Wet hunting', and he is supposed to be near. They are marching day and night, little sleep and up before daylight, 'anyhow a healthy life.'

Another family connection, the Duke of Norfolk, had joined Lord Robert's staff with the rank of captain in the Imperial Yeomanry.[59] The Duke of Westminster and Duke of Marlborough were also on his staff, 'in one capacity or another.'[60]

In the meantime the ubiquitous Talbot had no sooner returned from Africa in January 1900 than - determined not to be left out of the fun - he sailed again for Beira from Marseilles in *S.S. Oxus* on February 25th.

He went out as a war correspondent and had instructed James Fair to contact the Blackpool papers as to terms for his dispatches. Talbot considered they should be worth nine guineas per column, but the papers thought anything in excess of three guineas would be too much, and pointed out that by the time his copy had arrived in England it would be – to use a modern expression – 'old hat', as news from the front was being received by telegraph and appeared in the daily papers without delay.

He did, however, have some arrangement with the *Daily Mail* and pushed on undaunted. During the passage to Beira, he suspected some of his fellow passengers – Dutch, Irish and French – of being in collaboration with the Boers, and, losing his temper one day about anti-British comments, thought that he was in danger of his life.

There was a Russian musician on board, who, being a gullible individual, scoured the markets and shops of Port Said in search of a hippopotamus hide coat, which, he had been assured, was the only suitable rainwear for Africa!

Talbot had taken with him a groom called David and at Beira engaged a German servant called Willy. They travelled by train to Umtali, about 180 miles west of Beira, and there he busied himself buying horses, wagons, harness and provisions, and generally preparing for the road.

The start on April 4th was not propitious. A wheel came off one of the wagons and another had to be procured, together with a Cape boy to drive it. They had only proceeded two miles when the wagon nearly capsized, throwing out the boy, who sustained a badly cut head and an arm broken in two places. Finding that the horses were not broken to driving, Talbot abandoned the carts and harness and used the horses as pack animals. This, too, was not completely successful, as the packs slipped under their bellies and one intractable member of the team proved to be a racehorse called Barclay who, understandably, resented keenly the indignity of being used as a pack animal. On making camp for the first time and pitching his new tent he found 'it was an awful fraud and not quite seven feet long.'

He was determined to get to Rusape in one day, which be reckoned to be thirty miles away, but which turned out in fact to be forty-five, but by much hard riding and goading of a rebellious David and Willy, who doubtless in turn goaded on the pack horses, he arrived at Rusape at 8 p.m. having passed several lion spoors on the way, which probably helped to encourage David and Willy to make all speed!

> Having had little to eat for two days I was delighted to see a great steaming haunch of beef with potatoes and cabbage brought in; the mounted police kindly put up my two English horses in their stables; the pack animals arrived early in the morning (poor David and Willy!). I stopped at Rusape till Thursday waiting for a horse-box to take my cattle

to Marandellas, the line having been blocked for two days on account of an engine running off the line.

At Marandellas Camp preparations were being made to receive 4,500 men from England, and Talbot began writing his dispatches. Within a day or so, however, he and Willy were down with ague and fever and fearful retching attacks. As usual illness does not improve his temper; 'I find David a most intractable servant, wishes to argue on every subject and prefers his advice to me unasked for. Willy is willing enough but not very handy; being a German he is terribly slow.'

Willy is 'now and then off his head' and Talbot's fever is getting worse, so he decides to go to Salisbury for medical attention. Travel by train is difficult due to long delays and poor rolling stock, however,

> had my things taken to the station where after some trouble I managed to find a covered wagon and laid on my pillow, using my coat for the purpose and with my Scotch plaid was fairly comfortable, the unfortunate Willy brought a quantity of rugs, but could not make himself comfortable. About 1 a.m. we arrived Salisbury. I had telephoned Major Gosling to get a bed in his hospital for my German and I met a man at the station with the answer. I also found the hospital wagon, so put him in telling him to send me back a cap, which he forgot all about.

Talbot then found himself alone at the station with a temperature of 103 degrees, vomiting occasionally and clutching a tin box with £150 cash in it. Eventually he borrowed a horse and rode to the hospital, where, upon being examined, was found to have an enlarged spleen and his heart not in good shape. He remained in hospital writing up his diary, looked after by sisters 'by no means good looking', until he recovered and went back to Marandellas. On 1st May, General Sir Frederick Carrington arrived with his staff of eight officers, and Talbot was made a member of their Mess.

For the next two months he is at Marandellas, writing his dispatches but finding little to put into them, save accounts of the day-to-day events in the military camp. Horse races are organised, and Talbot takes part with considerable success, being praised by the General for his horsemanship. Barclay, who had suffered the indignity of being used as a pack animal, has his self-respect restored by being put in training. Poker and baccarat were played every night and Talbot gleefully records winning a 'very useful £140'. This success, however, is followed by the loss of £115 – 'a disastrous night' – but he won it back two nights later.

Many hundreds of horses had died from horse sickness and blue tongue; then glanders broke out and spread rapidly as all trucks and drinking troughs between Beira and Marandellas were infected. Talbot's 'dear little Brownie', a mare who would stand without being tethered, died. Then a message came from Major Mann, the veterinary surgeon: 'Sorry to say that Barclay had horse sickness and is dying.' Three of his horses died in five days and sixty others in the same period.

Talbot was impressed by the number of colonial troops passing through the camp - Canadians, Australians and New Zealanders - who had answered the Queen's call to arms. On 18th June, General Carrington and his staff left for Pietersbourg and Bulawayo, and the war correspondents were to follow later. After the relief of Ladysmith by Buller, Roberts reached Bloemfontein, on May 31st Johannesburg and on June 5th Pretoria fell, Mafeking was liberated after a siege which lasted for two hundred and seventeen days.[61]

After these events it was thought that the war was won, but guerrilla warfare dragged on until peace was made in March 1902.

Talbot did not leave Marandellas until 7th July and in the meantime he had sacked Willy, the German, and sent David, the groom, back to England. In their stead he hired a 'splendid Cape boy called Alec; he acts as stud groom, valet, boots, chambermaid and handyman for four pounds a month and food.'

The diary stops abruptly in the middle of a sentence, and on the 5th September, 1900 he cables James Fair from Capetown, simply, 'Returning'.

What he did in the interim is not clear, but from the *Book of Talbot* it seems that he joined Carrington's column and at last saw some action, which undoubtedly he would have enjoyed.

XII

BY October 1900 Talbot was back at Rhidorroch, having another go at the black game and stalking. Then, during February 1901 he was in London and just taken delivery of his new Daimler car, which he drove from Coventry and did twenty-one miles in twenty-five-and-a-half minutes, which pleased him enormously. It was also during February that he wrote to James Fair, rather mysteriously,

> I am sorely troubled old chap, really badly so, not monetarily, but otherwise, so probably next week I will write you, say Friday. It may astonish you to know I have become a great society humbug, if what I am about to do next week does not succeed I shall go to Sakhalin Island then to Vladivostok and on by the new railway across Siberia; if everything pans out as I hope, you will do me a great kindness to come up to town, however, that is in the future.

As we next find Talbot in Paris en route to St. Petersburg, things apparently did not 'pan out', and he is very downcast and melancholy. He has with him his valet, John Green - successor to Betts - and Sin, his dog - successor to Bob. He is very ill, with inflammation of the lungs, but on 16th March leaves for St. Petersburg, where he arrives three days later and meets his friends Prince Serge and Princess Orloff. As he now preferred to travel alone, finding a valet a nuisance, he sent John Green back to England from Paris.

For the next six weeks he studies music, putting in long hours of practice on his flute, and had a piano brought into his hotel room and a lady music teacher to play it. He meets Patrick de Bath, the brother of Hugo de Bath, who became the second husband of Lillie Langtry. He became pally with Bernhardt, Director of the Opera, as he saved him from being crushed in a lift. He also met a Dutchman who had £20,000 to spend but was not sure how to; Talbot suggested that he could help him as well as most people!

He played polo and broke in Caucasian ponies for Prince Serge. He supped beer and sausages with Prince Stolberg and two other Germans: 'the room reeked of beer and sauerkraut, capital fellow!'

He was greatly honoured by being permitted to attend a private review of the Gardes-à-Cheval, the Czar's bodyguard, in the presenceof the Czar himself. This was arranged by Princess Orloff.

On 8th May he leaves St. Petersburg and commences the 4,000-mile train journey to Irkutsk, from where he proposed to travel by road and river to Bulkur, where the River Lena empties into the Arctic Ocean. His main interest was in the wild sheep that inhabit the region, but he would bring back specimens of any other species of wildlife that aroused his interest.

During the train journey, which took nineteen days including stops, he met Professor Otto Hertz, a German, who was going in search of a mammoth that was known to be frozen up in a glacier somewhere near Yakutsk, in the hope of bringing it back for his museum in Germany. He also had an assistant, whose looks Talbot does not like, and a 'baby faced geologist'. The last part of the journey from Krasnoyarsk to Irkutsk was in a train which trundled along at twenty miles per hour, but had a piano on board, which the ladies played accompanying Talbot on his flute.

Arriving at Irkutsk, Talbot cabled to England for £1,000 and purchased a Mauser rifle with 800 cartridges. He hoped to catch a river steamer at Ust-Kut, 250 miles away, but was delayed waiting for his money and a road pass. With only three days left, off he goes in a two-horse, non-sprung carriage with a hood, his baggage in a troika, and no road pass. As he has no pass he has difficulty in getting post horses and is furious to see other passengers for the steamer pass him on the road. He pushed on day and night, hiring open carts and one carriage with wooden springs – 'a great luxury'. At a ferry he espied a boat and after a lot of haggling hired it and three 'cut throats' to take him 140 versts by river. Four other travellers joined him and they drifted and rowed for four days, provisioned with black bread, meat and a few duck that Talbot knocked down with his gun.

The steamer seems to have been delayed as Talbot and the others arrived in ample time before it sailed. Small, dirty and crowded, the wood-burning steamer proceeded on its way to Yakutsk, Talbot practising his flute, reading Shakespeare and trying to learn Russian as no one spoke any other language.

At Yakutsk the Governor General told him that the locals of some of his districts had complained that there were too many bears about and would he send the Cossacks to kill them? 'What price rabbits and farmers in England!', notes Talbot.

Boarding the steamship *Lena* for the next leg of his journey down the river of that name, the crew are 'all drunk and fighting like demons.' Some are taken to the police and some bound with ropes – 'altogether disgraceful.' For six days they travelled downstream, making frequent stops to pick up wood for fuel. Talbot slept on deck because of the heat, but burning embers from the funnel and mosquitos eventually drove him below to his cabin. The further north they go the fewer the hours of darkness until he is not sure when to sleep or what day it is, as his watches and Siberian clocks are unreliable, so he sleeps when Sin sleeps as he seems to know best!

They arrive at Bulun, where he buys a tent and equipment as he intends to go in search of *ovis nivicula*, the wild sheep. A Swede called Torgenson is a local magnate who trades in furs and employs the locals for fishing in the Lena delta. He speaks German and helps Talbot in purchasing a boat and engaging three Tungus as crew. For seven days he camps and hunts and again has violent attacks of dyspepsia, for which he blames tannic acid poisoning from tea, but his own baking of bread without baking powder, '[which] is not very wholesome, too heavy, but good food', would hardly help matters.

Wild sheep are at last sighted but he misses a fine ram he wanted as a specimen. He shot a wild reindeer, which made for a change of diet from the fish they had netted daily; the three Tungas ate twenty fish, all over ten pounds weight, in forty-eight hours!

Having scoured the terrain in the vicinity of Bulun for the elusive *ovis nivicula*, without success, Talbot decides to return to Yakutsk to re-equip himself more suitably for the conditions he found prevailing and to obtain letters of authority to continue his hunting near Verkhoyansk. As he left the hut in which he had been living to board the steamer, a bullet whistled past his head, fired by one of the men he had hired and whom he had not tipped for being lazy.

The steamer took nineteen days to cover the 800 miles to Yakutsk, steaming against the current and making frequent stops for fuel, cargo and accidental groundings. The food was abominable and the cabin full of tea-drinking and smoking Russians. All the time he worked away at his Russian, compiling his own little dictionary. One day the engineer gave a wild discourse with waving arms, shrugging shoulders, beard tearing and breast thumping. To quell him, Talbot quoted Shakespeare in a stentorian voice, to the indignation of the man who thought he was being insulted. His overwrought condition may have been attributable to Talbot having practised, that morning, five hundred and thirty-six scales, flats and minors on his flute.

At Yakutsk, his dog Sin was killed 'by a brick or something', and Talbot was very distressed. 'I am much out up about it, he was a friend in need indeed. Goodbye dear old Sin. May we meet again.'

Next day he informed against three men for 'murdering' Sin.

He stocked up with wines, spirits, pâté de foie gras and other luxuries, having experienced the paucity of such items – except vodka! – in Bulun. To replace Sin, he bought a dog he named Nick, who 'seems a first-class sort of type, wild as Hell and thin as a scarecrow.' Nick was a pointer and had 'great difficulty in learning English.' He also engaged a Cossack named Dmitri as his servant at a rouble a day and paid two months in advance.

Boarding the steamer for the return journey to Bulun – from where he proposed travelling overland to Verkhoyansk – he found crowds of people, including six priests, who went round with bottles and glasses in their hands, 'their drunkenness and the people all round beggared description.'

Having observed that some of the islands they passed were inhabited by bears, he became very eager to shoot one, and during a refuelling stop persuaded the captain to let him take a boat and four sailors to land on an island said to abound in bears. After a scramble through the undergrowth with Dmitri, during which they heard a bear but could not see it, Talbot returned on board and asked for volunteers to act as beaters, rather as one might organise a day's pheasant shooting. To Talbot, it seemed 'hardly credible, amongst forty young men they all refused, saying they had no ambition to be chewed up!' Then, the captain charged him fifty roubles an hour for the delay. 'Having towed the boat through shallow water for a mile, [he] returned wet, hungry, disappointed and fierce!'

The captain had also complained bitterly about Dmitri, who refused to eat with the crew, and incurred Talbot's wrath by allowing one of the sailors to be savagely beaten by his drunken crew: 'a man with a stentorian voice and no more blood in his veins than a flea, my unfortunate Cossack can get nothing to eat as this damned oopravliayooschyi refused to sell him anything.' The next morning, 'Woken up early this morning by entrance of Cossack wanting me to give him leave to stick the oopravliayooschyi, I said certainly not!'

Returning to Bulkur, Talbot went again in search of wild sheep and this time killed two, the head of the ram being cut off as a hunting trophy and specimen to be taken back to England. Nick disgraced himself by not coming to heel, putting up wild geese, driving off five reindeer and finally chewing up the precious skull of the ram! It was the Cossack who got the greater part of Talbot's wrath, however, by forgetting the dog's dinner and going to bed. 'I woke him up all right!'

Torgenson had provided him with a small wooden house and he soon entered into the social life of the community. The priest was a frequent caller and, though drunk most of the time, was an agreeable sort of person. Talbot 'bucked up' his Cossack in the matter of household chores and the duties of a man servant. The policeman's daughter was given a birthday party and this called liberal amounts of alcohol – Talbot was surprised to find she was an infant in arms. 'If they do not have a Saint's day in Siberia, somebody manages to have a birthday, and that means much drink.'

Nick went up in his master's opinion by biting a Tungus – 'Nick bites another Tungus, he is getting rather dangerous; it keeps people at their distance.'

He had deposited 500 roubles with Torgenson for safe keeping but soon finds that the Swede is trying to swindle him in the price of various items Talbot has bought through him and will not account for the balance he holds. 'Will have to look after my throat', is his conclusion on the matter.

Winter was now closing in, with heavy snow and the Lena freezing over. There is no hunting and Talbot is restless, 'mewed up in a stuffy little room with an atmosphere of stale cooking.' His flute is out of action: a full day of practice - major and minor scales and arpeggios - was too much for it, and he can find no one to repair it.

Being on good terms with the local doctor, he asks him to dine with him on 'breaded medallion of venison and champagne.' The Cossack in attendance 'skips about like a two year old'. No wonder, as he is full of vodka, which he drinks a bottle at a time; next day he is madly drunk and has to be thown out.

Encouraged by the success of the dinner, Talbot gives a supper party which was a success, until the good doctor called another guest by a foul name and the policeman had to restrain the priest from smashing a glass over the doctor's head.

The following day a sad and contrite doctor came to apologise and asked Talbot to supper, during which he spoke about the priests who, he said, owned about one third of the wealth of Russia and Siberia. The local priest had not preached to his flock for five months and on one occasion had come out of church with others carrying glasses, bread and holy wine, asking their friends to have a drink with them.

After an eight-day debauch, Dmitri, the Cossack, came back having found a wife, spent all his money, and in debt. Suffering from D.T.s and attempting to knife Talbot, he was again flung out and this time locked up by the authorities.

After a showdown with Torgenson, during which Talbot called him 'swine' and in consequence was in some fear of his life, he went about armed with his revolver and a stout walking stick. By now the Lena had frozen over and was safe for travel, so he decided to go on to Verkhoyansk. The priest provided him with three sleighs, reindeer and drivers at a cost of 100 roubles and Talbot generously gave him 250 roubles for his trouble. The priest gave him a farewell bottle of vodka 'which I wanted muchly' - Bulun had by now apparently been drunk dry and further supplies were anxiously awaited.

Before leaving, Talbot signed, in the presence of the doctor and policeman, a document requiring Torgenson to refund 365 roubles, which was to be given to the local hospital.

It was about 900 versts from Bulun to Verkhoyansk and the reindeer went at a fast trot between the posting stages; the best time he made was 135 versts - about ninety miles - in twenty-four hours. He rode in his kalutka wrapped in a Cameron rug and the rabbit skin blanket that had served him so well in Hudson Bay.

On arrival he stayed in the house of a Cossack where he was attacked in bed by mammoth bugs that even dropped from the ceiling and leapt from the floor.

In Verkhoyansk, as at Yakutsk, there were many political exiles, with one of whom Talbot made friends. His name was Martin who said that, having taken part in an insurrection, he was imprisoned for two years and not permitted to speak. A new doctor arrived - apparently the town had been without one for a year, and the last doctor had spent seven years without seeing any patients because he was never sober. Talbot continued learning Russian, 'with the Cossack's pretty daughter and gave her a lesson in flirting, a most apt pupil!'

By now he had given up any idea of hunting in the area and was eager to return to civilisation, and on 21st November his sleighs were packed ready for the journey. During his stay he had become friendly with the chief of police, who gave him skins, relics of mammoths, a bottle of cognac and one of sherry. Talbot gave him his medicine chest, which generosity nearly cost him his life afterwards.

Before leaving, word was brought to him of a bear that was terrorising a village on his route to Yakutsk, and he was asked if he would shoot it. Whilst the Yakuts would trap bears, they would not shoot them, as they believed they contained the spirits of their grandfathers. He set off, accompanied by the starosta[62] of the village near where the troublesome bear had his den. He also took Martin, the political prisoner, and that night slept at the house of the starosta, who by now was nearly frantic with fear and excitement. The next day they travelled a further forty versts, through a forest with deep ravines, breaking sleighs and with reindeer floundering about in all directions. Night coming on early added to their difficulties before they arrived at a miserable povarnia with no door, just a reindeer skin over the entrance and consequently bitterly cold.

> November 23. Early start, after 14V. got out of sleigh and walked to bear's den, the Yakuts pointed it out and stopped behind. I went fairly close and halloed, no success. I waited there with a pole, I poked inside, suddenly two deep growls, I sprang back but no bear came, waited, then order Yakuts to make a fire which they did, but would not come close. I was then helped by Martin and we carried the fire to the mouth of the den with plenty of moss to make a smoke.
>
> Suddenly another growl, dropping his rifle Martin ran, I went to the den and gave him back his rifle; just in time as out came the great brute with a rush and I put several bullets through him. He weighs about 400 lbs. . . . I am looked on as a hero; first bear shot here.

The bear's mighty corpse was loaded on one of the sleighs to be taken back to England and mounted. For years afterwards it stood, seven feet high, in the entrance hall at Lytham, arms spread menacingly.

Entering the Lamont country, Talbot decided to hunt again for the wild sheep, this time with success:

> After spying and seeing nothing walked on, at last saw far off one apparently enormous sheep. After a very long difficult stalk, and as there was a big precipice in front, we slipped the dog; the poor old sheep looked in front, but there I was, he looked down, there was a yawning precipice; by this time the dog was baying him. I took a long shot and got it right through the heart. A splendid specimen unknown to the British Museum, so I will call it 'Ovis Cliftonii'.

And so the ram joined the great bear on the journey back to civilisation and Talbot pressed on for Yakutsk as fast as the reindeer could trot. At Yakutsk a cold he had caught developed into inflammation of the lungs and he became so seriously ill that the Governor sent a message to Irkutsk that he was likely to die. From there the news was relayed to St. Petersburg and telegraphed to Lytham. John Green, his valet, was immediately sent off to meet him at Irkutsk.

Talbot was nursed by a political exile who stayed with him day and night and massaged his chest with oil. The doctor insisted that he should have a certain, very ugly nurse 'with eyes like a cat', at whom he hurled bottles of medicine.

By Christmas he had recovered sufficiently to give a dinner party which included bear soup from the one he had shot, mutton from the ram *Ovis Cliftonii* and a young capercaillie, followed by a Russian version of a Christmas pudding – 'very good, but no more like plum pudding that beer to wine.'

Whilst he was up and about, he could not turn his head or raise his arm. As he had given away his medicine chest at Verkhoyansk, he had no salacin to take for the rheumatic attacked that was to get worse. He pondered on his ability to endure the 2,000-verst journey by sleigh to Irkutsk, but set off and, after considerable suffering and hardship, arrived there, where John Green was waiting for him. Nick, his dog, had been mauled in a fight and had to be left behind at Yakutsk, and his last diary entry for the day of departure January 26th, 1902, is 'Goodbye Nick, old manny.'

XIII

AS Lytham Hall was let, Talbot intended to live at Rhidorroch upon his return from Siberia and warned Fair of his arrival by a succession of telegrams commencing on March 14th from Irkutsk, Warsaw, Berlin and London. The purport of these messages was that Fair should arrange for Talbot's French chef, hill ponies and other necessaries to be ready on his arrival and that his automobile was to be waiting at Inverness station on Saturday the 22nd. This last wired instruction from Warsaw was received on Thursday, 20th March.

The automobile, driven by Wilmhurst, a chauffeur and former sailor - whose knowledge of cars, it transpired subsequently, had been gained principally from washing them - duly left Lytham on Thursday afternoon and vanished for the next four days.

After Wilmshurst left Lytham another wire arrived from Berlin - 'Expect to meet autmobile Inverness station Saturday morning.' Fair, knowing the uncertainty of motor travel in those days and that Inverness was some 350 miles from Lytham, wired a Mrs Graham at Carlisle, where Wilmshurst was supposed to spend Thursday night, asking her to 'tell him to push on.'

Unfortunately Mrs Graham was away from home, as Fair was informed by the Lytham postmaster and, to add further to Fair's disquiet, the French chef telegraphed from London; 'Impossible to leave tomorrow; doing job; letter follow,'

Inverness

To: Fair, Lytham
Feel disgusted not finding motor here; telegraphed from Poland and Germany; would like to know why it is not here.
Talbot Clifton. March 22nd.

To: Chief Constable, Perth
Will you kindly instruct Wilmshurst, driver of Mr Clifton's motor car, who is on his way to Inverness to rail car to Inverness if he has not already passed through Perth.
Fair. March 22nd.

Ullapool

To: Fair
No French chef; have wired from Irkutsk; could not do more; most disappointing; absolutely nothing ready; the next time who can I wire in order to get a little comfort?
Talbot Clifton. March 22nd

c/o Mr Duncan,
169 Causewayside,
Edinburgh.
23rd March, 1902.

Mr Faire,

Dear Sir, Just a line to let you know that I only arrived in Edinburgh last night at 8 o'clock and the shops were all shut and I could not get any oil to go on with, nor could I get any one today, Sunday, so shall have to wait on till 8 o'clock Monday morning. I don't know when I can get to Inverness as the car is going very badly. I did not get to Carlisle until 10.30 Thursday and as I had such a lot of trouble and had to stop there and take the water pump off. I got my electric charged while I was there I could not get away until Saturday morning I am working on the car today and shall start as soon as I can tomorrow but if the car does not go any better I shall not finish the journey tomorrow; the roads are very bad I had two punctures on the back wheels so shall run until dark tomorrow night and then put up.

Your obedient Servant
Wilmshurst.

To: Superintendent of Police Perth

Understand Wilmshurst, driver of Mr Clifton's automobile, left Edinburgh this morning for Inverness. Please instruct him on arrival at Perth to rail car to Inverness and him to wire me.

Fair Lytham, March 24th.

To: Talbot Clifton Rhidorroch, Ullapool

Received wire from Wilmshurst that he left Perth by rail with motor last night. Please wire him your instructions to Station Hotel Inverness.

Fair.

Ullapool.

To: Fair, Lytham.

Wire received. Not having coal or motor, have had to put off people that were coming here. Decidedly unpleasant the whole business.

Talbot Clifton.

Rhidorroch Lodge,
Ullapool.
Sunday, March, 1902.

Dear Jim,

I am disgusted, I could not have given more time to order the cook than I did but yet he is not here.

To send the motor 700 miles by road with only the driver is the most foolish business I have ever heard of; it has not yet arrived and when it does it will require about a week's overhauling after a long journey like it is doing now before it can be used again, of course it will have to have new tyres which cost £30. If I go away again who the hell can I expect to deliver my messages, having in the past been a damned sight too slack. It is probably my fault nothing was attended to. Ponies arrived looking damned thin, I could only expect that as they came from Lytham. Kindly send all details of expenditure of last year to me, repairing and building of farms, roads etc. amount of income, also mortgage and expenses generally; you have plenty of clerks there to do it. I hope to see you here the end of this week to talk over business. Place to my account at Coutts £300.

V. truly,
J. Talbot Clifton.

This letter does Talbot no credit, as Fair had undoubtedly tried to carry out his instructions, but owing to a chain of circumstances he could hardly have foreseen, everything went wrong. The motor car in those days was still a sort of infernal machine to most people, and the workings of an internal combustion engine a complete mystery, as it is to not a few today! Wilmshurst, the driver, was a sailor whose engineering ability – it later transpired – had been gained as a car washer at Coventry, and it was not long after his arrival at Rhidorroch that he got the sack. Undoubtedly, Talbot still suffering with his chest and rheumatism, still perhaps brooding over his blighted love affair, and looking forward to the comfort of his own home, was bitter and disappointed, but it was unfair to vent his spleen on James in this manner.

Such trantrums, however, were of short duration; Talbot and James had grown up together and knew each other perfectly. Talbot well knew and appreciated James's ability and dedication to the management of the estate, but could not resist unleashing his – sometimes savage – sarcasm on James when a suitable opportunity arose. This was because Fair frequently reminded Talbot of the need for economy and tried to restrain his spending in an effort to repair the great breaches his former prodigality had made in the family fortunes. Whilst Talbot knew in his own mind that Fair was in the right, his was a nature that would not easily brook criticism, direct or implied, and when some matter arose wherein his knowledge was superior to Fair's – as with motor cars – he took full advantage to 'put down' poor James!

Fair did go to Rhidorroch and doubtless placated Talbot by being an attentive and appreciative listener to Talbot's stories of Siberia, whilst taking the opportunity of stressing the need for expenditure on roads and sewers at Lytham and St. Annes in order to encourage the building of new houses, the ground rents from which were sadly needed. During his visit he was, as always, treated as a member of the family and enjoyed the stalking the shooting and the lavish hospitality the Cliftons have always shown to their guests.

Talbot remained in Britain until the end of the year 1902, staying at Rhidorroch, visiting Lytham – on one occasion accompanied by Winston Churchill, then Member of Parliament for Oldham – making frequent journeys to London, and visiting his mother, Lady Drummond, at Edwinsford.

He was now a keen motorist and many of his journeys were made by car, not without incident, as revealed by his letters to James Fair.

Going through Carlisle I did not average more than eight miles an hour, I should think I could get witnesses. You might write to the people *re* their dog and say if they had not been so sharp in sending to their soliicitors I would have paid them £10 for the dog, but as it is I will certainly fight the case and bring in a counter action, if possible, for damage to the framework of my motor.

I have just returned, having had a desperate three days to get the motor as far as Coventry where it is going through repairs, mainly owing to Wilmshurst.

Telegram, July 3rd.
My motor arrived second in Paris Vienna race.

What did they do in Scotland about my summonses? [No details!].

Re: Summons for furious driving at Tintagel; when going through the small village there were two or three ladies walking in front of me and having a very small horn to signal with they could not hear it which necessitated my going very slowly until quite close. After reaching my hotel I told my chauffeur, who I have taught to drive, to bring something from the village. After coming back I drove again to the village when a policeman asked me to stop, which I did; he then told me my chauffeur had driven furiously through the village and after asking me my name, another man in shirt sleeves – a dirty looking tramp – began cross questioning my driver. I told him he had nothing to do with the case, when he said he was an under constable. Having no King's uniform on, kindly have a counter summons taken out against him. I personally have no idea what speed Williams went through the village, but I did not exceed ten miles an hour.

Chippenham, 27 February, 1903.

Dear Sir,
We have referred to the article in the *Field* newspaper of the 14th under the heading of *Convictions of a Motorist.* It is certainly an exaggeration that the fallen man lay pinned for a time under a fallen horse. The evidence showed that the rider's horse reared and the man fell off . . . Mr Williams the engineer would not say that Mr Talbot Clifton slackened his speed when told by him that an accident had occurred but that 'he prepared to stop the car and looked round,' but the man was

then up and grabbing for the other horse which was quite close to him.

Yours truly,
Wood and Audry.

Claud Lowther to James Fair

My motor driver tells me that he cannot drive the old car to London as it won't go up a hill and will have to be arranged. It will be as good as ever if a new motor is put in, which will cost £100 to £150 – otherwise it is useless. I am sending the driver up to Coventry with the other car to have a brake put on. As it is we can't stop it down a hill – which is most dangerous – Mr Clifton told me to have this done.

Talbot Clifton to James Fair

Carlton Club.

I got here yesterday, Williams in the Daimler skidded smashing a front wheel, I went on sixty miles to Lancaster where I had left the Mercedes with Adams to be boxed down. On emptying the petrol tank at the station the petrol caught fire and burst up the petrol tank and damaged the back. I have not seen Adams or motor, anyhow it is more than amazing.

Talbot Clifton to James Fair

Portiscliff,
Ferryside,
S. Wales.

Excuse pencil but having been in bed for a week I find it more convenient. Last Monday I was getting into my car when the board over the clutch wheel slipped precipitating my leg into the wheel that was rotating about 1,000 revolutions and before I could stop the engine the back of my calf was ripped up ten inches to the bone and all the muscle bulged out in a most unholy looking manner, however, I got it stitched up by the local doctor and it now progresses slowly but favourably but I am told I will not be able to walk for a month d..n it.'

Dear Jim,

Letter received absolutely false all through, the summons you got against me. Just off to India.

Talbot.

XIV

IT was during January, 1903 that Talbot departed for Colombo, accompanied by Dan, his valet, Gyp, a fox terrier and Nero, a Great Dane. His objective this time was to shoot buffalo. They set out from Hamandor: Dan and the dogs with an ox-cart and Talbot with his shikari[63] in a small bullock cart. After twelve uncomfortable days he returned to Matara having shot one cow buffalo. His temper had not been improved by having made a long and difficult stalk and was just preparing to shoot when two natives walked up to the herd and quietly drove them back to their farm!

Dan proved to be 'worse than useless' and was finally sent back to England in consequence of losing Talbot's luggage:

> Arrived Calcutta 6.30 p.m. and found that my portmanteau with all my clothes also saddle box that had been put in the guards van at Mhow, had not turned up; saw station master, Dan off his head of course, am going to make a searching investigation of it, Dam! Putting up at Green's Hotel, no clothing, Dam!

Despite having letters of introduction from the Duke of Norfolk to Lord Curzon (then Viceroy and Governor General) Talbot was unable to obtain any shooting, 'as the Rajas are stony broke after the Durbar!'[64]

He was also unable to get passes to travel through Tibet and China, so went on to Darjeeling, which he found very dull and filled with all the oldest ladies from Calcutta. He was not long in Darjeeling, however, before he succeeded in waking things up and getting himself in trouble!

In company with a man called Macnaughton, he entered Tibet through Sikim and the Jelap Pass, despite having been refused permits by the authorities. When challenged by the police, Talbot and Macnaughton coolly wrote out their own passes and signed themselves as Prime Ministers!

Soon after their return to Darjeeling, the news of their escapades leaked out and Talbot was visited by the Chief of Police and put on parole not to leave the town. Talbot did not improve matters by trying to send a cable to the *Daily Mail* saying it was an open secret that 300 men were to march to Lhasa and insist that the Tibetans should open out a trade route to India, but the Post Office refused to accept the message.

On June 2nd, Talbot notes: 'Mcnaughton had it out with the Lieutenant Governor, who is furious; so is Curzon, but they can do nothing to us, which makes them more peevish than ever.'

What Talbot and Macnaughton did not know was that the Viceroy, Lord Curzon, had obtained permission from the Cabinet in London to send a mission to Lhasa to try and establish diplomatic relations with Tibet, as he had forebodings that the Czar of Russia had designs on India, and if the Dalai Lama and the Czar made a deal, India's northern frontier would be exposed to attack. A Major Younghusband had been instructed to lead the mission under the guise of creating a commercial relationship and the utmost secrecy was considered essential. Only China's representatives had access to the Forbidden Land, and no one knew what was happening there.

Talbot notes in his diary on 18th June that Younghusband had arrived in Darjeeling and was staying in the annexe to the hotel and was 'very reticent in regard to the march into Tibet.'

In the event the mission got no further into Tibet than had Talbot and Macnaughton, and was held up at Khambajong for five months awaiting permission to proceed to Lhasa, which was refused. It was not until December that Younghusband with 8,000 men reached his objective by force of arms, and after killing over 600 Tibetans, only to find 'there was not a Russian in sight.'[65]

A local official also refused to issue passes to Talbot for use of government bungalows or to shoot, and Talbot attributed this to personal spite against himself.

> I was riding to the Amusement Club, saw Garrett who on seeing me smiled a very nasty smile, so I followed him into the Planters' Club and told him I considered his conduct childishly vindictive and showed him a letter from the Lieut. Governor saying that the whole business would have to be settled between Garrett and self; he lied to me; so I called him coward and offered to fight him privately with fists, wrestling or pistols; he bolted. Wrote to L. G. asking him to make Garrett apologise.

The next day Talbot was arrested. He was let out on bail of 500 rupees, again went to the Club and, meeting Garrett, called him a coward in front of two officers. Whilst the majority of members seemed to sympathise with Talbot, a special meeting of the committee decided that if he wrote apologising for using objectionable words within the club premises, he would be exonerated. Garrett, however, was not satisfied and wanted a full written apology to him personally to be posted in the Amusement Club, Talbot to pay 500 rupees to charity and to leave Darjeeling. After a friendly conference with the Advocate General for India, in Calcutta, Talbot agreed and wrote the apology, which was duly posted in the Club. This in no way dinished his very considerable popularity in

Darjeeling and he passed the time playing billiards and pyramids, roller skating, or rinking as it was called, and gave a grand ball for 150 of the best people in Darjeeling, but not including Garrett or those who favoured him!

He became very friendly with the Maharaja and Maharanee of Cooch Behar and was invited to shoot at Cooch Behar, where he stayed in the palace and shot from the backs of elephants. He later returned the compliment by entertaining Prince Hittendra Cooch Behar at Rhidorroch during October 1905.

Becoming bored with Darjeeling, Talbot left in August 1903, and during October we find him setting up home in a bungalow he has bought in Mandalay with a full retinue of servants. He had to change housekeepers as the first one smelt too much and he sent to Lytham for John Green to come and look after his establishment.

In March 1904, he wrote to James Fair from Hong Kong saying that he had been made war correspondent for the *Morning Post*, as war had now broken out between the Russians and the Japanese. He got to Japan, but was told that he would not get a pass for the front unless he waited a further three months, so he abandoned the mission and arrived back in England in July.

XV

AFTER Talbot's return to England he lived at Rhidorroch, as Lytham Hall was still let, and during the summer months devoted himself to yacht racing, as he had bought the fifteen metre racing cutter *Maoona,* with which he had considerable success.[66] He was also interested in motor racing and touring, acquiring a new batch of summonses for various alleged infringements of the 'Locomotive on Highways Act.'

It was during September 1905 that Talbot received the following letter:

Office of Agent General for British Colombia,
Salisbury House,
London Wall.

Dear Sir,

Understanding that you have taken an interest in the Cocos Island treasure which you are probably aware was placed there many years ago and according to records has never been taken away – it is valued at seven millions sterling. According to some very valuable information I received some few years ago I fitted out a small vessel in which I sailed from Victoria B.C., 6th July 1899, and arrived on Cocos Island 5th Sept., 1899. I surveyed the island and found traces where the digging had been going on, but according to information I had, it led me to a different place and on enquiring from the man put there by the Costa Rica government – who has lived there for many years and is the only man on the island – this man has the right to grant permits from the C. R. Govt., to prospect for the treasure. By this man I was told that this particular place had never been prospected and to do so was beyond my means as I only had three men besides myself.

After satisfying myself that this particular place was the most likely one I sailed to Callao to satisfy myself that the treasure was actually taken from Callao, which I found to be correct, after which I went home to Victoria. I was unable to raise money enough for a proper expedition, which would cost about £2,000.

My intention is to sail from England with two or three Europeans appointed by yourself for Guayaquil, Ecuador via Panama, as this place will give us a leading wind both ways to the island and back. At Guayaquil a sailing vessel will be chartered large enough to take the expedition consisting of about forty men all told. The working men will be natives who are acclimatised. The men will be kept on the island for three months if the treasure is not found sooner. The tools we should need on the island and the provisions would be bought in London and sent to Guayaquil in bond. I also need to provide the natives with a large tent to sleep in. The Europeans will sleep on board the vessel.

The conditions if the treasure is found – the C. R. Govt. claim one third, one third for yourself if you find the necessary money and one third for myself.

Cocos Island is located in the Calm belt and therefore rains nine months out of twelve. Jan, Feb and March are the three dry months which would be the most suitable time to prospect the island and we should start from here at the beginning of November to be there at the best time.

Any further information you require I shall be glad to let you have.

Yours faithfully
J. C. Voss.

The letter was written by Captain Voss, a Norwegian, who had made a namc for himself in maritime history by sailing round the world in *Tilicum,* a two-and-a-half ton Indian dug-out canoe, to demonstrate the capabilities of his sea and surf anchor. He had sailed from Victoria, British Columbia – crossing dangerous bars in breaking seas, and riding out gales with the aid of his sea anchor or 'drogue'. He had arrived in England during November 1904 and his invention was on show at the Earl's Court Exhibition.[67] He seems to have been introduced to Talbot by George Kelly of C. H. Tapp & Co. of Mark Lane, London and Charles D. Berry of Berry Bros. & Rudd, the famous wine merchants of 3 St. James's Street, and Kelly wrote to Talbot vouching for Voss's integrity.

Talbot was, of course, just the man for such an adventure, and James Fair was instructed to send for Voss and obtain further details, from which he compiled a detailed report including the following historical information: During the Peruvian Chilean War in 1827, the Chileans were marching on Lima and the Peruvian Government, becoming alarmed, placed the treasure on board the British ship *Mary Dyer* for safe keeping.[68] The master of the vessel, Captain Thomson, made a bolt for it, however, and sailed out of Callao harbour and, despite being chased by a Peruvian man of war, succeeded in reaching Cocos Island.[69] Somewhat unwisely it would seem, the *Mary Dyer* returned to Callao and being seized by the Peruvians, the crew were hanged with the exception of the Captain and mate, who were spared on promising to give information as to the whereabouts of the treasure, but they managed to escape without doing so. Some time later, Thomson managed to make a further visit to the island and secured a part of the treasure and while doing so made a rough chart or plan showing where it was buried. This chart he gave to a friend who later, according to Voss's statement, passed it over to him.[70]

Captain Voss, however, did not produce the chart during his interview with James Fair, but said that when he visited Cocos Island in 1899, and, from bearings he took from the chart and information he had been given, was convinced that the treasure was there, buried on a sand spit which was covered with each tide. He further stated that the spit of sand was about 150 acres in extent, of hard sand about ten feet thick lying on clay, and that the treasure would not have sunk through it. He had not taken any borings. He proposed that the treasure should be searched for by probing the sand with metal rods wired to a galvanometer, the probing being done by the thirty-five natives who would be able to work for seven hours between each tide.

Talbot, after studying the foregoing information, considered that the chance of success lay between fifty and one hundred to one, but as the estimated cost did not exceed that of buying a new motor car and running it for twelve months, he thought it a worthwhile venture.

Voss was duly authorised to purchase the necessary equipment in London, proceed to Guayaquil, charter a schooner, engage the thirty-five natives and make all other necessary arrangements for sailing early in January. An agreement was drawn up for signature between Talbot and Voss and finance was arranged whereby Voss would be able to draw money in Guayaquil. He appears to have had no funds of his own as he had to be sent the rail fare to travel from London to Lytham.

Talbot became very security conscious and wrote to James Fair from the Carlton Club:

> Thanks letter but in regard to things in relation to travel I go to experts or people that I am dealing with to discuss the pros and cons with them. I sincerely hope you have not made public my intentions to go treasure hunting as I asked you to keep it quiet so of course you have not let your wife know about it, that of course goes without saying; as you *must* regard this as *serious.* I cannot say more but if on arriving at this island or somewhere about the mainland and hear people talking about the expedition I shall feel more than annoyed.
>
> V. truly
>
> Let me know here if you have *not* told people or *have* told people or any one person about the expedition either by wire or letter as some one I hear has heard about it.

As transpired later, Talbot had already taken not a few people 'into his confidence'.

Kelly and Berry had no financial involvement in the expedition, but seemed so convinced of its success that they became most concerned that precautions for the safety of the treasure and the white members of the party should be taken to prevent hijack. Fair accordingly wrote to Sir James Drummond – Talbot's step-father –

asking if he could advise on contacting the British Admiralty with a view to obtaining surveillance of the expedition by any British warship that might be cruising in the area and Sir James suggested that Sir Ian Macgregor, Secretary to the Admiralty, should be written to.

Early in January, 1906, Talbot sailed for South America, and it was on the 23rd of that month that Kelly wrote in panic to James Fair, enclosing a copy of a telegram published in the *Daily Mail* –

> Valparaiso, Chile 21/1/06. The yacht *Rosemarine* belonging to Mr Harold W. S. Gray has put in here for the purpose of forming another expedition to the Cocos Island in search of the buried treasure which is supposed to have lain there undisturbed since 1820. Mr Gray's hunt for the treasure last year was interrupted by his dispute with Lord Fitzwilliam's expedition in the *Veronique.*

In his letter to Fair, Kelly urges him to cable Talbot at once to sail as soon as possible: but things are not going smoothly in Guayquil:

> Mr Dear Jim,
>
> I got here two days less than the month and found Captain Voss, it was lucky I arrived when I did as he is the most unutterable ass in matters of organisation, he expects to cram thirty-five natives and five white men in a vessel built for five men and wanted to buy this vessel for £260 in the hopes of re-selling. Instead of being 380 miles from Cocos Island, as he informed us in England, it is over 600 from here; he wanted to buy tins of food for the native labour and yet he had not found out what their natural food was, he engaged another man whom I am not taking but have to pay all the same. In one word Voss [may be a good sea captain] but knows nothing whatever about things on land. Now, this is what I did on arrival – I squashed the idea of his small boat as forty men so cramped up would have been certain to bring out yellow fever and have got the late chief of police to take me and labourers and party to Cocos Island via the Galapagos Islands – as he has to go there – for £100 and to call for me in two months and so bring us back for another £100 in his vessel, being about 300 tons. He is also getting my native labour for me as he knows the blackguards and the best men in this country. I am arranging the food for self and white men, while the cook for the labourers will give me a list of what they require and hope to start the end of the week. The revolution here was hell, 150 people killed, 450 wounded, many bullets went through the wooden hotel I am staying at, but no one was hurt. I was deliberately shot at in the street. It is all over now and the revolutionists have won; all the late officials are in hiding. We had the worst passage on record to the Barbadoes, nine days tempest. Send me papers, overseas *Daily Mail* etc. Yellow fever rampant here.

Talbot's next letter to Fair is dated February 16th and contains the news that the Costa Rican government had refused to grant permission to land on Cocos Island,[71] so he had paid everyone off, including Voss, who had returned to Victoria. Talbot further castigated the unfortunate captain, who 'turned out to be a regular scamp, said he could speak Spanish - not a word! The expedition should have left from Costa Rica, not Guayaquil', - and more in the same vein.

Talbot had brought a professional photographer with him who also incurred his displeasure - 'the photographer was in such a funk of yellow fever, red herrings, or anything with or without colour, that he was delighted to go back to England - I have had yellow fever since my contingent left, but not badly, it left me yellow and weak. Had a nasty earthquake in Guayaquil lasting four minutes, one of the worst they have had for years, my photographer was one of the first to run, the rest of them were on his heels . . . and the hotel was deserted. I felt as safe in the hotel as out, the building being made of wood.'

As the treasure hunt was off Talbot went to Riobamba, which lies near Mount Chimborazo, 20,577 feet high, and then on to Quito, the capital of Ecuador, passing Cotopaxi, 19,344 feet, the highest active volcano in the world - a journey by mule taking three days. Quito is only fifteen miles from the Equator and there he met the new president, General Alfaro. He was now thinking of making an expedition into the mountains, as he had heard of a new species of bear, also deer, jaguar and puma. Telegram to Fair: 'Cable immediately if two Irish setters shipped Guayaquil, send also first class bull terrier. Clifton.'

On May 13th, Fair received another rather mysterious cablegram from Quito: 'Send urgent hundred polo balls thirty clubs two pairs riding boots and breeches.'

Talbot did not go on the hunting expedition, since he was still suffering from the effects of yellow fever and feeling weak. It was from Quito that he wrote to Fair saying that he would like to return to Lytham Hall at the expiration of the lease to the present occupier. He also wanted to buy Rhidorroch as he thought it would be a good investment and bound to increase in value, but Fair counselled him against this and again preached economy. As usual, this aroused Talbot's ire, which always resulted in his criticising Fair for spending - in his opinion - too much on maintenance of the Lytham property and road and sewerage works for building development - 'certainly get the pictures at the Hall fixed up - just as necessary as rebuilding farm houses and making roads!' He also wrote mockingly to remind his agent that he considered his knowledge of certain matters vastly superior to Fair's. Referring to the management of the grouse moors at Rhidorroch - 'I know more about wild animals and birds than you can ever hope to know unless you take to a wandering life!' and, about Quito: 'I have about exhausted this country having studied it from an ethnological point of view, which is, of course, a subject you know nothing whatever about!'

Having thus disposed of Ecuador to his own satisfaction, Talbot travelled into adjoining Peru and arrived at Lima, from where he wrote during November to his uncle, Wykeham Clifton, announcing his engagement to Violet Mary Beauclerk, daughter of the British Consul.

Upon Talbot's arrival, Nelthorpe Beauclerk had made him welcome, looked after him, put him down for clubs and introduced him to the President. Talbot lunched with him many times and considered that he had 'one of the best chefs I have ever struck.'

In his letter to Wykeham, Talbot writes 'She is very tall and dark and just twenty-three years old, extremely clever and beautiful.' He would be leaving for England with his betrothed about 5th December with Mrs Faraday as duenna; George the groom and the two golden setters; and hoped to arrive about 7th January. He was not looking forward to chaperoning a couple of females up the Pacific and across the Atlantic. 'Violet's father has been ill and having positively no one to help me I have had to arrange entirely on my own. When it came to legal matters such as marriage settlements etc. 'Papa' Beauclerk – to be – cut up mighty rough, I stuck to my point, so he finally gave in. If you can conceive the most violent tempers imaginable you then get near the point: we are friends again.' Wykeham sent the letter to James Fair with a note in which he comments – 'Old Beauclerk seems a bit of a Turk . . . by the way he went about settlements he seems to have had some inkling of Talbot's pecuniary habits . . . To judge by the letters the young lady did not "jump" at him, and this is in her favour.'

Telegram. 'Lima. – To Fair: Tell Justice to make ladies boudoir last bedroom facing Loch Achall immediate. Clifton.'

The courtship seems to have been swift but, having proposed, Talbot departed to the mountains 'to say goodbye to liberty' and so that they might both think deeply on what they were about to do. The first present he gave her was his beloved volume of Shakespeare.

In *The Book of Talbot* Violet writes: 'But all the time in Quito, at the back of Talbot's thoughts were some words which had been spoken to him by Ashton in Guayaquil.[72] They had left him somehow haunted: "Now that you cannot go to Galapagos, why not go to Peru?" Unless Ashton had asked him this, unless he had spoken of Violet as he did speak, Talbot would perhaps not ever have gone to Peru. Smoking a pipe, Ashton told Talbot of how with her father she had come to Guayaquil. Of how she had ridden his pacing horse, using, pressed against its neck, the rounded rein which was never to be pulled against the heavy bit. She used a side saddle from up-country, the leather being decorated with silver; she used a silver shoe for the stirrup. The horse was young and wanton. One day it threw her twice into the dusty road, but she laughed and mounted again.

Shaking the ashes out of his pipe, Ashton said that when Violet had left Guayaquil he had shot the horse she had ridden, because she could not have faced seeing anyone else riding it.[73] Then getting up and turning away to look out over the river he said: 'perhaps here is your hidden treasure. Anyway go to Peru and see.'

XVI

AFTER their marriage Talbot and Violet made Lytham Hall their principal residence from 1908 until 1922. He was thirty-nine years of age when he married her and apparently decided that the time had come to settle down as squire of Lytham and live on his estate. This must have been a matter of much gratification to James Fair and his father, Thomas, and what may have pleased them even more was that Talbot entered into a deed of settlement whereby the estate became entailed once again. This meant that he would have to curtail his spending and live within the limit set out in the deed and abide by the decisions of the trustees of the settlement.

He became a county councillor, although he hated public speaking due to the hesitation in his speech. It is difficult to realise that he had this impediment after reading his letters and diary entries in which he expresses himself so fluently, and it may be that he enjoyed setting down on paper what he could not get out in words. His apparent aptitude for learning other languages and his determination to make himself understood in them may have been due to his feeling that a listener would consider any hesitation in his speech due to difficulty in expressing himself in a tongue foreign to his own. Frustration caused by this speech difficulty may also have brought on his blazing tempers: Violet Clifton says, 'He himself was appalled at his wrath. Don't answer with anger; help me instead.'[74]

While in residence at Lytham he busied himself with orchids which he and Violet had collected travelling to Burma, Malaya, the Andaman Islands and the Nicobars. The flowers were kept in the orchid houses which he had built within the walled gardens. He loved to play the organ which he had built in the Hall until 'the house shook with music.' Shooting parties were organised and many important guests enjoyed the hospitality of the Hall, but pheasant shooting was tame sport to a man who had faced and shot charging water buffalo and a furious Siberian bear.

Among the guests that visited Lytham were the Grand Duke Michael of Russia, the Duke of Norfolk, Mark Hambourg (who played the organ to Talbot's delight), Anna May Wong, the Chinese actress and many other notables.

In his autobiography Mark Hambourg writes:

My friend Talbot Clifton, with whom I used to stay near Blackpool, was

> an eccentric chap of many tastes, mostly expensive ones, and of considerable ability. He had that queer kind of humour which enjoys finding out other people's foibles. I shall never forget the time I met him. He came to fetch me in Blackpool in a fast racing-motor, and then drove at ninety miles an hour down the public road and in through his extremely narrow lodge gate without slowing up for an instant. I was terrified, though I must say that he was a magnificent driver. As, however, I perceived that he intended to give me a shock, I looked quite unconcerned, as though it was the usual thing to drive at racing speed along tortuous roads, and through narrow gateways. I enjoyed his company notwithstanding his peculiarities, because he was genuinely fond of music and art, and appreciated the savour of life. He had installed an electrical organ in the hall of his house, on which he would strum for hours at a time. As the instrument was a large one, the stops had to be distributed in the various bedrooms, which ran round the gallery of the hall. Actually, they were hidden under the beds themselves. Once when a relation of ours was staying in the house, to whom for some reason my friend had taken a dislike, he got up in the middle of the night, rushed down to his organ and began to play 'Nearer my God to Thee', as loudly as he could on the trumpet stop. The unfortunate guest, rudely awakened, was nearly blown out of bed by the sudden outburst of sacred music directly proceeding from under his bed. Needless to say, that guest left the next morning, pale and shaken.[75]

Another view of the squire's hospitality comes when, in 1922, after the Irish Rebellion, Talbot gave sanctuary to and entertained Oliver St. John Gogarty and his family at Lytham, in gratitude for his assistance when Talbot himself had to flee Ireland, as recounted a little later in this chapter. Gogarty in *As I was going down Sackville Street* writes:

> How wonderful was his Lancashire welcome! The Clifton gold plate was out in our honour. We feasted long and sumptuously. Our host wore a scarlet tail-coat faced with lapels of light blue silk. It was a uniform he had designed for the President of the Lytham Golf Club, over which he presided.
>
> I gazed at him as he sat in scarlet at the head of his table in the great dining hall hung with old rose velvet and gold. Golden candelabra expanded all around. He sat magnificent and munificent. And for all its arbitrariness, the uniform in which he was attired was not bizarre. It well became the scene. I watched his long, bony hands, golden from many suns . . .
>
> He imagined that he had an impediment in his speech, but it was not a stutter, only a little halt now and again which gave it emphasis and the charm of distinction.[76]

As country houses rank, the Hall is not unduly large and Gogarty's 'great dining hall' is something of an exaggeration. It is a pleasant rectangular room, the main feature of which is a semi-circular alcove containing a handsome mahogany sideboard or servery, specially made for the house by Gillow of Lancaster. In Talbot's day the guests sat at small tables for two with individual table lamps: Talbot with the wife of the principal guest and Violet with the husband, other couples being similarly disposed around the room. Dining protocol also extended to the domestic staff. The butler ate by himself in the steward's room; the senior housemaid, under housemaids, ladies' maid, parlour maid and footman in the servants' hall. The cook and scullery maids regaled themselves in the kitchen.

The staff were paid a board wage of fourteen shillings per week plus 1s 6d washing money and 1s 6d beer money, in addition to which they received an annual salary - paid monthly - of about £20 in the case of a scullery maid, and upwards in accordance with rank. The board wage was paid to the senior housemaid, who bought in the food for the staff who had free milk and all left overs from the dining room. I suspect that, as in the Royal Navy, a form of 'mess savings' existed whereby with shrewd buying and careful management a cash surplus could be made for the benefit of the staff - nevertheless, they ate extremely well!

During the late-1800s, the butler at the Hall was John Float, one of whose understandable dislikes was the expression, 'I don't mind if I do'.

In those days a cask of ale stood in the steward's room with a tray of horn mugs beside it, and tradesmen or others delivering goods or messages were usually asked by the butler, 'Will you have a horn of ale?' If the person replied 'I don't mind if I do', the butler would proceed about his duties and, perhaps, returning after about twenty minutes, the thirsty one might summon up enough courage to ask, 'What about my beer, Mr Float?', who would reply, 'You said, "I don't mind if I do" and *I* don't mind if you *don't.'*

Inevitably, many stories are told about 'John Talbot' by the people of Lytham, some of which may have gained in the telling.

Once, upon arriving in London after one of his journeys abroad and being short of cash, he telegraphed the estate office: 'Send me five thousand pounds,' The reply came back - 'Regret no funds available; suggest you wait till rent week.' Reply from Talbot - 'Sell Lytham!'

As rent week was only a few days away he decided to return to Lytham, and, to show James Fair that he could exercise economy if necessary, decided to travel by train, third-class instead of first. Upon arrival at Euston, however, it occurred to him that he had never seen a third-class compartment in his life, so, buying a platform ticket, he went through the barrier and peered into the carriages of the waiting train; having satisfied himself that, after all, they were not so bad, he returned to the booking office and purchased third-class tickets for himself and valet. Upon reaching the barrier again he found to his fury that the train had gone. So he booked a special!

The estate office staff had the privilege of using the private golf course over land that is now South Park, Lytham. One day John Bagot was knocking a ball about when he was joined by the squire, who began telling him a story. Owing to Talbot's difficult enunciation Bagot had much trouble in following what he was saying, and when the squire finished his tale by saying quite clearly 'Would you, Bagot?', John replied 'Yes, Sir.' The squire looked at him in amazement and horror, and said 'You would? By God, I wouldn't!' Poor John was so terrified that he did not dare ask the squire to repeat what he had said, and to his dying day never knew to what enormity he agreed he would have been a party!

The Mayor of Blackpool, visiting the Hall, arrived in his chauffeur-driven car and was greeted at the front door by Violet. Talbot, who loathed such formal occasions, was in a sulky and mutinous mood and skulked about on the north side of the house. Peering surreptiously round the corner he observed the Mayor's chauffeur – a tall, well-made man – standing beside his car, and suddenly said, 'Hey, you, come here.' Upon obeying Talbot's summons, the man was greeted by him saying, 'You're a big fellah aincha, can you box?' The surprised chauffeur replied, 'Well, I can, a little, Sir.' 'Right', said Talbot, 'take your jacket off!'

In the meantime Violet had ushered the Mayor into the Hall and having made him welcome said, 'Oh dear, I wonder where my husband can have got to; let's go and look for him.' Coming to the north entrance hall, she said, 'I wonder if he could be out here,' and opening the door, there, to her horror, on the north lawn, was the lord of the manor knocking seven bells out of the Mayor's chauffeur!

Before the motor car had ousted the horse as a means of transport, Talbot, during one of his usual morning visits to the stables to inspect his 'cattle', suddenly said to the coachman, 'Have you ever had a black woman, Sanderson?' Somewhat surprised, Sanderson replied, 'No, Sir, I can't say I've ever had a white one.' Talbot looked at him pityingly and said, 'You bloody fool, you bloody fool!', and continued his inspection.

It was Christmas Eve and in the gathering dusk a small figure was trudging up the Church Drive to the Hall carrying a huge basket. As he neared the Curtain's Pond the boy became aware of the tall figure of a man in the shadow of the trees with a gun under his arm. Suddenly, a deep voice said, 'What have you got there, boy?' and out from the shadows stepped the squire. 'Pots for th'All, Sir', replied the boy, and upon closer examination Talbot found the basket was filled with crockery for the servants' hall. 'What a damned shame making a little chap like you carry all that weight. Here, give it to me!' Taking the basket, he swung it three times round his head and sent it crashing into the murky depths of the pond! He then produced a pound note which he gave to the boy, saying 'Here, take this, go home, and a merry Christmas to you!'

Walter Snalam, a well-known local butcher, told the story of Violet Clifton telephoning his father saying, 'Mr Snalam! Chops, for the love of God, chops; there are none for the Squire's breakfast!' Walter, basket on handlebars, apron flying in the breeze, pedalled furiously up the main drive with chops to appease the raging squire.

On the occasion of the last Lytham Agricultural Show, Violet, as President, had asked Lord and Lady Kinnaird to attend.[77] After lunch, his lordship said to the writer, 'Did you know Talbot, Kennedy? Damned funny fellow. We were staying at the Hall once, and after dinner he said to another chap 'Come on, let's go and see Lonsdale, I'll race you to Lowther Castle! Well, he gave this chap ten minutes start and we hadn't gone more than fifteen miles when we came to his car upside down in the ditch, with the fella underneath and smoke pouring out. Talbot said, 'By God, the silly fella's ditched himself, we shall win! He never stopped. Damned funny fella.'

As soon as war was declared in 1914, Talbot travelled to London and at the War Office offered his services in any capacity. His speech debarred him from command, but the offer of his fast cars for dispatches was accepted and one of his earliest missions was the delivery of letters to the King of the Belgians, who with the Queen was staying at a small house at La Paune. Violet at the same time worked at Dunkerque helping to provide clothing and tending the wounded coming in from Ypres.

In 1917, Talbot was commissioned lieutenant R.N.V.R. so that he could wear naval uniform whilst patrolling the west coast of Ireland in his own yacht on the lookout for enemy submarines. It was while carrying out this duty that Talbot bought Kylemore House in Connemara, as the lease of Rhidorroch had expired. To enable him to buy Kylemore and because of his past prodigality, the Clifton with Salwick Estate was sold to the Magees of Bolton; a sad transaction as the land had belonged to the Cliftons for many centuries and they took their name therefrom. They now had five children and lived at Kylemore until, in 1922, they had to leave as Talbot was in trouble with the Sinn Feiners.

A car full of armed men had come and taken Talbot's Lanchester car; they said they would return it in a day or so but, as time went on, it became apparent that they had no intention of so doing. Talbot swore to get his car back and when one evening the Lanchester was seen passing on its way to Letterfrack with two men and a woman, he made his preparations to ambush them on their return journey.

His motor mechanic and Conboy, the skipper of his yacht, were to take the Ford car and place it on a bend in the road. When the Lanchester approached, they were to switch on the headlights to dazzle the driver. Talbot took the Austin and, parking it beside the Ford so as to block the road, took up his position on a knoll that commanded the road. Violet, who accompanied him, had rushed upstairs and put on her diamonds under a high dress, she also equipped herself with rope and pepper with a view to apprehending Coneely, the leader!

All firearms belonging to loyalists had been impounded by the police during 1921, so that the Sinn Feiners would not be able to increase their armament from this source. Talbot, however, had smuggled in one of his shot guns, which he now carried with him. After an hour's wait the moon came out, which spoilt the ruse of using the Ford's headlight – but when the Lanchester arrived they could see by the moonlight that it now contained seven men, and not two as before.

As the car came to a halt Talbot called 'Get out of my car. Leave your rifles in it.' Six men and a prisoner they were taking to Westport got out of the car and one of them ran back down the road. A shot from Talbot's gun rang out in the darkness. The leader of the party shouted, 'Gilan, are you covering him behind with your revolver?' But there was no reply from Gilan.

After much parley it was agreed that the men would return the Lanchester next morning and that they would not take revenge on Conboy.

'Come on home, Vi,' said Talbot. As they drove back she asked what had happened to Gilan. 'I shot him.' 'Oh, no, surely not? The light was too dim. How awful if you did shoot him!' Talbot laughed. 'I don't shoot at a fellow without hitting him, and it would have been more awful if he had shot me in the back.'

They were back at the house. Conboy spoke now, and he, usually so full of easiness, became suddenly forcible. He said that Gilan would be found wounded, that the men would take revenge upon Talbot. 'You put no promise on them for your own safety, but for mine, and all the rest of us. You must go or you'll bring a doom on the lady and on the house!'

Talbot pondered; he saw that Conboy spoke with reason. 'Yes then, I'll go. Will you come, Vi?' She would not go, his going would make it safe for them all. With the mechanic he drove right through to Belfast and sailed from there, glad that he did so, because the next day and for days afterwards, because of Talbot, all boats sailing from Dublin were searched by order of his enemies.[78]

Sure enough, the next evening, Coneely with armed men entered the house and ordered everyone out while they looked for Talbot, saying, 'We'll search for him, and we'll shoot him here and now.' Not finding him they left and the next morning Violet drove a horse and trap fifteen miles to Recess and then by train reached Galway where a friend telegraphed Talbot telling him on no account to return to Ireland. That night, after her return to Kylemore, the men were back and handed her a letter.

Oglaigh Na H - Eireann,
Headquarters
4th Western Division,
Castlebar.
14/4/22.

To:
Mrs Clifton,
Kylemore,
Connemara.

On the night of the 12th April, 1922, your husband, Talbot Clifton, with others who are known to me, lay in ambush at a point on the main road between Kylemore and Leenaun, and fired at officers of this division who were proceeding to Castlebar.

As a result of the shots fired, Captain Eugene Gilan of the Irish Republican Army is now hovering between life and death in Mr McKeown's Hotel, Leeaun. I am satisfied, from information received, that you also participated in the ambush, and this is to notify you that an armed guard will be placed on your premises, and that you, Mrs Clifton, are to leave Connemara before noon, Monday, 17th, 1922. Otherwise other steps will be taken.

If you desire to make any statement it will be necessary for you to come to Castlebar, and I promise you a safe conduct.

Signed, Michael Kilroy,
G.O.C. 4th Western Division, I.R.A.

The nursery governess, Elizabeth Taylor, tells how four or five armed men remained on the premises occupying the servants' hall. The previous day had been the eighth birthday of Easter, the youngest daughter, and she and her mother handed round the cake to the astonished Sinn Feiners, saying, 'Do please have some cake; but really you must!'

The next day with the aid of the nuns, who sent her a car, Violet left and returned to England with the four children who were in Ireland, a maid and Elizabeth Taylor.

Talbot was successful in recovering most of the contents of Kylemore, which were shipped in a small coaster to Islay where he had bought the Kildalton Castle estate. The crew of the vessel were so painstaking in emptying the house that when the things were unpacked, sticks of gelignite were found amongst them, the crew not having had any idea of what they were. The Lanchester car was also recovered and a message came that people wished Talbot to stand as member for Galway.

Gilan long afterwards sent word to Clifton through Conboy, saying that he had long lain on his back and bethought him, son of a sometime police constable, of his jolly end - how easily he might have been killed unconfessed. He said that if Talbot Clifton ever needed a faithful servant, he Gilan, was his man.[79]

XVII

THE Kildalton Estate, lying at the southern end of the Isle of Islay, Queen of the Hebrides, comprised, with the castle, policies, demesne, deer forest and farms, about 16,000 acres. The castle had been built in the mid-1800s by Ian Ramsey, a successful Glasgow grocer and distiller, but stood on the site of a much earlier building, a fortress which more appropriately had borne the name of castle.

With the purchase of the estate in 1922, Talbot automatically acquired the formal legal title of laird, and with his Scottish ancestry - on his mother's side - slipped easily into the role. He had always wanted to own land in Scotland and never returned to live in Lytham, preferring the unspoilt beauty of the island hills to the flat lands of the Fylde of Lancashire. The Kildalton stags were famous and there were grouse and blackgame in the hills and pheasant in the bottoms. Woodcock abounded in winter owing to the mild climate and there were myriads of wild fowl. Whilst Talbot was a big-game hunter and a first-class shot, he was also a naturalist with an exceptional knowledge of natural history and was a Fellow of the Zoological Society.

He paid little more than a pound an acre for the estate, and the disposition whereby it was transferred to him was drawn in the meticulous phraseology of Scotland, describing each boundary in detail until it reached a point marked by a stone cairn on the top of a hill - 'and thence along the skyline' - what a glorious description, in very fact, to own as far as the eye could see - and Talbot loved to live and look out upon the land he owned.

Steeped as he was in tradition, there was only one way of doing things and that was the correct way. On formal occasions his piper played during dinner and highland courtesy and hospitality were always shown to his guests and to the needy.

Soon after taking up residence he found he required a secretary, and a young man named Barrow was sent up from England. In Glasgow he had to pick up a brand new Ford van filled with paintings of wildlife by Archibald Thorburn, for whose work Talbot had a great admiration, and by road and by steamer travelled to the island.

On the morning following his arrival, Barrow came down to breakfast, and, helping himself to porridge from the sideboard, sprinkled on sugar, added cream, and sat down to enjoy it, when in came the laird.

'What on earth do you think you are doing?', he roared.

'Having my breakfast, Sir,' replied Barrow.

'You can't eat the porridge sitting down, in Scotland!'

Helping himself to a generous portion, the laird salted it, and, pouring milk over, said: 'Come, on your feet!' and he and Barrow marched up and down the room side by side until 'the porridge' was consumed!

Some days after, Barrow was instructed to buy a cow in calf as a potential source of fresh milk for the household. Not being well versed in animal husbandry, he sought advice from the factor and, having decided on what appeared to be a suitable animal, reported back to the laird.

'Good, when is she due?'

'Oh, they're sending her round tomorrow, Sir.'

Surprised at the laird's immediate merriment, Barrow again sought the factor, who explained the necessity of the cow being delivered of the calf before becoming the household milk donor!

It was from Kildalton he wrote to his agent in Lytham, 'Yes, I shall be pleased to let the town have the mill as a museum, I think the Lytham Town Clerk as a fossil would look well in it!'

During 1925, Talbot and Violet went to Baghdad, as he wished to meet Gertrude Bell,[80] and while there also met King Feisal. Afterwards, they travelled on to Bahrain, where they stayed with the Sheik who took such a liking to Talbot that he gave him one of his Arab mares, saying, 'I will bring her to you when I visit the King of England'.[81]

The Sheik kept his word and Talbot returned the compliment by entertaining the Sheik, his brother, and two of their eight wives at Kildalton. The castle is surmounted by a tower which – likening to a minaret – they used for devotional purposes. Prayer mats were spread there and, although there is no record of the muezzin's call echoing over the hills of Islay, Allah may have been mildly surprised at receiving worship from the battlements of a highland castle!

Instead of the mare, an Arab stallion named Hamid was sent to Lytham where he enjoyed a quiet life in the Hall stables and later at Lowther Castle, as, after Talbot's death, he was given to Lord Lonsdale by Harry Clifton.

During March 1926 Talbot arrived at Kano, Nigeria, preparing to cross Africa, travelling first by car and then with horses and bullocks, to El Obeid, a distance of 1,500 miles, and then on another 400 miles by train to Khartoum.

He seems to have undertaken this journey to prove to himself that he could still endure hardship. He was now fifty-eight and probably found life at Kildalton rather tame.

He was not particularly well, and was, indeed, suffering from blood poisoning and had been warned against going by his doctor. Having made up his mind, however, nothing would stop him, and during the journey he wrote to Violet, 'It takes a certain amount of will power at my time of life to leave my native country, but to gain an insight into one of God's great worlds is a privilege granted to few.'

For 350 miles he travelled by Ford car through the forest of Bornu and arrived at Maidugari. It was here that he engaged as his servant, Mahomed Noa, the son of a chief who came from near Lake Chad. They drove on in tremendous heat, the temperature in the car sometimes reaching 140 degrees Fahrenheit. The country they passed through was, according to Mahomed, the land of the leopard men and crocodile men who preyed upon children and ate human flesh.

Arrving at Fort Laney in French Equatorial Africa, Talbot met the Governor, for whom he was carrying official letters, and who he said looked exactly like Napoleon. Having been given comfortable quarters by the police, Talbot was provided with a car and petrol by the Governor to travel to Bokoro, a hundred and fifty miles further on. A Greek called Marco Poulos called to see him and said that he had learnt English at Lytham!

Being fuelled with petrol for the car, and six bottles of champagne and two of brandy for himself, Talbot travelled on in the intense heat and, on reaching Bokoro, wrote:

> Terrible day. Motor broke down one mile beyond Fort Laing, two wheels broken during day. Too tired to eat having been in the open tumbledown Ford all day in the awful sun. Slight touch of dysentry owing to bad water tea is made from. No sleep as boy upset scalding tea over my ankle. The continuous throbbing pain kept me awake. Pitched my bed outside camp.[82]

From Bokoro to Adre, Talbot trekked with bullocks and riding ponies, a distance of 400 miles, encountering heat, torrential rain, thunderstorms, voracious mosquitoes and the wind sometimes like a blast from a furnace. Scarcity of water was one of his great worries and usually it was foul and, even when boiled to make tea, was unpalatable. His interest in wildlife was unabated, however, and he saw hartebeest, antelope, giraffes, buffalo, lions and many other creatures. He shot occasionally for the pot, and guinea fowl made a welcome addition to the fare. Mahomed, who wrote his own account of the journey for Violet many years after, claimed that unicorns also inhabited the area, but there is no record of Talbot seeing one!

Progress was slow with the bullocks – about three miles an hour he reckoned – and sometimes they lost their way. Ramid, his guide, was too fat and very stupid; Talbot thought he was a eunuch.

Mahomed relates that at one place they stopped there was no water and many goats were dying of thirst: 'the master was having a water bottle filled with tea. And he started to share the tea amongst the goats. And it finished. And none remained, not even a drop for him.'

At a place called Am Gereda, the bullocks were replaced by camels as transport for the baggage. Here Talbot went down with fever and dysentry – 'Ipecacuanah, quinine and brandy may get me away.' He managed to ride on, although he 'vomited all the way; seasick from the back of a horse for several hours – most wasting process. However, we went quickly and my horse bucked, which did me good.' For the last part of the journey he was accompanied by Masalit Arabs who gave him shelter by night, shade during the hottest of the day and provided him with sheep, guinea corn, and milk and water.

At Violet's request through the Colonial Office in London, a car was sent from El Obeid to Adre – a distance of six hundred miles – to collect Talbot who was still a very sick man. After a rough six-day journey with two cars, with delays caused by burst tyres and bad roads, Talbot arrived at El Obeid where the rail head was. Taking Mahomed with him, Talbot entrained, and by way of Khartoum and along the Nile, he travelled homewards once more.

Two years later, in January 1928, Talbot was taken very ill at Dakar, where he had arrived with Violet intending to go Timbuckto, thus satisfying a long-held ambition. Violet had some misgivings before they left, as he was far from well. The deadly malady that was to kill him now rapidly gained ground, and to spare him as much suffering as possible, it was necessary to get him out of Africa quickly. Violet was then unaware of the nature of the disease, but knew that he was unfit to endure the stifling heat, the poor accommodation, the rough roads and the noise of African towns and villages. He agreed to give up any idea of going to Timbuckto and instead wished to go to Dahomey via Bomako, and when Violet suggested that instead they should go to the Canary Isles or Madeira, he said, 'I do not go back.'

Another object of the expedition was to get a wife for Mahomed who accompanied them, and when they arrived at Bamako he was 'ordered to look for one.' The railway inn – where they slept in their own camp beds – was run by a Frenchwoman who, with Talbot and Violet, formed a small selection committee to inspect possible candidates brought forward by Mahomed. The first girl did not qualify as she was not a virgin – in the opinion of the Frenchwoman – who, apparently, could tell by her eyes! The second girl, though seemingly suitable, had to be refused as her father did not approve of her going to England, so the matter was dropped and Mahomed was apparently quite happy to remain in his master's service without a mate.

Despite his desperate condition, which worsened daily, Talbot still kept his diary and recorded with grim amusement how Violet, meeting an Arab with a girl for a French client, courteously escorted the pimp and his charge to the correct room at the inn!

Paralysis now set in and the doctor persuaded Talbot that he must go back to Dakar, where they arrived after fifty hours of agony in the train. They embarked in a vessel for Las Palmas, but owing to a change of instruction, the ship put in to Santa Cruz. Here x-rays showed that he was beyond any hope of recovery and he died three weeks later.

His embalmed body was brought back to England by Violet on the boat deck of a small Norwegian steamer, the *San Jose*, and then to Islay, where he was buried on the Green Hill at Kildalton.

Oliver St. John Gogarty, near neighbour to Talbot when at Kylemore House, Connemara, his guest at Lytham Hall and Kildalton Castle, his merciless critic but devoted friend, says of him:

> Of what use were all his expensive and spasmodic excursions? What did he achieve? Nothing. Nothing in the hucksters' view or the view of the solicitors' clerk. He was noble, aimless, irascible, bullying, dauntless, extravagant, generous, scorning craftiness or thrift, golden-hearted, golden-fisted, fast to his friend, sadistical and successful - a figure unhorsed into our humdrum days from Roncesvalles or Fontarrabia.
>
> Let us give up the pretence of wishing for the times of Charlemagne again if we cannot admire in our own time Talbot Clifton.
>
> My greatest tribute to him is that he is incredible in these, our times.
>
> It is no use cavilling, 'His Life' - What was it all about? I can answer. He is the figure of an ideal predominant in the mind of the yeomen of England. A friend of the people, a Robin Hood. A man they choose to represent. A man they hail, acclaim and depend on. Because he is to be trusted to obtain and maintain for them that indomitable freedom he impersonates and represents.[83]

Chapter Four

Harry

ORN on 16th December, 1907 at Beaumont Street, London, Henry Talbot de Vere was the first child of Talbot and Violet.[84] The name de Vere came from an ancestor on his mother's side, the first Duke of St. Albans, who had married Lady Diana de Vere, eldest daughter of Aubrey, 20th and last Earl of Oxford. St. Albans was the natural son of Charles II and Ellen Gwyn (the famous Nell) and so a dash of the Royal Stuart blood was added to the Cliftons' of Lytham by the arrival of Harry, the heir apparent to the estate.

In his own words he was 'gently nutured until the age of nine', when he went to Downside, which he seems to have loathed and suffered under a strange sense of injustice done, not only to himself, but to others. This resulted in his leaving after six years without having distinguished himself scholastically, but with his natural love of literature sharpened. He was then sent to Bonn, where a tutor made further efforts to prepare his mind for entry to Oxford, until Harry was sent back to England during March 1926. An ex-Christ Church professor had recommended that he should be under a good tutor before taking a special paper in history for entry to the college.

Harry's bookishness irritated Talbot, who declared that a gentleman did not have to work to enter the university. 'Simply drink a glass of sherry with the Dean - and I suppose you can do that all right - or you aren't my son.'

Talbot, however, insisted that he should go to Grenoble for his French - which was Harry's strongest subject - and where he and foreign students 'did great drinking and listened to the nightingale, with scent of roses blown over.'[85] He did manage to get a vacancy at Christ Church, having passed in French, and in October 1926 commenced what seem to have been the happiest three years of his life. His home life was not happy, though all the family loved

Kildalton. Talbot was ill and intolerant of the 'damned bookworm', so different from himself, and tried to make him into a tough, outdoor man as a 'worthy' successor to his estates. Harry genuinely wanted to work and become a scholar or journalist, but, when with his father during holidays, life was sometimes unbearable. There were short periods when Talbot was more charming and interesting than any man Harry had ever met; but then there were long periods of gloom, suspicion, anger and bullying. He insisted on billiards every night and Harry was severely rebuked for missing an easy shot, yet woe betide if Talbot got beaten. This compulsory play created in Harry such an antipathy to the game that when taking up residence in Lytham Hall as squire some years later, a message was sent to Lytham Conservative Club that they could have the billiards table but must remove it that very day - which they did.

So it was that Harry found Oxford so delightful; to have his own rooms and to study and talk and drink with his friends. But:

> More important and precious than any parties the excitement of cards and wine and motors, and that first thrill of anything to do with women, was the store of wisdom and knowledge one could dive into.

It was while at Oxford that the correspondence between Harry and William Whinnerah, now agent to the estates, commenced. William had become agent with the retirement of James Fair in 1919 and like his predecessors - three generations of Fairs - became the confidant and advisor of all members of the family.

Upon his return from Germany, aged nineteen, Harry received his allowance of £400 a year, paid quarterly, from which he was to pay all his personal expenses, except college and tuition fees. Upon informing him by letter of this arrangement, William took the opportunity of warning him against the dangers of getting into debt and the necessity of keeping a strict watch on expenditure so as not to become overdrawn at the bank. 'I hope your expenditure may keep well within your allowance if for nothing more than the extremely comfortable sensation it will afford you, but in any event do not, I beg of you, ever make application to any outside agency for monetary assistance.' Words that might have been written by Thomas or James Fair to the young successor to the estate of their day, and Harry responded as courteously as they had done and vowed to become a model of moderation.

Running equally true to tradition, however, Harry is overdrawn within four months and writes to William asking for a loan in expectation of his next quarter's allowance. He has bought an etching for £100 on speculation and Christie's are trying to sell it for him 'but they have not as yet mentioned a reserve price.'

William, of course, sees the danger signals flashing and delivers the first of many mild rebukes – he is speculating with money which is not of his own saving, but money he is anticipating by borrowing from the bank or his father – 'It seems to me to be a case of, heads you win – tails father loses.'

Harry seems to have taken William's gentle chiding to heart and managed to straighten out his finances to such an extent that William, writing to James Fair, who was now a trustee of the estate, says, 'It is a matter for the greatest satisfaction that Harry is naturally careful in all money matters . . .'

How fortunate for William's peace of mind that he could not see into the future.

Harry also succeeded in making William purr with pleasure by turning down a suggestion by Fair that he should have a car:

> [Fair] . . . very kindly but wrongly suggested he put it to father, and I answered,
>
> (1) That I could not afford it.
>
> (2) That I did not want it.
>
> Both of which are quite true and I do hope he says nothing to father altho' he has already mentioned it to mother . . . I have lots of money.

William replied by return: 'Thank you very much for your letter which if I may be permitted to say so, is an excellent one and to the point.'

During the summer vacation Harry wrote from Kildalton: 'We are all alone here which is marvellous, like birds released from a cage of gold.'

Father and mother were away on their travels.

On 19th September, 1927, Harry wrote the following letter to William from Kildalton Castle:

> Please forgive my almost always writing what may be termed business letters.
>
> The other day father replied to a question of mine – that it would be better if Micky were to be heir – that it would be unfair to the other children.[86] But surely the death duties which father said would be heavier in that case, could be arranged, could they not? This is what I would like to know and also since this involves the coming of age, to try and avoid it. I realise that you are already making arrangements in which I do not personally wish to concur. I write to you instead of speaking to father as you are such a good counsellor and I have tried mother but she always makes specious arguments against my views. If only I could get father to agree with my plans everything would go simply. But although this is no sudden resolve (over a year old in this form) when I suggested the Metamorphosis of Michael and myself he just said that I was speaking, without thinking, the first thing that came

into my mind; not understanding that I had been thinking without speaking for a long time. I am afraid he would think I was being ridiculous and might be very angry and therefore I am asking your advice as I would prefer not to idle away the time till I was twenty-one pretending I was the perfect Clifton.

I do not know how much independence I will have after I am twenty-one as my idea is that if I have enough money after that I will give up sport, cease being a gentleman (at which I am very bad) and become a student. I am trying to draw you to the main argument that if father would accede to my wish and put Michael in my place, postponing the coming of age festivities for another nine or ten years I could begin my career as a student straight away. At least, could I? *Would* father agree? or do you think he would consider it very selfish and prevent my ever becoming a student. I am neither learned, talented or a genius. But I am no sportsman and never will be one and if allowed to work now I may be able to fill some position, perhaps even make a little money later. The only reason I asked to go to Germany was to have an opportunity to do a little work for I am a bad worker and there are too many other things here. I realised when I went to Oxford how hard men do work and realise I know nothing compared to others. And the worst of it is that my sisters, who have never worked – I had almost said my whole family – think that I (an inveterate idler, hardly able to get into Oxford, hardly able to stay there) work hard.

It is a queer and unpleasant situation, I see almost no prospect of getting a degree and yet my family think I work hard. In many places, the atmosphere, the conversation is worth a book a day to the young man who is at the same time diligent in himself. Here there are no books in the atmosphere and no diligence in the undergraduate. And yet the irony is I am considered to work hard. I wonder what your advice will be? I tremble that you will wish me to do the (for me) twenty-one-ster farce. I hope you may think my projects reasonable.

Good bye, your affec.

Harry.

P.S. Forgive my troubling you – take it as a tribute to your wisdom. May the preparations for December year and the attendant difficulties [about the house] both vanish and melt for nine years, I pray and hope.[87]

William replied in a nine-page letter; had he taken his father's critisicm too much to heart? As a matter of fact he had been quite pleased with his progress over the last three years. There was the natural anxiety of parents to see their children succeed in life. His father had been pursuing the 'usual method of gingering up, successful in ninety-nine per cent of boys', but when he realised that the hard line would not succeed he would not persist. His father had not realised Harry's extreme sensitiveness and he had not been well for two years. It was the duty of all young people to obey their parents until of age, but after, Harry had every right to shape his own life and could be a creditable squire as a man of letters instead of an outdoor, robust, bucolic John Bull. In the natural course of events he might marry and his wife and family never forgive him for abdicating in favour of his brother.

> Your extreme sensitiveness and modesty are liable to become a burden unless you watch them but you can never be anything but a gentleman, whether you elect to wear the purple or prefer to earn your living quite independently of your great birthright. By virtue of your birth alone you are a personage of importance without taking into account your own charming personality, and what might be quite a proper choice for one of your age in an ordinary position in life, is not always permissable to the eldest son of an old County family - *Noblesse oblige.*

Soon after the foregoing correspondence Harry wrote from Oxford saying he was trying to join the Air Force Squadron and William replied saying that if he was being influenced by a desire to propitiate his father it was unnecessary as he was not now averse to his becoming a scholar and thinks a bookworm in the family might not be at all a bad thing.

On 30th January, 1928, Harry wrote to Whinnerah saying that he had seen his parents when they passed through London on their way to Dakar, 'We all kissed one another goodbye last Wednesday, which was a surprise.'

He never saw his father alive again.

II

TALBOT having died in March, 1928 - nine months before Harry came of age on 16th December - meant that Harry could disentail the estate after the trustees of the settlement had discharged all the death duties for which they became liable. Harry does not seem to have raised again the matter of his abdication in favour of Michael, but for the next six years he was subject to the control of the trustees, whose problem was to raise the money for death duties with the least diminution of the estate. This meant the strictest economy being exercised by all and was a repetition of the state of affairs which arose after John Talbot's father dying before he, Talbot, came of age. Due to the greatly increased burden of death duties, the increased cost of living and depressed financial state of the country, the need for economy was now infinitely greater than when Talbot came of age. Harry's allowance, whilst still under the control of the trustees, was not ungenerous, nor was Violet's jointure: the younger children's portions, however, were no greater than those settled on the brothers and sisters of Talbot fifty years previously.

As we have already seen, when members of the family exceeded their allowances and got into debt, they had usually been bailed out by the trustees who dipped into the reserves set aside for maintenance and improvement of the property. Talbot's reckless expenditure - before his marriage and re-settling the estate in 1907 - had resulted in the enforced sale of the Clifton-with-Salwick estate and the trustees of his settlement resolved that, as long as they remained in control, no major sales should take place.

Lytham Hall was still let and Kildalton Castle was the family home and, whilst smaller and with lower outgoings than Lytham, had to be kept up in a manner appropriate to the standing of the family: with housekeeper, butler, cook, maids, chauffeur, gamekeepers, stalkers and gillies, which, coupled with the frequent entertaining of guests, constituted a considerable drain on the exchequer.

After the death of his father, and his own coming of age, Harry's modest requirements and earlier indications of care in money matters, which had so pleased William Whinnerah, began to change, as he became increasingly aware of the financial potential of his position. Was he not the possessor of some eight thousand acres of prime farmland in Lancashire, sixteen thousand acres of shooting and stalking in Scotland and his estate receiving ground rents and rack rents from the towns of Lytham, Ansdell and St. Anne's-on-the-Sea? It was hard to be the owner of all this and receive a mere £2,000 a year for spending money.

Within a year of his father's death, Harry – still at Oxford – is the possessor of an Alvis saloon car which he sells and buys a new Chrysler, has a racehorse – and an overdraft of £854. Whinnerah is horrified and exhorts him to stop the excessive spending and remember his great obligations as the present head of the family. Harry writes back, agreeing that he has been overspending terribly and feels that he ought to start doing some work other than literature, such as estate work or going into business. In reply, Whinnerah takes the view that a business or commercial life would not be suitable and he should be very careful not to enter into any business partnerships, but consider diplomacy, the Bar or Parliament.

It was during September, 1929, whilst visiting Barcelona, that Harry was introduced to a representative of Jerez (the house of Domecq) who, he alleged, dined and had tea with the King of Spain and his courtiers at the Pabellon Domecq, as the Prime Minister was a cousin of Domecq. This gentleman was prepared to enter into business with Harry for the importing into England of a fruit syrup known as Agraz, composed of orange and grapes or lemon and grapes, which, diluted in six parts water, produced a most delightful drink which could not fail to sweep the British Isles. Agraz was supplied in twelve litre carafes and sixty were being sent to Lytham to start business at a cost of £126. Would Whinerrah kindly send Harry that amount to the Banco Hispano Americano.

> I have now £84 in the Midland Bank and £20 in my pocket to carry on. So if you would allow me £100 on my horse, I could start *business* straight away out of *income* and I could sell my samples anyway, so I am not risking much for a wonderful drink and perhaps a splendid business, for an agent of Jerez is an envied man in Spain and I am now my own profit maker. Here is my chance and of my own making. An apprenticeship even would cost much more in a big firm.

The money was sent and in due course the consignment of Agraz arrived at Lytham, where the sixty wicker-encased carafes were stored in the estate office stables where they remained for many months. Alas – no one was interested in this exotic drink and preferred English beer and pop! After more than a year had passed Whinnerah wrote to the House of Domecq asking if they would take the fruit syrup back and received a letter saying that they had never heard of the man who sold it to Harry and who dined and took tea with the King of Spain!

As a good let of the stalking and shooting at Kildalton to an American party had been arranged for the season 1928-29, it was necessary for the family to vacate the castle until the following March. This arrangement was to provide badly needed additional funds and Violet, exerting herself to make it a success and having arranged for local staff, transported her own establishment to Lytham with every regard to economy. 'Staff arriving Preston at 4 a.m. with rugs and cushions, will lie down in waiting room, to avoid expense of hiring cars or rooms in hotel – please ask station master to have good fire in waiting room.' This, of course, was long before the days of British Rail!

Returning from Barcelona, Harry took up residence in Oxford and bought a half share in another racehorse. By all appearances he was living fairly quietly and making some effort to curtail his spending, although he was overdrawn £750 at the bank and owed the trustees a further £1,250 for cash advanced, and Whinnerah – who had now replaced James Fair as a trustee – admonished him mildly but without serious alarm.

On 24th March, Harry's new horse won the hurdle race at Colwall Park and Whinnerah sent him a telegram, 'Well done, may Chocolate and Yellow prevail'.[88]

Violet was also pleased with him, as his tutor had said that although he would never pass exams, nor learn very much, he was full of literary promise and may add something to English letters. This tranquility was rudely shattered by Whinnerah receiving a telegram: 'In terrible debt like last year – writing Harry Clifton.'

The telegram was followed by a letter from Harry enclosing accounts for payment from three turf accountants amounting to over six hundred pounds. The letter was contrite and after trying to show something on the credit side – he had refrained from buying a picture in Paris, he had about £250 worth of books with a dealer and the half share in his new horse was worth about £300 – he finished by saying: 'My plans for the future are to live, probably in London, and learn music. I am as you can imagine, thoroughly repentant, but the same thing happened last year, so perhaps that is not much good.'

Whinnerah wrote him a restrained but plain speaking letter on the evils of betting; 'You appear to have betted persistently over an extended period and that your gains should show such an infinitesimal proportion of your losses may convince you of what everyone else was previously aware, that betting is a Mug's game – spelt with a capital MUG!'

The accounts were paid and the bookmakers written to, with Harry's consent, informing them that they were to accept no more bets from him.

During November 1930, Harry embarks at Marseilles and visits Egypt, Djibuti and Colombo. He makes Saigon [89] his base for several months and visits Angkor-les-Ruines, writing two long articles on the ruins which he sends to Whinnerah with instructions to submit them to newspapers and journals with a view to publication: but despite numerous submissions, no editor is disposed to use them.

He wrote from Mang-Prabang in Laos during February 1931 in serious mood to Whinnerah, who, he felt, might be wondering what he was going to do when 'this gadding about is over'. He considered that his future life might be one of work and perhaps anxiety and before he embarked upon it he would like to spend some time as follows: 'A month or two learning the highest horsemanship, perhaps with Rodzianko, a Russian colonel in Dublin and perhaps a month or two learning to fly.[90] After that I fix myself somewhere in London and for the next few years learn singing and music.' He felt he was too young for politics but in the following years he might be able to 'fill a part'.

His next letter to Whinnerah was from Tokyo where he was having an audience with the Emperor's brother, Prince Chichibu, and it was from there that he sailed for Los Angeles. A later letter from Nikko, Japan, contains the news that 'I was defrauded of over £500 in Indo-China so I have been thoroughly plucked and proved myself an utter fool, but I have not been extravagant.'

Whilst at sea in the *Tatsuta Maru,* bound for North America, Harry wrote the following to Whinnerah:

> I think it is the only reasonable traffic solution for roads to cross one another, like the railway crosses a road, either by a bridge overhead or a tunnel underneath, therefore if it lies in my power will refuse to sign leases for any road on my property unless this be made a condition, even if I have to lose a portion of the lease rental money thereby. We must not be behind the times and this will preserve life from accidents and also accelerate the traffic, after all, no one makes a road *through* a river but over it.'

As Harry did not scruple to sign building leases in the future without covenants as to the carrying out of such engineering works his agent must, after all, have convinced him of the probable cost and consequent diminution of the returns from the development of his estate.

Having visited Hollywood Harry proceeded across America, saw Chicago and sailed from New York in the *Bremen;* he arrived back in England at the end of July. Whilst abroad he made a number of purchases of curios which were duly dispatched to Lytham, including a life-size stone eagle from China, considered to be extremely rare, provided it was genuine. The eagle carried an inscription which, being translated read: 'Made in the Ta-Yeh period [AD 606] ninth month, fifteenth day at an auspicious moment for the house of the Governors. Yu Jen made it. Made for use at the Ping-an Fort'.

In order to have its authenticity confirmed, the eagle was again crated up and dispatched by rail to the Ceramics and Ethnography Department of the British Museum, where grave doubts were expressed as to its antiquity and the inscription was pronounced a forgery. From this it would seem that the eagle was not made at an auspicious moment for the House of Clifton and that Yu Jen had not made it!

Harry had returned to Kildalton where, owing to the fall in value of the sheep flocks and consequent low returns by way of rent, efforts were made to obtain the most advantageous lettings of the shooting and deer forests, while keeping the castle, with policies and demesne, as the family home. From there he wrote enquiring about taxation, the payment of death duties and the distribution of the available surplus to meet the outgoings of the estates, the family allowances, and housekeeping at Kildalton. He proposed that the latter item, housekeeping, should be cut drastically and that the losses on sheep should be offset by silver fox farming.

In Scotland the sheep are usually 'hefted to the hirsel', which means that they are acclimatised to the land on which they are born and if sold off and moved away to another hirsel or sheep range, will, like homing pigeons, make every effort to return. When a farm is re-let or comes back into the hand of the owner, therefore, the incoming tenant, or the owner, must take over the sheep stock at a valuation. At Kildalton, two large farms had come in hand and the sheep had to be purchased by Harry, which, despite the prevailing low prices, involved a considerable outlay.

Whinnerah replied in a long letter setting out clearly the financial obligation and the position regarding the farms. He made the point that it would be unfair to his mother, sisters and brother to cut down too much on housekeeping – to which Violet contributed a quarter of the cost out of her jointure – and suggested that whilst silver fox farming might be an excellent investment, its commencement now would entail further unwelcome outlay of capital.

The laird of Kildalton's reaction to this letter was that he himself was taking over the running of the estate; Kildalton was his.[91] 'And, Mr Whinnerah, if you consider an expense inevitable and I do not, it is surely for me to decide, and I will. On the other hand being under trustees for my debtorship of the death duties, if I consider an expense expedient and you are absolutely against it, you have full powers in vetoing it, as I shall veto whatever I think unnecessary expenditure at Kildalton, even if I were to veto *all* expenditure of my money here. I intend to retain Kildalton for the time but as it is mine

I intend to run it as I wish, and I wish every account to be submitted to me. If I dismiss everybody it is my business.'

To put his authority into effect he had already given instructions for reducing staff, ceasing to insure the farmsteads, reducing his contribution to housekeeping, selling off all the sheep on one of the farms in hand and buying silver foxes instead. Socially, as 'Clifton' was in some measure an established name, he did not consider it necessary for the family to seek acceptance by 'show'.

All this was contained in four letters received by poor Whinnerah on the day before he commenced his annual holiday, and he wrote to the laird so informing him and saying that he would reply more fully upon his return. He received a telegram: 'Good holidays; dismiss care; Affectionately, Harry Clifton.'

Harry's increasing frustration and rebellion against the irksome rule of his trustees and the advice of his agent can to some extent be gauged by the way he concludes his letters to Whinnerah. Up to his leaving Oxford he had always written 'Yours affectionately, Harry', now it was usually 'Yours sincerely, Harry Clifton', or just 'Clifton', if he was in a really bad mood.

He also began to develop an unpleasant trait of giving instructions to members of the estate office staff without reference to or informing his agent. Whilst Whinnerah was on holiday he instructed Dean, the cashier, to alter the insurance cover on all the Kildalton properties, either cancelling or substituting absurd figures. Dean, of course, did nothing until the return of Whinnerah. Unfortunately, in years to come, Harry continued this practice to the embarrassment of all concerned and sometimes to his own detriment; it was an almost childish way of getting at his agent behind his back.

On Whinnerah's return from holiday he found another letter from his principal instructing him to send all the Lytham estate accounts and particulars of mortgages to a firm of London Chartered Accountants; he was, he said, 'Acting upon advice in the present exchange situation.' Which really meant that he was receiving advice from one of the first of many unscrupulous financial buzzards who regarded him as one of the plumpest pigeons ever to come out of Lancashire to be plucked.

As the company with which the Kildalton properties were insured was also the mortgagee for a very considerable sum, the directors were not amused at Harry's proposal to insure the castle only - which was a bad fire risk - and not to insure the farmsteads which were a good risk, and regarded the proposal as an unfriendly act. This was a serious matter, as the company had mortgages on the Lancashire estates to the amount of £182,000 and in the past had always acted most reasonably, and there was also a most advantageous provisional understanding for further advances to pay off the death duties that might now be jeopardised. Upon receipt of this intelligence the matter of economy on insurances was dropped by the Laird.

Nothing daunted, Harry next wrote saying that he wished the bankers who had handled the estate's accounts for over a hundred years to be changed for bankers who had no local office.

The long-suffering William Whinnerah wrote again, pointing out the advantages of the old bankers, who knew the family and the estate and gave accommodation far in excess of what other banks might be prepared to extend in such difficult days. Again, Harry conceded that the reasons put forward were excellent, but in his next letter casually mentioned that a friend of his had accepted the position of family solicitor in place of the old firm in Preston who had acted since the late-1700s. Another reasoning and placating letter pointing out the disadvantages of such a change at the present critical time for the Estate produced reluctant agreement that the matter might be shelved for 'several months or years if necessary.' The change did in fact take place later on.

Violet, not unnaturally, objected to Harry's sweeping proposals for staff reductions, as Kildalton was the family home for the present, and living there would be quite impossible without an adequate number of servants. Whinnerah suggested that a reasonable number would be six indoor servants, odd man to attend to fuelling etc., chauffeur to attend cars and mechanical appliances, two gardeners and two keepers. To this proposal and the suggestion that the economy measures need not drastically reduce the family's lifestyle Harry commented: 'I feel like being sarcastic and saying I am delighted there is no urgent need for economy, only that would be extremely light headed when I know that there is.' He had, of course, won a very valuable point in his skirmishing with the trustees. He had, in his own mind, been prepared to go to great extremes to save money, to suffer inconvenience, to deny himself things that a wealthy young man of his class would normally enjoy. All this self-denial was being turned down as unnecessary, so why should he be taken to task in the future if he went over the edge a little?

The death of Talbot had been a shattering blow to Violet, from which she never fully recovered. By upbringing and position, she was unused to, or unaware of, many of the practicalities of ordinary life and had, of course, always been waited upon hand and foot. She was a person of great courage, and upon receiving hard knocks – of which she had more than her fair share – always rose up and faced life again with great dignity and fortitude. She had been intensely aware of her duties and responsibilities as the wife of the squire of Lytham and laird of Kildalton, and, as his widow, continued to attend the many engagements she was asked to fulfil with grace and meticulous punctuality. 'There is nothing more rude', she contended, 'than to be late for an appointment.' She was highly intelligent, a romantic, authoress and poetess, and had a way of expressing herself on paper or by word of mouth which was entirely her own, and which sometimes confounded the reader or hearer! Her output of letters and cards was enormous and, like so many of the ladies of her day, wrote down the sides of the paper, across the top, sometimes across the already written page. One letter arriving at the estate office had written on the back: 'On second thoughts I think they ought to be pink' – which must have aroused the postman's curiosity considerably! It was, however, only a reference to the colour of some bedroom curtains. It is understandable that in some matters she should be utterly impractical, as when trying to help out at Kylemore, she attempted to milk a cow into a cut glass salad bowl. The cow, unused to such refinements, kicked savagely, smashing the bowl and cutting Violet's hand so badly she had to be taken to hospital!

One could always learn from Violet; many years after – when the writer was agent to the estate, and she was living in Lytham Hall – the guest guns at a shoot were taking tea in her boudoir. A Portuguese couple were her household staff of butler and cook and the latter had made a rather ominous looking cake. 'Mr Kennedy, do ask the guests to have some cake.' The guests, however, preferred the pâté Beauclerk and other savoury items; noticing this, she suddenly said, 'Oh dear, what *are* you doing, let me show you.' Taking a decanter of sherry she poured a generous dollop over each piece of cake, put a teaspoon on each plate and said 'There, try them with that.'

The cake disappeared in three minutes flat.

'My father, Nelthorpe Beauclerk, always said, "It is impossible to eat cake without sherry," she informed the guests.

She was very tall and held herself straight. Her nose and chin were pronounced and proclaimed her aristocratic ancestry. She was dark, but her hair greyed rapidly with advancing years and worry. Her clothes were often out of the ordinary; she favoured cloaks and sometimes wore a tricorn hat which took her appearance back a couple of centuries. She never wore jewellery after Talbot's death. When she entered a room or passed people in the street every head would turn. One of her trials was that she did not care for tea, and, when visiting, was offered tea by rich and poor alike. She much preferred a glass of wine – in the strictest moderation – though she enjoyed a glass of green chartreuse at ten o'clock in the morning.

Harry's sudden economy measures at Kildaton caused her great concern, as she loved to entertain there and felt that some of the shooting and stalking should be retained for social purposes and – as all the family did – turned to William Whinnerah for advice and help.

> We should retain the castle and let the stalking and shooting annually on best terms, but retain the grouse and one forest if possible. Harry causes me some distress by his strange attitude to life. He said the other day that taxation being so high it might be well to share this house; I agreed, but with whom? – with Augustus John, the artist, a man who is entirely immoral (he made proposals to a girl here to be his mistress). Harry knew it, and he drinks, they are entirely common! Well, I just said I'd prefer to leave Kildalton; to that Harry – always kind and generous – just said, 'Oh well, just as you like, of course.' Now he says he *may* never return but live in the East for ever; all this makes it absurd spending a good deal of his money to keep a home he evidently cares nothing for. Avia is cured and she hopes for some London next year in which case we could not afford to entertain here as well.[92] The year after, 1932, Easter will 'come out'.[93] I tell you all this, as all the shooting might be let on terms of years unless you realise that it is well to keep some back as a lure to young men.
>
> Harry's friends are often too high-brow to shoot, but then the young men who would propose to the girls, do shoot. Harry is very intellectual, very unconventional, and I'm sure his views are [as] good as mine, only different.

The housekeeper at Kildalton was Blanch Cormier, who was French and very easily upset if things did not go to her liking. Milk, butter and eggs were supplied to the castle by one of the farm tenants at fair market value, as one of the conditions of letting the farm, and Madame Cormier questioned the quality and cleanliness of some of these products. This enraged the wife of the tenant farmer, who held qualifications in dairying, and was proud of her certificate and knowledge of milk production and cleanliness. This feud broke out whilst Violet was in Egypt with Avia, and Whinnerah, in keeping her posted of events, writes:

> There have been occasions when a good deal of bad French and broad Scotch has been used with considerable heat with the usual result of unfriendliness and repayment of grudges on both sides. As a mistress of long standing, none will recognise sooner or more clearly than you, how these feuds develop and persist, even when the individuals are of one race and religion; but when different races and different faiths are involved, the heat generated becomes quite appalling . . . I have no fault to find with Mrs Cormier, but it does not require much imagination to suppose that on occasions she can scathe with unusual force and effectiveness; in fact, tradition says she is wonderful in many respects!

During June, 1931, Violet held a reception at the Hotel Majestic, St. Anne's-on-the-Sea, to which one hundred and thirteen people were invited. As usual, Whinnerah had to advise on the guest list, and to her suggestion that more of the 'smart set' of Lytham St. Annes be invited, he replied: 'My personal views are that the smart set of this district has become extremely attenuated, if not entirely extinct, I think your time and efforts could be much more advantageously spent in extending hospitality to the many voluntary workers in the Borough.'

She was now writing on notepaper bearing her own coat of arms as a widow; instead of a shield, a lozenge, which bore the arms of Clifton impaled with those of St. Albans.[94]

> At last I've got my correct paper (the lozenge for a widow and no crest) is it not pretty?
>
> The season is over, the visitors have gone, economy can reign! I hope Harry won't 'do things over my head.' I was surprised the other day when I talked to him. I said 'I've told Baird I'm willing to move out if the winter shoots would give you more with the castle thrown in.' [95] Harry said coolly 'Oh yes, I've told him [the tenant] he can share the house (a P.G. or some such plan! And that an Easterner!) I said nothing and am waiting to see Baird but if I find that I am expected to make a boarding house of our home, I'll probably go off as really it is not good enough!

The proposed guest was a Maharajah and his entourage.

Harry had become engaged to be married during 1931 but in May the next year the wedding appears to have been called off by mutual agreement. 'I gave the girl the engagement ring as she was fond of it, and so my £600 had gone.'[96] He was becoming increasingly interested in racing and considered that the money devoted to the upkeep of Kildalton would be much better invested in more horses.

In June of the same year he sailed in *R.M.S. Makura* for New Zealand and while at sea wrote a number of letters to Whinnerah. He still could not understand why his trustees could pay the government many thousands and he only a few. 'I wonder why you would not let me touch my capital – you stopped my learning music and flying, besides not being able to reward people or start business. Tell Ancil [97] not to win a race with Brunel until I return, and buy a couple of well bred colts for the flat races. I have never been any good at games, indeed I have always been, and am, rather weak and the thing that has done me the most bodily good is horse racing. It is the only thing of that kind that I will ever be able to look back upon. And the time for it is very short as I am already almost too heavy.'

Like his father, Harry was very tall, well over six feet, dark and with the pronounced features of his parents. In his later years he grew a beard.

Writing of his intentions when the death duties had been paid and he was free to disentail, he said:

> To you, however sensible I may appear, you will always think of me as a

boy, which is natural, which I both fret at on the one hand, and like on the other.

And I shall always regard you with affection, but now as a man with his life to make (according to financial and social considerations and position) whether I do right or wrong, is for me to bear the penalty, or reap the reward.

And I continue to cut my suit according to the length of the cloth and if I think that my property is equal to my taking up a certain line at a certain time it upsets my balance if this line of action be blocked, reacting on my mental life.

This has been emphasised by my belief, and it has often been told me, that even under my flightiest moods there is a profound commonsense, which I think will always stead me in material matters, whilst my will and learning and power of thought, will, I hope, make me my career in destiny.

By May, 1933, a marked coolness towards each other is apparent in their correspondence, instead of 'Dear Harry' and Dear Mr Whinnerah'. it is now 'Dear Mr Clifton' and 'Dear Whinnerah'. In a memorandum made by Whinnerah after a meeting at Lytham, Harry blames him for not raising money, independently of the trustees, for him to spend. He had not provided money to buy silver foxes or thoroughbred foals. By Whinnerah's actions he had caused inconvenience and loss at Kildalton to Mrs Clifton and the employees there. He refused to sign any more leases of building land until financial matters had been arranged. He wanted ten thousand pounds raised that week and threatened to go to money lenders if he did not get it.

And so, as in the past, we have the reigning squire kicking against the pricks, but now with a viciousness completely foreign to his predecessors, who would never have dreamt of trying to impeach their agent.

Whinnerah's co-trustee was William Duckworth, a wealthy industrialist, who lived at Ribby Hall, near Lytham. His commonsense and experience in the realm of business and finance made him a powerful adviser and comforter to William, exemplified by the following telegrams:

Whinnerah
Estate Office,
Lytham, England

Have not time answer your letter today. Have wired H. C.; don't worry more than can help hope for the best.

Duckworth.

Henry de Vere Clifton Esq.,
Travellers Club,
London.

Advise cancellation of letter to *Whinnerah competency, honesty* and *service* deserve better and more considerate treatment. I claim a good deal of the undeserved blame bandied about; *don't don't don't try to rule* your little *world* by making everybody miserable; when everything is put right come [to] Montecarlo for a change.

Duckworth,
Cap Martin Hotel,
Menton.

III

ONCE freed from the restraint of his trustees by the discharge of the duties payable after his father's death, Harry lost no time in setting about the dissipation of his heritage. He returned to live at Lytham Hall and once again the clatter of hooves was heard in the cobbled stable yard, as he had added to his racing string by further purchases and taken them to Lytham to train. The saddle room door has painted on it the names of previous winners, from 1788 to 1795, and John Clifton winning the St. Leger with Fyldener in 1803 and Citizen in 1805, were perhaps inspirations to attempt similar victories.

As trainer he engaged Colonel Paul Rodzianko, the noted horseman, who had for four years previously been Director of the Cavalry School at Dublin. Rodzianko had as a boy been enlisted in the Corps des Pages and then in the Russian Chevalier Guards, as had his father, who married the Princess Marie Galitzin.[98] Having escaped from Russia during the Revolution, he returned in 1917 and had the gruesome task of visiting the Ipatieff House, Ekaterinburg, and preparing a report on the murders of the royal family that took place there.[99] It was at Lytham Hall that the Colonel met and later married Anita Leslie, the writer, though they subsequently parted.[100]

His stay at Lytham was of comparatively short duration and in 1936 he was succeeded by the famous Charles Carter, whose family had been associated with horse racing in France since its earliest days as an organised sport.[101] Two exercise galloping tracks were laid out in the park and the grooms' quarters over the stables again came into full use.

Success on the course was sometimes jeopardised by Harry taking a horse - trained to perfection for a particular race - out for a gallop himself on the day before the event, 'just to see how he goes.' This did not improve relations between owner and trainers and perhaps accounted for the usually short duration of the latter's engagements.

Whilst he may have sometimes driven his trainers to despair, Harry was not lacking in pluck and during November 1935, he rode in the Molyneux Steeplechase over the Grand National course at Aintree and came in fifth, though a stone overweight. This won him acclaim from the press, fellow riders and owners, as he had never raced over fences before.

The Colonel schooled young horses, two at a time, over low jumps inside a small corral or enclosure, he, like a ringmaster, standing in the centre with a whip to encourage them to jump. Harry decided to have a go at this himself, but instead of holding the long lines attached to the halters in his hands, tied them around his waist and then touched up the horses with the whip. Both animals immediately bolted in opposite directions and Harry in the centre almost suffered self-inflicted 'death by wild horses!' He got off with a double hernia but the consequences might have been much worse.

After his visit to Hollywood he became intensely interested in film production and went into the business with Brian Hurst as 'Clifton Hurst Productions' One of their first films *Nora O'Neale,* a musical, got quite a good write-up in the press, but a more serious story, Edgar Allan Poe's *The Tell Tale Heart* did not do so well.

The latter production had a special showing at Lytham's new Luxor Cinema, to which all the Estate tenants were invited. Harry himself appeared on the stage to introduce the show but the audience, whilst 'captive' was hardly captivated. Poe's story is extremely short and consists of a homicidal maniac telling how he murdered an old man because he could not bear looking at one of his eyes, which resembled that of a vulture – 'a pale blue eye, with a film over it.' Having dispatched the old man he dismembers the corpse and, having carefully drained off the blood into a tub, conceals the remains under the floor boards. As someone had reported a scream during the night the police call and are shown round by the over-confident murderer, who invites them to sit down in the room with the body under the floor boards. His composure begins to wane when he imagines he can hear the old man's heart start beating, a sound which increases in intensity until his nerve breaks and he shrieks, 'Villains. Dissemble no more! I admit the deed! – tear up the planks – here, here! – It is the beating of his hideous heart!'

Lytham had seen nothing like this since, perhaps, the *Murder in the Red Barn,* and unfortunately most of the audience, not having read the story and the film being slow moving and bereft of dialogue until the arrival of the police, were quite mystified when the heart started up. The sound increased from a gentle throb to a loud thump, not unlike the idling diesel of a fishing boat and provoked hoarse whispers of 'What's yon bloody noise?' – 'Nay, ah've never heard owt like it!'

One morning the squire arrived at the estate office and informed Whinnerah that he considered a menagerie at Squire's Gate, St. Annes would be a very good idea, and finished by saying, 'As a matter of fact I've ordered a few animals', and threw down a letter on the desk in front of William.

This was from Chapman's, the wild animal dealers, who confirmed that they were sending to Lytham two Bengal tigers, four African lions, elephants, giraffes, zebras etc., and a final item of 'fifty assorted monkeys!'

William's scant hair nearly stood on end: 'God bless the Queen, where are we going to put 'em?'

Harry replied, nonchalantly, 'Oh, I don't know, can't you get something knocked up? Not too expensive you know.'

William Gregson, the chief surveyor, assisted by the author, set about the unusual task of designing an animal park, with due regard to safety, as should the Bengal tigers or the African lions escape they might consider the estate's new camping ground adjoining as a convenient snack bar.[102] The final plans were approved at a special meeting of the Lytham St. Annes Borough Council and the site was staked out on the ground, indicating the position of the various enclosures and buildings. Harry arrived in his car, took one look and, without even getting out, said 'No, I don't think it would do: let's forget about it', and drove off. And that was the end of the animal park, except that Chapman's began proceedings as arrangements for delivery of the animals had been put in hand.

IV

IT was during 1935 that the first major sale of land - now Blackpool Aerodrome - took place. £175,000 was raised, which was in part used to pay off a number of mortgages.

A generous amount was, of course, set aside for Harry's own use, and from now on he began to live on a grand scale, which quickly earned him the reputation of being a millionaire. As well as a town house, he had an establishment at Cowes on the Isle of Wight, where he entertained Rosa Lewis, for whom he had considerable affection; she, in turn, had an affection for Lancashire cheeses, which were duly sent to her from Lytham.[103]

The Hall was fully staffed and when in residence Harry made some effort to carry out the duties expected of a local squire. Public speaking did not come easily to him and he was inclined to talk over the heads of his audience, using classical similes which where beyond the comprehension of many of his listeners. Sometimes he forgot to make the point he originally intended, as happened once at the crowning of the local Rose Queen. In referring to the girl's father - who was one of his tenants - he said that he always reminded him of 'a certain pig', but omitted to add that as a child he had been given a ride on this animal in the tenant's farmyard! An unfortunate lapse that caused considerable indignation.

He now had a Bentley car and an American Buick roadster with a left-hand drive, in which he drove furiously round the estate, sometimes accompanied by Whinnerah. The latter, who at the best of times did not care for cars, sat beside the squire holding his bowler hat on with the crook of his rolled umbrella, and, as he faced the oncoming traffic from what is usually the driver's position on English roads, was in a state of mortal terror!

On one of these occasions, whilst crossing Lytham Moss, Harry suddenly stopped in the middle of the road and proceeded to explain to William some new project he had in mind. Another motorist drawing up behind was unable to pass and after a minute or so sounded his horn. The squire took not the slightest notice; the motorist again sounded his horn and, getting no response, suddenly shouted: 'I say, you Sir! Do you think you own the road?'.

The squire turned his head and said coldly, 'As a matter of fact I do!' and went on with his discourse to William.

He had a disconcerting habit of not always making his requirements quite clear. One day he entered the estate offices carrying his Cairn terrier, Cora, and said to one of the staff, 'Do you think I could possibly have a drink of water?'

The staff member rushed into the caretaker's quarters and said 'A glass of water for Mr Clifton, please.'

The caretaker's wife took a glass, polished it, ran the cold tap until the water became cold enough to mist the glass, spread a clean napkin on a silver tray, upon which the glass was placed, and then borne out to the waiting squire. 'Ah! Thank you so much, little Cora was rather parched.' Placing the tray and glass on the floor, he put down Cora, who gratefully and splashily slurped up her drink!

During June 1935 Evelyn Waugh was a guest at Lytham Hall and wrote the following letter to Katherine Asquith:

> Dear Katherine,
>
> A very beautiful house by Kent or someone like him with first-class Italian plaster work. A lap of luxury flowing with champagne and elaborate cookery. Mrs Clifton, Easter (or so she seems to be called), Orsa, Michael, a youth seven feet high with a moustache who plays with a clockwork motorcar and an accordion. The above all Cliftons all are tearing mad. The children bright and giggling. Mrs C. more sombre and full of soul. Tom Burns who is a great favourite with these. Then there is a po-faced debutante walking out with Michael. Large park entirely surrounded by trams and villas. Adam dining room. Five hideous Catholic churches on estate. All sitting at separate tables at meals. Two or three good pictures including a Renoir. Went to Blackpool yesterday evening. That is a good place. Missed Rector of Stiffkey by two days. He had been starving in a glass case.[104]
>
> Appalling heat. All sitting in sun with a dozen aeroplanes overhead and the gardens open to the public.
>
> Evelyn.

The letter is included in Mark Amory's *The Letters of Evelyn Waugh.* It is likely that Tom Burns, Director of *The Tablet* – to which Violet contributed – introduced Waugh to the family.

'Orsa' would be Aurea, the eldest daughter.

In January 1936, Harry is again off on his travels and invoices began to arrive from Delhi's Ivory Palace proprietors, Fakir Chand and Roughnath Das, and Delhi's Fine Art Jewellery Store's proprietor, R. D. Ram Nath, amounting to nearly twenty thousand pounds, for jewellery, ornaments, ivories and many other items, all on their way to Lytham.

From India he travelled on to America and from New York cabled to Whinnerah:

> I wish Lytham Hall not to be used by anyone for three months servants can have vacation.

This was followed by a further cable from San Francisco which was received on 25th May:

> Close Lytham Hall; sell horses; dismiss all staff. Stop. Absolute order. Stop. Cancel sisters' allowances. Stop. Raise mortgage ten thousand pounds in case I need capital; cable Royal Hawaiian Hotel five hundred pounds. Stop. Cancel subscriptions all my Clubs; advise me orders carried out.
>
> Clifton, *SS Lurline.*

Whinnerah immediately cabled back:

> Money transmitted; carrying out all your orders; assume sales include those [horses] Ancils training. Greetings.

He probably sent this with his tongue in his cheek, as none of the orders were carried out. He knew full well that his principal would quite likely cancel the instructions in the course of a few days and it was best to play the waiting game.

By December 1936, Harry was back in London and there was no further reference to the drastic measures he had ordered in May. His next move, however, was to instruct Whinnerah to sell all the ground rents in Lytham St. Annes, which included the three towns of Lytham, Ansdell and St. Annes-on-Sea and comprised about half the rent roll of the estate, and had been carefully built up over the last hundred years.

All the head lessees were written to, informing them that they could purchase the freehold of their properties. This included houses, shops, offices, factories, schools, and in some cases, churches and chapels.

In giving his consent to an aircraft demonstration at St. Annes, he wrote to Whinnerah saying, 'Make it clear that I will tolerate *no accident* upon my ground like the one last year through *Sheer negligence.*'

One cannot help wondering what steps he considered the organisers should take to prevent such a mishap without the aid of Divine intervention!

The year 1937 saw the Coronation of George VI and to make the event Harry displayed his generosity by a gift of land to the borough for playing fields, a sovereign each to three hundred cottage tenants, gifts of cash to the estate office staff, and sufficient wine from the cellars of the Hall to enable every patient and member of the staff in the borough's two hospitals to drink the health of their Majesties.

V

THE proceeds from the sale of the ground rents amounted to £700,000 which Harry proceeded to 're-invest' in more racehorses, an Anson 'plane, objects of virtú made by Fabergé, including an easter egg in gold presented by the Tsar to the Tsarina in 1895. Chinese objets d'art, among which were many beautiful creations in jade and porcelain, and fourteen pieces from the Imperial gold desk set of Emperor Chien Lung (1736-1795). He also bought paintings, which included pictures by Gauguin and Tissot. From India, a dealer whom he had met in Agra, wrote offering 'fourteen paintings on ivory of all the Mogul ladies in their 'Natural bodies which includes our own Noor Jehan'. He considered that Harry would 'adore them and love to have them hung in your own private chamber', but, 'these paintings should only be seen by you and your friends and not by respected mother or sisters'.

Inevitably there were some fakes among his purchases, as, for instance, the de Tanner jades, but these turned out to be such good fakes that they had a special value.

Whinnerah was of course shocked to see what was then considered the almost bed rock security of the Lytham St. Annes ground rents exchanged for works of art, but had the collections been kept until today and sold at current prices, the Clifton fortunes would probably have been restored several fold; whereas the 999-year ground rents had little prospect of rental growth and would have diminished in value.

In addition to art treasures, other strange purchases arrived at Lytham, usually without prior warning or instruction. Packing cases consigned from America, with air holes and slow rustling sounds from within – revealed, when cautiously opened – what appeared to be tortoises. These creatures – about twenty in number – were put into a loose box in the stable yard and offered lettuce, sliced apple and other succulent items which they spurned. When several died, the curator of the Blackpool Zoo was sent for and pronounced them to be terrapins or water turtles. At Whinnerah's urgent request they were taken to Blackpool, where they probably ended their days in more congenial quarters.

The arrival of about four tons of Indian stone gods at Lytham goods' station also created some anxiety, as, not being clear to whom they were addressed, they had lain there for some time and demurrage was accruing. The station staff were also in some trepidation lest their unusual charges should resent this unceremonious treatment and lay a curse upon the railway company and all connected with it. Ownership having been established, the goods were immediately re-dispatched to the Clifton town house in London.

During his travels in the United States, Harry met many unusual people and, as he was reputed to be a millionaire and was a member of the aristocracy, he was courted by society hostesses and crooks alike. Some people genuinely liked him and did their best to keep him out of trouble without any thought of personal gain.

Unfortunately he thought that he could outwit the crooks and if told that a certain person was a dangerous acquaintance would reply 'Oh, I know, but you see I like bad types!'

He also had a strong leaning towards the occult, astrology, spiritualism, fortune telling and their practitioners, to whom he always seems to have given a ready ear.

It was in Los Angeles that he was introduced to the Reverend Violet Greener, known as the Ghost of Hollywood, who had such a profound influence on him that he provided £40,000 to assist in the building of the Agabeg Occult Church. A pamphlet which was circulated prior to the opening of the temple extended the sincere thanks and appreciation to those who had assisted in its creation and heading the list of names in block capitals is 'Mr Henry Francis de Vere Clifton'.[105]

Services were held at 8 p.m. on Sunday, Tuesday and Thursday; the Reverend Violet was pastor and consultations could be had by appointment. She had violet tinted hair and green painted eyelids because her spirit voice, 'likes it that way!' [106]

As an added token of Harry's appreciation of the Reverend Violet, he gave her a diamond encrusted gardenia brooch worth ten thousand dollars.

One of the slimiest letters Harry must ever have received was apparently from one of the supporters of the temple:

Hotel Taft, New York.

On May 5th last I had a long talk at Agabeg Temple with Mr ...., Director of Relations – I presented the *Temple with one of our silver plated 'Tecklite' illuminated* Switch Plates and they say they are delighted with it.

While I was there I showed Mr.......... one of the most beautiful strings of pearls in all the world – (I have a letter from him) 103 of them and weigh 773 grams – lustrous, inconceivably beautiful and rare, it is thought it took one hundred years to find and assemble them.

They are over 500 years old, graded perfectly from large size to smaller – It thrills everyone who has an opportunity of seeing it.

> 103 irridescent, *Rare Green Pearls* - that seem in different light exposures to have all the beautiful colours. My thought is some noble and grand person should own these pearls - and personally I think the wonderful Pastor of Agabeg Temple should own and wear them - she would treasure them beyond all words - I will be here several days at the hotel - *May I show them to you? before you travel on?*

Harry does not seem to have bought the pearls for the wonderful pastor, and, in fairness to her, she may not have known about them.

On 5th October 1937, Harry was married to Lillian Lowell Griswold at 72 Mount Vernon Street, Boston. She was twenty-eight and divorced from her first husband, Merrill Griswold, a Boston banker and attorney, during the previous February. She was a descendant of James Russell Lowell, a writer and one time Ambassador to the Court of St. James. She was a great-niece of Amy Lowell, the poetess, and of Emeritus Professor A. Laurence Lowell of Harvard.[107] She had been a professional actress for several years and met Harry about a year previous to the marriage, in London. She had once visited Lytham. Soon after the marriage she was taken so seriously ill that she did not arrive in England until 22nd December, and even then was confined to a wheelchair with two attendant nurses and was put to bed on arrival at Lytham Hall.

Harry did not accompany his bride and stayed in America 'writing plays and absorbing American atmosphere', as she put it. A certain amount of mystery surrounds their marriage, which does not seem to have been the outcome of a passionate love affair and is said to have taken place after an all-night party. Years after, Lillian's daughter by her first marriage told me, 'When those two woke up and realised what they had done I guess there wasn't a sorrier couple in North America.'

Left to his own devices Harry returned to Los Angeles and during April 1938, was invited to take part in a poker game with Lew Brice, a retired 'hoofer' and brother of Fanny (Baby Snooks) Brice, the famous comedienne - Tommy Guinan, brother of Texas Guinan, nightclub proprietor - Jack Reynolds and George Lewis. Two years previously he had met these gentlemen in Hollywood and played a friendly game for small stakes, 'losing only ten thousand dollars.'

Meeting in Lewis's hotel room the game started: 'using matches as fifty cent chips.' Then it was suggested that 'things be livened up' and a telephone call was made to Brice who was invited to 'come over' and bring some girls with him. Brice arrived alone, saying the girls would be there later. When Brice got into the game, cheques and I.O.U.s were substituted for matches in the stud game, with the dealer's choice on antes. On the first hand Clifton said he lost $1,000 and on the second, $500.

On the third hand, Clifton said he had a king in the hole and Brice had a seven. As the game progressed Guinan and Reynolds withdrew, Clifton drew another king and Brice drew a nine. The betting continued; Clifton drew a jack, a ten and another jack. Brice drew a six and two sevens. That ended the game.[108]

Brice's three sevens having beaten Harry's two pairs, kings and jacks, made him the loser to Brice for $150,000, as he had placed in the pot a cheque on a New York bank for $50,000 and a draft on a London bank for $100,000 – in English money, £30,000. The total pot won by Brice, made up of I.O.U.s and cheques, amounted to $340,000.

A gay champagne party followed the game, in which the two beautiful young women – who in the meantime had arrived – took part; but Harry soon departed to seek comfort and solace at the Agabeg Temple from its high priestess, the Reverend Violet Greener.

> 'I knew as soon as I saw him – before he could speak a word – what had happened', she said. 'The first thing I said to him, before he told me any names at all was "Who is this George Lewis?", and he said to me "My God, how did you know it was George Lewis? How did you know anything about it at all?" From a vantage point thirty miles from the game the Reverent Violet had closed her eyes and listened to 'the voice' and knew that the 'Millionaire Squire of Lancashire England' was being gypped, she said. With her occult powers – 'It's a God given gift and I am wonderful', she explained – the Rev. Violet divined that the game was stud poker, illegal in California, and not the legally recognised draw poker.
>
> She told off all the names and told the amazed Clifton further that he should stop payment on the cheques he had written to cover his loss.
>
> 'She deserves a big reward, doesn't she?', Clifton commented fondly as the mystic finished.[109]

Following the reverend lady's advice Harry reported the matter to the District Attorney's office and obtained a temporary court order halting payment on his cheques and charging conspiracy to obtain money by fraud and device. He also charged that Brice, Guinan, Lewis and Reynolds had represented themselves as men of great wealth, able to pay the huge poker debt if they lost. The District Attorney's office also assigned guards to surround Mr Clifton after he had said he had received a threat over the telephone that unless he ordered payment on the cheques, 'the boys would take it out of your hide', and at the same time detectives were ordered to pick up his poker opponents.

The D.A. also ordered a search to be made for the two beautiful young women who took part in the champagne party, as Harry alleged that they were brought in to keep him in a 'carefree state of mind', while Jack Reynolds flew to New York to try to cash his cheque. As the *Daily News* headlined it:

Hunt two queens who held hand of poker loser.

Lew Brice had to drop his claim to the winnings, but he very nearly got the money according to Jerry Geisler, Harry's lawyer: 'Brice was waiting at the bank to cash the cheques when we got the court order'.[110]

Fortunately, before leaving New York for the west coast, Harry had appointed Dr Armand Hammer - now the world famous philanthropist and head of Occidental Petroleum Corporation - as his financial agent with power of attorney to scrutinize any large cheques Harry's New York bankers might receive in case of forgery.

When the cheque for $150,000 drawn in favour of Brice arrived, they telephoned the Doctor, who knew Brice's reputation as a gambler. After much difficulty in locating Harry's whereabouts, he found him at Violet Greener's home and having convinced him that he had been duped, the police were informed and the cheque was stopped.

Brice attributed his success to Clifton's wild playing. 'I'd like to play with him every day', he told Chief Inspector John Klein.

Tommy Guinan commented sourly: 'If you ask me I don't think Clifton is an Englishman after all, I think he's a Welshman!'

Harry first met the doctor at the Hammer Galleries in New York, where he and his brother Victor were in business and their store of objets d'art and paintings had, of course, drawn him like a bee to a honeypot. At first the brothers were suspicious of the young Englishman with his often dishevelled appearance and eccentric behaviour, but, enquiry revealing Harry to be a man of substance, they became firm friends.

Some idea of how Harry's reputation for great wealth had spread is given by the mention of a prominent Fifth Avenue jeweller whose name he gave to Hammer as a referee:

'Is Harry Clifton's credit good?'

Incredulity vibrated down the telephone line, 'He's good for everything you've got in your store and everything in ours as well. He's one of the richest men in England. His family owned the whole city of Blackpool and he has tremendous holdings in real estate on which he gets an income of ten thousand dollars a day or more.'

Sometimes the brothers would join Harry at his favourite Chinese restaurant and he amazed them by his method of investment. Having ear-marked a few stocks he called the Chinese waiter and asked him 'should I buy or sell?' The man, who could hardly speak English, gazed at him uncomprehendingly until pressed by Harry 'just tell me, buy or sell'. Finally the waiter ventured 'buy' and Harry went to the 'phone and instructed his broker to buy 10,000 of the particular stock. Such eccentric behaviour had the New York Stock Exchange in turmoil.

Harry arrived back at Lytham on 22nd May and joined his bride at the Hall. News of the poker game had, of course, been flashed across the Atlantic and was eagerly taken up by the national press. For years after he was known as the 'Poker Squire'.

Some of his friends and relations were not so amused and felt that he had sullied his good name and did not hesitate to let him know:

Guards Club
Brook Street, W.1.

We are - all of us here in London - so sorry for you and your name which should remain honoured.

I again caution you against immoral old women passing as fortune tellers - card sharpers and the like - they will lead you to complete destruction.

Yours and very frankly,
.....................? [111]

VI

WHEN Lillian recovered from her illness she set about putting things to rights in the Hall. Out went the mounted heads, stuffed animals and birds - all the trophies of the huntings of John Talbot. Hidden from sight in the stable lofts, they remained at the mercy of moths and mice, until, after the Second World War, they had to be committed to the flames.

In came new furnishings, china and glass for the table and smart green uniforms for the maids; probably the first face lift since the completion of the Hall in the 1760s, as mercifully it had escaped any Victorian alterations.

With her American awareness of the importance of fire escapes, she pronounced the Hall a death trap and had patent spring loaded rope and harness escapes installed on the upper floors and, when the staff showed their reluctance to test the equipment, had no hesitation in taking it on herself and jumping out of one of the topmost windows.

Coming down one morning, she heard Blanch Cormier - who had come as housekeeper - dressing down one of the maids, who was sobbing hysterically.

'She has broken one of your best wine glasses, Madam,' Blanch informed her.[112]

'O.K.', said Lillian to the girl, 'You bring me one just the same, right now.'

Taking the glass, she said, 'Now you're sure this one's the same?'

'Yes, Madam', sobbed the girl, 'I'm very sorry.'

'Right!', said Lillian, and hurled the glass straight into the dining room fireplace.

'There! Now I've broken one, too, so stop making that goddam noise!'

She was a shrewd woman and possibly had more business acumen than her husband, but the role of lady of the manor did not rest easily on her shoulders and to a great extent she shrugged it aside.

Sometimes their public appearances resulted in considerable surprise for their hosts. The secretary of one of the local golf clubs, upon receiving a telephone message from the Hall, rang up the captain and members of the council saying that the squire and his lady were calling round that evening.

Harry clad in dinner jacket and Lillian in evening gown and jewels duly arrived, were welcomed, and introduced all round.

The club members were intrigued by a newspaper parcel Harry was carrying under his arm, until he said to the steward, 'Could you please bring me two plates and some forks and knives. Oh, yes, and some vinegar and pepper and salt. That table will do nicely.'

The slightly stunned steward having complied with this request, Harry and Lillian sat down and opened their parcel in front of the now goggle-eyed members, revealing fish and chips!

'I do hope you don't mind, we thought we'd just bring our supper with us,' explained Harry.

It did not, seemingly, turn out to be a very successful marriage as their personalities clashed in many ways and rows were frequent. Seven months after their wedding, in the early hours of the morning, Lillian fell some thirty feet to the ground from the first floor window of the south dressing room.

Harry explained to the press: 'It was just one of those stunts that did not come off. She was trying a feat and thought she was able to walk along a certain place, but unfortunately she could not do so.'

The truth of the matter seems to have been that during a blazing argument after a not completely teetotal evening, he had rushed into the south bedroom locking the door behind him. She, pursuing him, and finding the door locked, went into the adjoining dressing room, opened the window, and tried to edge her way towards the bedroom window along the stone string course which only projects about one inch from the face of the wall.

In the fall she suffered severe injuries to the chest, a damaged spine and fractured her right arm in two places.

Once again, Lillian lay for many weeks in the principal bedroom attended by nurses and visited by eminent doctors and surgeons. Here she held court, received friends and took a keen interest in all that went on. I – then chief surveyor to the estate – was one day summoned to her bedside to take a glass of sherry and have a chat. During the conversation she said, 'I guess you're wondering what all those crates are.' Down one side of the room were about twenty stoutly made wooden boxes, which could not fail to attract attention in such surroundings.

'Yeah, we've cornered the world emerald market', she said with a slight note of sarcasm in her voice. 'Go on, bring one over and dump it out on the bed.'

Her instructions being complied with, out came a quantity of pale cloudy green fragments, somewhat like the green chippings used for filling inside the kerbs round a grave.

'That's dross from a South American emerald mine; if you can find a clear bit, that's an emerald. You have a look!'

An anxious search through the dross not revealing any piece of the required transparency she said: 'We can't find any either. I guess we've been done again.'

In 1943 they were divorced, Harry getting a decree on the grounds of her adultery with a naval officer. Lillian cross-petitioned on grounds of cruelty, but this was dismissed and Mr Justice Hen Collins, in giving judgement, said:

> As to the window incident the husband said he was in no way responsible for it, and had no part or lot in it. There was no corroboration of the wife's allegation that her husband pushed her.

The foregoing account of their married life, culminating as it did in divorce, leaves one with the impression that there was little real affection between them. Several years after the divorce, however, Lillian wrote to Harry from New York in terms leaving no doubt that, for a while at least, they loved each other and that she still had a deep affection for him, though living together was impossible.

She starts by asking if he had received a letter she wrote the previous year and asked if it was true that he wanted her back as she had been told.

She felt that the reasons for the failure of the marriage were that he thought she had married him for his money: his mother and William Whinnerah disapproved of it and conspired together to separate them: the local gossips shredded their characters – 'every act we did or thought was discussed and twisted.' She mentions another woman:

> Why you ever married me and fell in love, while [she], giving you the royal run around, still fascinated you. No doubt you thought you could outsmart her. You should know that those women have lived an entire life of mean paltry greed and their entire mentality is given to improving their technique in separating the male from his wallet. Any man who thinks he can outsmart a woman at her job of more and more security is not thinking . . . believe me, had I been after money, I'd have demanded more pay for playing nursemaid to a brat who had his candy and broken his chains.

She states that Whinnerah and Harry's mother approached her to assist in having him certified and claims that she managed to thwart 'this last piece of human horror.'

Whilst protesting that she still loved him she castigates him:

> I know I could have controlled the ghastly mess but I didn't want to then. There was no happiness in it for me and if you were so insistent on destroying your happiness and your possessions I'd be darned if I was any old school teacher to a stubborn mule who thought he was a hell of a smart guy who could out-clever professional crooks. The only way you'd ever learn was when your check bounced and there was no more land to sell and the art collection swindled out of you. To tell the truth I

> didn't care. A nasty little boy can be spanked but a grown man who has no more self respect than a lot of cheap vanity is just a plain nuisance. I was bored with a silly pest who was so sure he was God's original genius . . . I knew you were acting like a nut from hurt pride, but I had nothing to do with it and I got the brunt of your entire thirty-four unhappy years.

She finishes her letter:

> I can enjoy you while you don't have me in your collection, but when once bought, quickly forgotten. That wasn't a nice experience.
>
> As friends we might be happy in each other's company, but not as one of your possessions. I just wanted to make sure you understood why I asked you to visit. I want to see a very dear friend of whom I'm terribly fond.
>
> Please come over Harry. I can think of nothing which would so please me.
>
> Affectionately yours,
> Lillian.

Those who knew Harry Clifton will appreciate the letter as an extraordinarily true assessment of his character; her merciless criticism is leavened by repeated reference to an underlying kindness and generosity which sometimes surfaced.

Some of his acts of apparent meanness may have been occasioned by forgetfulness. He would promise to reward or recompense people for carrying out some task or assignment and then refuse to make good his promise. He sometimes gave money or valuables and then asked for them back. He was adept at leading people on - some rascals, some genuine - by agreeing to take part in schemes which would, so they believed (and he also at the time probably believed) make their fortunes. When the persons had gone to endless trouble to get things moving and came back to him, like good dogs with wagging tails, expecting a pat on the head, they were surprised to find their patron had gone cold on the project and, having no further interest in the matter, had left them flat.

He loved playing at being a big businessman and formed several companies for film making, construction and land development, importing and exporting, from which evolved a number of projects.

One of his schemes was the creation of a new Garden City to cover some two hundred acres of the township of Westby with Plumpton, which he owned. Plans were prepared by an eminent professor and conformed to the then most up-to-date conception of how a complete residential town should be laid out. It had a shopping centre and public buildings, the dwellings were to be of good quality with large gardens, and an extensive lake was proposed as a feature of the landscaping. This Utopia was to be named Saint Christopher after the patron saint of travellers.

Whinnerah, who was just retiring as agent, refused to have anything to do with the idea, building land was hard enough to let or sell in Lytham St. Annes without creating opposition on the doorstep. This was prime farm land, the lake would cause many problems, the matter of sewage disposal seemed to have been left to the imagination and war had just been declared on Germany!

Not even Hitler could deter Harry from his purpose, however, and he instructed a local firm of architects to have erected on the site a foundation stone in the form of a large concrete block bearing the following inscription:

> St Christopher
> In commemoration of the foundation of the town of St. Christopher, this stone was laid by Harry Talbot Clifton, 29th November 1939.

This pedestal was ultimately to be finished off in granite bearing the carved figure of the saint.

The ceremony was attended by many local dignitaries and representatives of local authorities. Whinnerah presented the squire with a silver trowel with which to lay the stone, who in doing so, said:

> I hope that St. Christopher will get near to what he is supposed to have carried one day in human form . . . God.

After the ceremony the guests were entertained to luncheon at the Clifton Arms, but unfortunately it had not been made clear *which* Clifton Arms. Some people repaired to the Clifton Arms at Marton, some to Warton, some to Clifton, but luckily most went to the hotel at Lytham where champagne flowed and speeches were made.

It was about a fortnight later that the Fylde Water Board telephoned the estate offices, complaining bitterly about the concrete monolith which had been erected precisely on top of the fifteen-inch water main to Blackpool!

And so it came to pass, that men with heavy hammers and pneumatic drills came and smashed the stone to pieces. All that remain today are a few fragments of concrete rubble lying on the roadside as a reminder of the town that never was!

During 1938 Harry had purchased Rufford Abbey, ancient seat of the family of Savile in Nottinghamshire. All the farm land had been sold off previously and the purchase consisted of the house and parkland, with a number of cottages and other buildings. The house was vast and had sheltered royal personages over the centuries, including Edward VII, who was accommodated in the royal suite when he came for the shooting. Why Harry bought it is something of a mystery, as to live there was out of the question: all the furniture had gone and to staff it would have required a small army of servants; to develop the park as another garden city presented many problems due to lack of services and, in any case, the war had commenced and the abbey was requisitioned for military purposes.

One day Harry arrived to inspect his purchase and, calling at the Hop Pole Inn at Ollerton, enquired of the landlady if he could have lunch for himself and his baby. She, not knowing who he was, told her cook that 'Such a nice young man' was coming to lunch accompanied by his little baby and a consultation ensued on the merits of a little fish or chicken for the infant. At one o'clock Harry and his 'baby' arrived, the latter proving to be a beauteous and fully grown damsel whose luncheon requirements ran more to smoked salmon and Chablis than minced chicken with mash and milk!

As the war years dragged on the property began to suffer from neglect and the effect of troops being quartered there. The gardens ran to waste and the deer fence surrounding the park was broken down and the timber used for various purposes. This allowed the herd of deer to escape and ravage the crops of the adjoining farms and resulted in the deer having to be hunted down and shot.

At the end of hostilities the place was in a very rough state, the last occupants having been prisoners of war, who used the tapestries to make handbags to send home to their girlfriends, and similar acts of vandalism.

In order to prevent any further damage to the property and generally look after the place, Joe Hodgkinson, one of the Lytham Estate workmen, was sent to Rufford to take charge.

Joe was the kind of man who would tackle anything, brisk in manner and with ready Lancastrian wit. The abbey was reputedly haunted and there is a headstone in Ollerton churchyard recording that the occupant of the grave 'died of fright upon seeing the Rufford ghost'. It is a fact that the previous caretaker would not go his rounds of the house without a large dog on a leash. When the dog refused to go along a passage or into a room, whimpering and cowering, the caretaker would not go any farther and hastily departed with his dog. One day Joe was visited by a mystic who wished to spend the night in the sewing room immediately over the main entrance, said to be haunted by an old lady in black.[113] Joe was most co-operative and ushered the man into the room, where, equipped with torch, coffee and sandwiches, he settled himself down for the night.

Later on, Joe, who did not fear ghost or devil, quietly stole upstairs to the room above the watcher, opened the window, and, as the stable yard clock struck midnight, gently lowered down, on a piece of twine, a stuffed owl he had found, so that the beak tapped on the window. The watcher hearing the tapping shone his torch on the window and saw two orange eyes glaring at him out of the darkness.

'Eeh! the bugger did skrike,' said Joe afterwards, 'he went down them stairs six at a time. I never saw him again. His coffee and sandwiches were all right, though![114]

The property was finally disposed of by piecemeal sales of the land, houses and cottages, and the abbey itself, being the subject of a preservation order, was sold to Nottinghamshire County Council under purchase order as it was incapable of beneficial use.

VII

UPON the declaration of war Harry made every effort to join the Air Force 'as a mechanic like Lawrence of Arabia', but without success.[115] He then applied himself to farming, purchasing Anstey Hall Farm in Hertfordshire and Clavering Hall Farm in Essex. The home farm at Lytham was taken in hand, and efforts were also made to increase food production at Kildalton. To co-ordinate the farming effort, the Clifton Agricultural Company was formed, with offices at 40 Buckingham Road, London.

Early in the war, Archdeacon Fosbrooke[116] became Harry's attorney and when John C. Bills - who had succeeded Whinnerah as agent - accepted an appointment as a valuer with the Air Ministry, William Latham, Chartered Accountant of Lytham, took over the management of Harry's affairs.

Lytham Hall became a convalescent hospital for soldiers; all its furnishings were removed into store and very little ever came back.

Harry was not without funds. The sale of the Lytham St. Annes ground rents and other parcels of land between 1935 and 1939 brought him just over one million pounds. Of this sum, however, over four hundred thousand went to pay off mortgages, and a substantial amount went to the trustees of the marriage settlement of John Talbot for re-investment. Despite these realisations the rich farmlands were left and, in Lytham St. Annes, land with an enormous development potential for building.

In January 1941, Harry - like his great grandfather, Thomas Joseph, brought up a Catholic - was received into the Church of England, which meant that he became patron of the benefices of five churches in Lytham St. Annes and Blackpool with the power of advowson, or gift of the living, of each church. This had lapsed when his father, John Talbot, became a Catholic in 1898, when the patronage was administered by the University of Cambridge.[117] In deciding to change his faith Harry was probably influenced by the Archdeacon.

In June 1941 Latham journeyed to New York to set up an art gallery at 44 East 57th Street, to offer for sale Harry's now very considerable art collection. This was with the consent and encouragement of the Ministry of Economic Warfare and was intended to help Britain's currency. While he was in America he went to Hollywood and saw the Reverend Violet Greener and - with Harry's consent - persuaded her to return the valuable jewel he had given her, which was sold in New York for $21,000.

During 1942, Harry had patented the design for a craft driven by an air screw and rising up on skis or pontoons, which he thought could be developed into cargo carrying vessels that would defeat the U-boat sinkings, and he advertised in the *War Time Trading Bulletin* – '30% rights in invention from patent for sale: £150,000. Stops ships sinking, increases speed by twelve knots. Shipbuilders and aircraft manufacturers willing to help this country will find interest. Partial air principle. Highest credentials required and given.' Whilst no manufacturers seem to have availed themselves of this intriguing offer, it is remarkable that the idea, in essence, has since been developed in the form of the hydrofoil and hovercraft.

One matter of estate administration Harry endeavoured to settle in his own way. In 1850 Thomas Joseph Clifton had agreed that Lord Derby should have the right to drain 258 acres of his Weeton estate into the recently cut main drain through the adjoining Clifton estate. In consideration of this right, Thomas received a corn mill and house at Freckleton. In 1932 it was found that 577 acres of the Weeton estate was being so drained and some new arrangement should be made. Nothing was settled, and in 1942 Harry, remembering the matter, wrote to Lord Derby:

> I point out, in my estimation, the many hundreds of acres you drained for many years through our land is equivalent to seven thousand pounds reparation . . . As my ancestor took a windmill I will close the matter in perpetuity for something in kind, like a horse, foal or mare.

Derby apparently replied courteously but suggesting the matter be left until the war was over, and Harry, in replying, said: 'Your mention of a racehorse gave me great joy, but if the difficulties are too great, a simpler device will have to do.' And there the matter seemed to rest.[118]

In addition to the Archdeacon and William Latham, Harry now had as counsellors, a psycho-therapeutist and natural orthopoedist, named St. George, and a diamond merchant, Weiss. This unusual quaternity applied themselves diligently to such matters as agriculture, film production, fine art, building development, the foundation of a clinic for the eradication of phthisis in the Glasgow district, naval architecture and other matters in which their principal was interested, as well as trying to keep him out of trouble.

The Archdeacon received no payment save expenses for his efforts and the considerable worry and responsibility he shouldered, and the sometimes unpleasant situations in which he found himself.

Harry was again hard up and pressing his attorney and agent for more money, but not content to leave matters to them gave F. W.

Rickett authority to seek a buyer for the Lytham estates. Rickett had connections with a number of business concerns; stockbrokers, marine patents and the promotion of companies. He had also taken part in negotiations for oil-prospecting concessions in Iraq and Abyssinia, and schemes for handling oil output expropriated by the Mexican Government. He was regarded as a shrewd and capable negotiator and financier. During May 1943, Rickett visited Lytham with Rudolph Palumbo and his surveyor to inspect the property. Palumbo was a financier who Rickett described as a 'merchant prince whose father or grandfather financed Garibaldi.'[119]

Latham had prepared a schedule and rough plan of the estate, and after the inspection a trial valuation was made of £757,500.

On June 7th Rickett met Harry at Anstey Hall Farm, where he was staying the weekend, and had with him a draft letter which he asked Harry to copy and sign in his own hand to be evidence of Rickett's authority to negotiate and be regarded as a firm offer!

Dear Mr Rickett,

I thank you for the memorandum of the meeting held at the Clifton Estate Office, Lytham, on Wednesday, the 2nd June, and having read same, am prepared to offer you or your nominees my Lytham Estate for £600,000, on condition that it is definitely understood and agreed that the Lordship of the Manors remains in my possession. I also agree that a reasonable and sufficient time shall be granted to you for the examination and consideration of all the data and details necessary for the schedule of completion.

Yours ....

Before signing the letter Harry asked to see the memorandum referred to and Rickett produced a piece of paper on which a few lines were written in his own hand but which did not set out in detail the matters discussed on 2nd June. He explained that a proper memorandum would be prepared and Harry, accepting this, signed the letter.

Harry then went to Lytham and consulted with Latham and together they made their own valuation, arriving at a figure of £1,350,000, whereupon Harry instructed Latham to inform Palumbo that £600,000 was not enough and he did not intend to include the farm lands. He also consulted his solicitor, who wrote to Palumbo making it abundantly clear that no contract existed.

On August 18th, Rickett went to Harrow-on-the-Hill where Harry was residing at the home of St. George, the therapeutist, and during dinner told Harry that Palumbo was forming a company and that if Harry would sign the memorandum referred to in the letter of 7th June, Palumbo would pay him £300,000 in cash and the remaining £300,000 in shares in the company. He would also pay Harry the difference between the annual dividends and £15,000 *per annum* free of tax.

Harry was greatly impressed by this offer and asked Rickett to guarantee it there and then, but he demurred and said Palumbo would do this next day. He then produced the letter of 7th June, written by Harry, which had now been endorsed by Palumbo and Rickett, signifying their agreement. He asked Harry to write underneath 'I hereby agree and confirm' and again sign it. This he did, but wrote underneath, 'By Order of Rickett, Emperor of Lytham.'

This angered Rickett, who said he had spoiled the letter and asked him to write it out again. Harry re-wrote the letter three times before Rickett was satisfied and pocketed the third letter, leaving Harry the original.

Returning to London next day, Rickett gave the letter to Palumbo, by whom it was registered at the Land Charges Registry as an estate contract.

Harry's solicitor again wrote to Palumbo saying that he was prepared to proceed on the terms put to Harry orally at Harrow, but that the price should be £750,000 and Harry to be chairman of the new company. Not receiving a satisfactory reply to this letter and upon learning that the letter of 7th June had been registered, a writ was served on Palumbo's solicitor claiming, among other matters, that no contract existed and that the entry in the Land Charges Registry should be voided. Upon receipt of the writ Palumbo counter-claimed for specific performance of contract.

The hearing took place in July 1944 and lasted for fourteen days. The judge found in favour of Harry and granted a declaration that there never was any concluded agreement between him and Palumbo for sale of the estate.

In his judgement Mr Justice Vaisey said that Palumbo had relied on a letter 'extremely badly written' on a half sheet of paper and he could not hold that this property changed hands on a paper which came into existence in a highly haphazard fashion. He also ordered that Palumbo should pay three quarters of the costs.

Palumbo appealed against the judgement but the Master of the Rolls, Lord Justice Finlay and Lord Justice Moston dismissed the appeal. The Master of the Rolls, in referring to Mr Justice Vaisey's comments on the proceedings at Harrow on the 18th and 19th August, 1943 considered them 'moderate in the extreme', which comment was endorsed by Lord Justice Moston.

Had Palumbo won his case it is unlikely he would have been in a hurry to sell up the estate, as Harry subsequently did. Palumbo must have seen its enormous post-war potential, as he was already shrewdly buying up bombed sites in the city. Had he won and retained the estate it is not inconceivable that his son, Peter, who has aroused such controversy in London by his architectural proposals, and who is currently Director of the Arts Council, could have been the squire of Lytham.

The Archdeacon, whilst aware of the meetings and arrangements which had taken place, took no actual part in them. He had only met Palumbo once, but had seen Rickett several times. During October 1943, the Archdeacon had lunched with Harry at the Travellers' Club, and when leaving to catch his train back to Lytham, met Rickett in the entrance hall.

Without any preliminary, Rickett said: 'I have just been telling Harry that he ought to act like a white man and not cause all this trouble.'

The Archdeacon replied: 'Is the matter very serious?'

'It is very serious for me,' said Rickett, 'for I am between the devil and the deep blue sea.'

'In what way?' asked the Archdeacon.

'Why', Rickett replied, 'these people are going for me.'

'Do you mean Mr Palumbo?'

Rickett replied, 'Yes, and those associated with him.'

'But how can they be going for you?'

'They are charging me with misrepresentation.'

'Then you are indeed between the upper and nether millstones,' said the Archdeacon, and went to catch his train.[120]

VIII

EVEN before the outcome of the Palumbo case was known, Harry, during May 1944, was again becoming involved with another firm of financiers, and again schemes were being propounded to make great gain for all concerned. Harry remarked to Latham after one of his meetings with his latest advisors that it gave him a great thrill to be negotiating in millions whilst at the same time hard up for ready cash.

An approach was made to Harry's cousin, the Duke of St. Albans, to see if the St. Alban's Trust would take over his mortgages, but the Duke advised that they should have 'nothing to do with Mr Clifton or his affairs as no matter how much was made for him he would show no appreciation.' [121]

The truth of the Duke's opinion was soon brought home to Latham. At a meeting with Harry in Lytham he received a lecture on finance and his principal's dissatisfaction at Latham's handling of such matters, culminating in an explanation of the difference between a good agent and a bad agent. This was more than Latham could take and, telling Harry that he had done his best to hold the position during the war and had done all he could to assist, as his services were not satisfactory the squire could have his resignation just when he pleased.

This resulted in another meeting attended by the Archdeacon, St. George and Latham. The Archdeacon first told Harry that he could not continue as his attorney if Latham resigned and asked him to say if he had complete confidence in the persons assisting him in the managment of his estate. He also made it clear that if he desired to take the advice of those of whom he had little knowledge, in preference to those who had assisted him throughout a most difficult period, he was free to do so. Harry, having expressed his complete confidence in the Archdeacon and Latham, told the latter he hoped they would be together for many years.

The most important and far-reaching outcome of this showdown was the formation of a voluntary trust to manage Harry's Lytham estate, on 8th June 1944. The trustees were the Archdeacon, William Latham and John Barker Leaver, a solicitor resident in Lytham, who were authorised to adminster the estate in the most advantageous manner.

Within a few months, however, the trustees had a supplementary deed prepared to provide for the succession in case of their beneficiary's early demise! This they considered necessary as he had been thrown and savaged by his grey stallion Flag, which he had unwisely attempted to ride whilst at stud. He had also, on one visit to the home farm, entered a loose box to pat a fully-grown and rather dangerous Friesian bull which had his head down, and was pawing up the sawdust and roaring.

'What a nice fellow, I'll just go in and talk to him.'

Entering the box, despite the farm manager's entreaties not to, he walked up to the bull, gave him a hearty smack on the rump and walked out. The bull was so surprised that he stopped roaring and pawing and sheepishly looked after him!

There were many problems for the trustees to deal with. Neighbouring Blackpool comtemplated acquiring five thousand acres of the farm lands on which to build the world's biggest airport. There was also to be a seaplane base four miles in diameter and fifteen feet deep, constructed in the Ribble estuary between St. Annes and Southport, connected to the airport by an underground tunnel. At a modest estimate this could be done for ten million pounds, but a later estimate suggested thirty million. The trustees thought this would be disastrous for Lytham St. Annes and were greatly relieved when the Air Ministry vetoed the proposal.

Harry soon found the restraining hand of his trustees irksome as his demands for more and more money did not meet with immediate response and he resorted to what might be described as 'trustee baiting', a pastime to which he applied himself assiduously and with, one suspects, a certain amount of pleasure.

He proposed that he should have a personal representative, appointed by himself, who would sit in on the trustees' deliberations, who could promote Harry's point of view and if necessary veto any decisions that might be contrary to his ideas. Learned counsel, however, quashed this without hesitation, whereupon Harry turned on St. George and blamed him for advising him to agree to the trust!

Harry was still desperately anxious to make his name as a producer of motion pictures, particularly documentaries, and, in order to have a mobile studio, tried to charter an aircraft carrier! Failing in this he lowered his sights somewhat and began negotiations for a tank landing craft costing £70,000. Latham, upon taking expert advice, was informed that 'Mr Clifton might just as well buy Euston Station for his park, for all the use the vessel would be to him!'

Again thwarted, but apparently determined to acquire a sea-going vessel of some kind, he bought the twin-screw motor yacht *Kihna.* This once magnificent vessel of 573 gross tons and overall length of

183 feet, had seen active service under the white ensign during the war. She required a complete re-fit before she could be classified by Lloyds and re-entered in their register of yachts; some work had already been carried out but not paid for and a lot more needed to be done.

Kihna, however, was sailed to Galway – where Harry was ill in a nursing home – to await his instructions, if not pleasure! Matters were not improved when the yacht – whilst shifting berth in harbour – went full astern into the quay owing to some misunderstanding between engine room and bridge! The final indignity was the nailing of a writ of attachment to the mast because of the unpaid accounts for repair. Finally she was sold to Trinity House, but left another account in the estate books listing heavily to the debit side.

It appeared afterwards that Harry and some of his intimate friends had the idea of sailing away in *Kihna* to some tropical island and creating their own Utopia far from the post-war world and there live a simple idyllic life – a proposal to which Harry's trustees would doubtless have given their wholehearted support.

The main target of Harry's attacks on the trustees was Latham, who, as personal agent, trustee and agent to the estate was particularly vulnerable. He was subjected to long telephone conversations – mainly one-sided – at any time during the day or night, during which he received the outpourings of his principal's discontent. 'He would never have dreamed of entering into the Trust had he realised that his Trustees, in addition to his agreed annual payment from the estate, would not undertake the expenditure known to be necessary for the maintenance of his personal estates; in particular Kildalton and Rufford.' He had also understood that the trustees would assist in his business activities.

He maintained that his farming, film companies and other projects had shown substantial appreciation under his control. He did allow that he had lost a few thousand on the pigs. This, perhaps, was not surprising as he had his own ideas on pig farming and did not like to see them penned. Irrespective of whether they were breeding stock or fatteners he would have them released and the pigs would joyfully scamper off, ravaging growing crops, woodlands and gardens. Whilst the pigs were literally bristling with health and energy, they became lean and fleet of foot, instead of attaining the obese proportions required for the ideal baconer.

During 1948, the Eire–Moroccan Company Limited, Director General, The Laird H. Talbot de Vere Clifton, was formed to stimulate trade between Eire and Morocco. The proposed activities of this company were many and varied, including the export of peat from Kildalton to Morocco, the construction of a harbour for Ceylon, and a French importer had placed on order 1,100 Irish tweed suits for the Arabs(!). Harry himself was in Marrakesh making arrangements for a documentary colour film about the Arab and Spanish civilisation, which he considered could be produced at the bargain price of £100,000. A local pasha and a cadi, who were interested in the company, were so rich they could afford to provide a palace for each of their eleven sons.

By 1948 the trustees, by judicious sales, had realised about a quarter of a million pounds, of which Harry had received about £100,000, but he still pressed for more, and they informed him that in view of recent legislation, sales of land must cease for the present.

This was the Town and Country Planning Act 1947, one of the most complicated pieces of legislation ever passed by Parliament, which sought, basically, to skim off for the state the rich cream of development value arising out of the sale or lease of land for development purposes, or arising out of certain changes in land use.

The measure provided for compensation to be paid out of a global sum to land and property owners who were mulcted of their profits by reason of the Act. This sum was so inadequate that it was considered by the professional bodies that the amount of compensation likely to be received by an individual claimant would be extremely small.

This appeared to be a body blow to the estate, as many acres of Lytham St. Annes were now ripe for development. The immediate effect was to slow down development almost to a standstill, as surveyors and solicitors grappled with the manifold problems created by the Act, and the general feeling was to delay further development in the hope that a change of government might bring about a repeal of the measure, or at least a modification of its impact on property owners and builders.

When this was explained to Harry, he immediately renewed his attacks on the trustees and said they should have made provision for such legislation by further mortgages and raising temporary loans. He would accept a reduced allowance if they gave him £30,000 now, as he was again short of money.

The Archdeacon and Latham were prepared to accede to this request but Leaver protested strongly and said that Latham's dual capacity of personal agent and trustee was an embarrassment to the proper conduct of trust matters. And so the seeds of dissention were sown within the Trust.

During 1949 Harry took up residence in the Irish Free State, staying sometimes in the Portmarnock Country Club but mainly in the Royal Hibernian Hotel, Dublin, and spending most of the ensuing two years in bed.

It is not clear what his particular complaint was; he seems to have become something of a hypochondriac. His hangers-on and toadies were summoned to his bedside but made to wait, sometimes for hours or even days, before being granted audience. Most of them lived in the hotel and ate and drank at his expense and some, having succeeded in pleasing their master or by putting over some plausible story, departed with fat cheques.

Sarah Hurst, sister of Brian Hurst, the film producer, who had been in partnership with Harry before the war, acted as Harry's secretary, nurse and confidante and 'screened' visitors before admitting them into the presence.

Latham made many journeys to Ireland to report on matters relating to the estate and Harry's private business. These visits became more and more burdensome as Harry became increasingly difficult and, indeed, vindictive in his criticism of the trustees' management of affairs. He was pressing all the time for the sale of the estate and, whilst the Archdeacon and Latham were prepared to continue the realisation of large sums of money by sales of land and property, Leaver was obdurate that they must implement the provisions of the trust deed to the letter.

Inevitably, Latham's health began to suffer under the strain of the visits to Dublin, the long telephone calls that sometimes became tirades, and the worry and frustration of it all.

Then Leaver resigned from the trust – without animosity and probably with considerable relief. He continued to act through his firm, however, as legal advisor to the trust.

Harry's war of nerves was beginning to pay off.

During one of his visits, in January 1950, Latham was informed by Harry that he had built up his art collection to such importance that it should be catalogued and that he had appointed Cyril Bunt, retired curator from the Victoria and Albert Museum, to do the work. He wished to vest the collection in a company that was to be named 'Lorenzo de Medici Limited'. Bunt's problem was to locate where the various items were lodged, as they were scattered over London, Lytham, Ireland and America, and Harry – squirrel-like – was not quite sure where! Poor Bunt became increasingly mournful as time went on and finally disappeared from the scene, as did 'Lorenzo de Medici'.

It was during the same month that Violet, Harry's mother, joined the Poor Clare Community at Arundel as a probationer for four years, paying £25 per quarter for her keep. She did this so that she could help other members of the family – who were also hard-up – out of her jointure, and took the name of Sister Seraphim. Auria, Harry's eldest sister, was ill and in need of urgent financial assistance, so Latham sent her £20 and £6 per week. Upon reporting this to Harry he was told that 'twenty pounds was not very generous but in time of need better than two hundred at other times.' Hearing that Tom Matthews, his old gamekeeper, was dying, however, he ordered that £60 should be sent to him. He had no desire to meet his brother's children and had no responsibilities towards them.

During one dreadful interview, he told Latham he wanted £30,000, of which Latham could have ten per cent commission and the Archdeacon a cut of £700. He was furious that of £50,000 borrowed by the trustees, part had been used to pay off a bank overdraft and part used to refund the trustees for money already advanced to him. He had not authorised Latham to take his salary as personal agent as he did not see why his agent should be paid when he was hard up. The accusations and harrassments continued the next day. Even when Latham retired to his room to seek some rest he was pursued by the squire asking why his personal bank account was overdrawn £10,000 without his being informed, the inference of which so shocked Latham that he could not afterwards recall what he replied. The crowning insult came when Sarah Hurst delivered a message from Harry that 'it would be nice to have a letter thanking him for his hospitality in Dublin!'

When Latham came back to Lytham his nerves were shattered and the Archdeacon said that as a duty to himself and family he must at once resign as personal agent and 'cease to be subjected to these intolerable attacks.' [122]

It was decided that the Archdeacon should go to Dublin and tell the squire that if he wished to go to the court to have the trustees replaced they would not defend such action in the ordinary sense.

On 9th March, though unwell, the Archdeacon travelled to Dublin, taking with him Lathom's written resignation, and booked in at the Royal Hibernian. The next morning he was found dead in his room. It is not recorded if he met Harry the night before, and it seems that the journey was too much for the serious heart complaint from which he suffered.

After the death of the Archdeacon, a Dublin solicitor, James McGarry, was appointed a trustee, and thirty farms, comprising about 3,500 acres, were sold to the tenants for £357,500, to raise cash for the insatiable squire and to pay off some of the mortgage debts. This was a sad business, as the Westby land had been in the family's ownership for at least 700 years, and in another thirty years time would have been worth six million pounds. The tenants did not appreciate then the potential of their purchases and were rather reluctant to buy. One old farmer remarked afterwards, 'Eh, deary me, once we were prosperous tenants and now we're poor bloody landowners!'

As Latham's notice of resignation did not expire for six months after the death of the Archdeacon, he continued to act as personal agent and still went to Dublin, though his health was deteriorating. Harry could not understand why visiting him made Latham ill and recommended walks in the country.

After the appointment of McGarry and the sale of the farms, life became more tolerable for Latham, though he still continued to be summoned to Dublin. Harry had purchased 160 acres of land near Nassau, New Providence Island, which he proposed to develop with houses. He was buying more works of art and jewellery, among which was a diamond – 'more important than the Junkers diamond' – for which he had paid £700 and was offering it to the Aga Khan for £300,000, but there is no record of the outcome of this transaction!

Harry, whilst taking the air in a chauffeur-driven car and stopping for a short stroll, lost his favourite talisman, a sapphire which he wore round his neck on a gold chain. Miraculously, the stone – reputedly of 200 carats valued at £100 per carat – was found the day after by Harry, with Weiss, his diamond merchant friend, apparently making its position known by emitting psychic signals to its owner!

McGarry accompanied Harry on one of these afternoon drives and afterwards related how, passing through a tiny village, Harry told the driver to stop at the post office as he had a telephone call to make. Entering, he gave the postmistress a number on a piece of paper, explaining that there might be some delay and that the call was to King Ibn Saud of Arabia. Undismayed, she got through and Harry, having had his conversation – probably with some court official – complimented the lady on her efficiency and asked her how much he owed. She replied: 'I don't rightly know, Sor, we don't get many calls to that gintleman in these parts, you will understand!'

As was to be expected Latham at last succumbed to the pressure and was laid up for eight months with a complete nervous breakdown and, as transpired later – a coronary thrombosis condition.

Early in 1953, Sarah Patricia Hurst, with apparently considerable reluctance, became a trustee. She was sixty-eight years of age, not in the best of health, and had returned to live in London. Harry came back during the same year and lived sometimes in Grosvenor House, sometimes the Dorchester, or the Ritz. He now had seven different firms of solicitors acting in his affairs, some of whom were probably unaware of all the others' existence.

William Latham died in November 1953, aged fifty-three. For nearly fourteen years he had devoted himself to the estate and Harry Clifton's affairs. He was a man of great ability, complete integrity and an almost fanatical attention to detail. As we have seen, he never spared himself and, whilst his knowledge of the technicalities of estate management was not great, he was quick to grasp a point and assess what action should be taken. The trustees had a number of professional advisors and consultants, as the estate and their beneficiary presented many problems, often beyond the scope of any one practitioner. Latham was most abstemious, but had one unusual gift - if one may so call it - alcohol had little or no effect on him. He told me that when in New York disposing of the Clifton Collection during 1941, he came up against several unscrupulous types, one of whom tried to get William drunk with the intention of 'pulling a fast one'. Having drink for drink, William saw his host under the table and had the satisfaction of delivering him back to his apartment in a state of complete oblivion!

With Latham's death the last of the original trustees had gone and McGarry, realising the difficulties of taking an active part in the administration of the trust from Dublin, wisely resigned.

Leonard Urry had, for a number of years, been associated with Harry's interests in the film world and he and Sarah P. Hurst now became trustees, whilst the writer of this story was appointed agent to the estate.

Leonard was a theatrical agent and had a long association with show business. He had been entertainments manager at no less an establishment than the Café de Paris, and, while there, engaged as hostess a young girl from India who became Merle Oberon, the famous film star. Her biography, *Merle,* describes how she could not get work until Leonard took pity on her and advanced money for dresses, which helped to put her fast on the road to stardom.[123] He also discovered Carol Levis, famous for his radio programme for discovering theatrical talent. Dining or lunching with him in a London restaurant could be fascinating, as he was often greeted by well-known people connected with stage and screen and usually had some interesting snippets of gossip about them.

Sarah Hurst was the daughter of an Egyptologist, full of mysticism and, I suspect, spiritualism, which suited Harry as he was very superstitious.

IX

AS I was personally involved in much of the remainder of my story, it is simpler to continue the story with myself in the first person. Having been with the estate for nearly twenty-five years as articled pupil, assistant and then chief surveyor – excepting the war years when in the navy as a mine-sweeping officer – I was well versed in most matters appertaining to its management and knew much more of its background than either the trustees or their advisors.

Soon after my appointment I was summoned to London to see Harry, who was then residing at Grosvenor House. He, very business-like, with pad and pencil, put to me a number of questions upon which I expounded at some length and elicited from him the comment that I had a very loud voice!

After an hour or so the squire said that, 'all work and no play makes Jack a dull boy', and we should adjourn to the Dorchester to dine; Leonard Urry, who had been present during the interview, went on first to secure a table. Left to ourselves Harry sat down and wrote out a cheque which he handed to me, saying London was a very expensive place. Without looking at the amount I handed it back and said, with regret, that as agent to his trustees I could not accept it. 'Ah, I thought you might say that,' he replied and tore it up. He now proceeded to dress for dinner by putting on an old trilby hat and winding a woollen scarf round his neck. He was wearing flannel bags and a Norfolk jacket, and completed the ensemble by taking a stout walking stick upon which he leaned heavily. Reaching the ground floor he said 'Do go ahead, Kennedy, I think you will find a taxi waiting.' Standing by the entrance I watched his slow progress across the lounge – a slight limp, his unusual garb for town, his greying beard and height, caused all eyes to be turned upon him. In the taxi he said, 'I know you must think me very extravagant taking a taxi such a short distance, but, you see, I have to be so careful.'

Arriving at the Dorchester the taxi meter had clocked up about one shilling and three pence, and Harry, producing a five-pound note from his waistcoat pocket handed it to the driver who said:

'Cor blimey Guv, I can't change that!'

'Did I ask you to?', snapped Harry, 'that's for you.'

Entering the hotel, I was instructed to proceed ahead to the restaurant where the head waiter would show me to our table. Looking back, I saw one porter divest him of his hat whilst another helped him to unwind the scarf, Harry meanwhile slowly moving forward with his stick.

The cabaret was about to start, but was delayed when Harry made his appearance, pausing to look all round whilst leaning on his stick and stroking his beard.

At the table - where Urry was already seated - on taking my place I noticed that the remaining chair had a cushion on it. Harry now made his entrance, moving across the room escorted by the head waiter, watched in fascination by the other diners, and on arrival at his seat looked down and said, 'Thank you Charles, I think two cushions tonight please.'

Summoned by handclap, a waiter rushed up with another cushion and Harry slowly and painfully sank down saying, 'You see, Kennedy, I have to be so careful.'

For the next ten years the piecemeal break up of the estate continued with increased urgency due to Harry's 'expressed fear that a change of political government may occur, or the possibility of war, may bring about a very undesirable position, and, in accordance with his wishes, the trustees are endeavouring to make his position financially more fluid.' [124]

This apparently was sufficient reason to justify the trustees authorising sales without being in breach of the provisions of the trust deed, which, as we have seen, had been interpreted by several learned counsel in differing ways, which seemed to indicate a certain degree of elasticity in its structure!

Whilst Harry professed to have strong leanings to Labour he had good reason to bless the Tories, who brought in the Town and Country Planning Act of 1954. At the risk of boring the reader, it is necessary to explain that this measure provided for compensation to be paid to land- and property-owners for loss of development value - due to the provisions of the Act of 1947 - at the full agreed valuation of their claims plus interest for seven years at seven per cent.

After careful study of the Bill introducing the 1954 Act, the trustees' advisors said it appeared that if *refusals* of planning permission could be obtained on the areas of land where the amount of development value had been agreed upon under the 1947 Act, the Central Land Board would be obliged to pay up in full.

Time was short because there was a deadline on this provision, but the estate office staff worked like beavers, preparing over a hundred planning applications, most of which were refused and the outcome of which was that Harry received over £600,000 compensation, whilst ownership of the land remained with the estate.

True, the compensation money would be re-payable to the Ministry if planning permission was received in the future, but the escalation in value of building land soon became so great that in the years to come such amounts became almost nominal.

This was a windfall that had not been foreseen before the introduction of the new Act; nevertheless, the development of the land for which planning permission had been granted was pushed forward and, with the relaxation of war-time restrictions on private house building and the scarcity of building land created by the Planning Acts, prices of land and property rapidly increased. The Lytham St. Annes estate had always been developed by the granting of building leases whereby the ground rents were secured by the property built on the land, and increasingly high premiums were now charged. Almost before the ink was dry on building agreements and before a brick had been laid, the ground rents were sold, and, with the premiums, money poured into Harry's bank accounts. Incredibly – considering the large amounts received – the mortgage debt remained, until, by 1962, it amounted to over £300,000, and the only way of paying the interest was by selling off more land and property, as the rental income from the estate had shrunk to just under £6,000 *per annum*.

As Harry was not prepared to part with – or had already spent – any of the near one and a half million pounds he had received since 1954, there existed, as John Spencer, the estate solicitor, said, 'a suicidal policy which could only lead to disaster.'

There was only one thing to be done, and the Guardian Assurance Company, the principal mortgagee, had made the best offer of one million, three hundred thousand pounds, for the remaining 2,500 acres of the estate, excluding Lytham Hall and the sixty-acre inner park, which were sold to the company two years after.

Harry had won. In thirty years he had received over three and a half million pounds, and liquidated, for his own use, the Clifton heritage.

X

DURING my ten years as agent to the Trustees I had little direct contact with the squire. Leonard Urry now acted as his personal agent and trustee, and was, to a great extent, buffer between us. Nevertheless, from time to time I received from Harry himself some odd or unusual instructions. One of the first was to send a certain Arabian monarch a young Ayrshire bull and two in-calf heifers. 'You see, Kennedy, the children only get a little goat or camel milk and are sadly undernourished. Now, good rich Ayrshire milk would be an inestimable boon to them.'

Upon my enquiring to whom I should send the cattle, he replied, 'Oh, I don't know, you'd better ask Mack.' The latter was a self-confessed communist who had promised to hang Harry on the nearest lamp post when 'The Revolution' took place; but, in the meantime, enjoyed a glass of champagne – from the cellars of Lytham Hall – and carried out little missions for his benefactor.

Mack said he had no idea and suggested the Prime Minister, if such a personage existed. As the intention appeared to be the establishment of a milking herd, I made, without success, tentative enquiries as to what the animals would be fed on, having a vague idea that goats and camels lived largely on thorn bushes, which diet would be unlikely to produce a satisfactory gallonage from the pampered ladies from Lytham. My own private feelings were that on arrival the cattle might become the principal item of a first-class barbecue.

However, 'to listen is to obey': two suitable heifers were selected with a young bull of good lineage to sire future generations, when suddenly, word came through to hold everything as the King had been deposed by his brother. Feeling greatly relieved, I thankfully stopped the arrangements being made for sending the cattle out by plane. In due course the heifers calved and the matter appeared to have been forgotten when the message came, through Mack: 'Carry on, the King is back and his brother has been executed.'

Once again two heifers were chosen and arrangements resumed for export when, to everyone's dismay, it was found on veterinary examination that the young bull was deficient in the matter of his reproductive organs and was unlikely to father sons and daughters in Arabia whose excellence would bring fame to the Lytham herd!

Fortunately, by this time, some other project had claimed Harry's interest and attention, and the matter was allowed to drop.

During 1957 on Harry's instructions – and be it said, mainly due to Urry's persuasion – Lytham Hall was prepared for Violet, Harry's mother, to leave the convent and take up residence. The first floor was adapted to make a spacious flat and here she lived until her death in 1962. Whilst she had little money to spend she had her small establishment of butler, cook – usually the butler's wife – housekeeper, and Lizzie Taylor, formerly the children's nurse, as lady's maid. The estate outdoor staff were always available to help and she lived very comfortably, entertaining her friends and relations in the manner befitting a dowager. Almost all expenses were paid by the estate office and, apart from her personal pecuniary embarrassment, she obviously thoroughly enjoyed the position. She was, of course, immediately asked to open bazaars and grace similar functions with her presence; this she did, 'as to the manner born' and this she was. Lytham responded to her dignity and charm and whilst the matter of donations to worthy causes caused her some embarrassment there were few situations with which she could not cope.

One such matter was going away by train, as – for the aforesaid financial reasons – she always travelled third-class. The ticket, having been purchased for her privately, was secreted in her handbag and she would arrive at the station to be met by the station master, who, escorting her to the train with due deference, handed her into a first-class non-smoking compartment.

As the train drew out, he would remove his hat and Violet would incline her head graciously from the carriage window. Little did he know that before the train had reached the next station she had collected her things and moved into the nearest third-class carriage!

Although Violet's establishment was small, everything had to be done in the correct manner, especially as regards food. One applicant for the position of butler professed to be an accomplished chef and said that with the aid of his wife he could act in this dual capacity and give complete satisfaction. His tenure was of short duration. One morning the telephone rang: 'Mr Kennedy, I have just seen packets of custard powder being brought into the house. I will not have custard powder in Lytham Hall. The chef must go, immediately.' And go he did!

In the north entrance hall stands a marble statue of 'Venus after the bath', and one morning as Violet was coming down the main stairway, Betty Lund, the Irish housekeeper, was dusting Venus, and, greeting Violet, said, 'Good morning, madam. Tell me, now, would this be a statue of yourself when you were a young woman?'

Telling me the story afterwards Violet said, 'You know, I really was rather flattered!'

Despite the large sums of money Harry was receiving prior to the sale of the estate, he still kept up the pretence of being hard-up, and during a telephone conversation he once said to me, 'You do not seem to understand, Kennedy, how poor I am. Do you know, I am living on soup, only soup!' Putting on my best sympathetic tone of voice, I said, 'Oh, I really am sorry, but where are you staying just now?' Came the reply, 'Oh, at the Ritz you know, still there.'

It was not long after this conversation that he again telephoned from the Ritz and said, 'I want to give George, the hall porter here, a nice tip, he has been so good and I think he is retiring soon. I know: let's give him a plot of building land and he can go and live at Lytham.'

Having selected a choice plot in a pleasant quarter of Lytham I had the conveyance drawn up and took it to London for execution by Harry, who presented it to George. That night I found myself installed in one of the most prestigious bedrooms in the hotel, with flowers, morning tea, newspapers etc. and savoured momentarily how those of great wealth manage to rub along.

George Criticos – known by many famous patrons of the Ritz – was himself a well-known character. Thanking me for my part in the matter, he said: 'Mr Clifton is too generous; I have a nice home in the south and want to retire there and grow my roses, which I love. Please, can you sell the land for me?'

After retiring, George published his memoirs and in them refers to the land as the most unusual tip he ever received.[125]

Sometimes I had to entertain visitors sent to Lytham by Harry for one reason or another, and a certain Dr Couch from America arrived one day. The doctor said he had discovered the cure for cancer and all he wanted from Harry was £10,000 to introduce it to the world. He was elderly, voluble and claimed to have controlled the elements and restored the dead to life. I suspect he was not unconnected with the Ghost of Hollywood and the Agabeg Temple. He was, of course, a mystic and spiritualist, and during dinner at the Clifton Arms expounded on the virtures of his wife and how helpful she was to him.

'Say boy, if I gotta' problem I just call her up and she tells me what to do.'

When I remarked on the expense of transatlantic telephone calls, he said: 'Aw hell, no! She's been dead for fifteen years.'

Seeing my look of incredulity, he said, 'You don't believe me? I'll call her up right now and you can have a word with her.'

'Not now, please, Doctor!', I said in alarm, 'not in the middle of dinner. What would the other diners think?'

Taking the point he got on with his meal, but I have sometimes wondered what would have happened if I had agreed that he should give his wife a call.

Like in many other towns, the war left behind in Lytham St. Annes a number of buildings erected in connection with defence and the war effort. Two large brick buildings behind St. Annes had been used for the repair of heavy military equipment, and thinking they might be used as barns, of which the estate was in need, it was agreed to take them over and not require their demolition and the clearance of the site by the Ministry.

Upon hearing about them, however, Harry had other ideas, and I received a visit from a French viscount who had persuaded Harry that large profits were to be made from the sale of canned beef to the French Foreign Legion. The home farm, newly stocked with Ayrshire milking cattle was to be switched to beef production and the buildings would be ideal for the cannery.

Town planning regulations, however, forbade the use of the buildings for any purpose other than agriculture and application for change of use would be refused.

Harry's long sojourn in Ireland had in part been for purposes of tax relief and he had not been long returned to England when he became a 'non-resident' of Britain for the same reason. He spent much of his time in Paris at the George Cinq Hotel, and at Monte Carlo, from where Sam White in his newsletter to the *Evening Standard* of January 26th, 1957 makes mention of Lytham's squire:

> Of the many eccentrics who pass through the gilded salons of the Monte Carlo casino, the most notable, as befits tradition, is an Englishman.
>
> He is fifty-year-old Harry Talbot de Vere Clifton, Squire of Lytham in Lancashire. Clifton has the reputation of being a mystic and a poet. He looks the part.
>
> Tall, bearded, always dressed in heavy tweeds with a heavy brown scarf wrapped around his neck, he wanders around the gambling tables as though in a trance.
>
> His abstracted air is something of a legend in the casino. He sometimes speaks to complete strangers under the impression that they are old friends, and ignores old friends under the impression that they are strangers. He is a bachelor and describes his family as 'The Royal Commoners' who can never accept a title because of their royal descent.
>
> Clifton is the author of several little-known volumes of poetry. In the casino, apart from his trance-like air, he is notable for heavy gambling carried out with the appearance of complete unconcern, and sudden outbursts of indiscriminate generosity.
>
> Recently he fished two pieces of jewellery out of his pocket and distributed them to two complete strangers.
>
> Clifton has lived a great deal of his life in India and it to this that he attributes his apparent sensitivity to the slightest chill in the air. During

> a spell of cold weather he will not leave his hotel suite for several days on end.
>
> India has also given him an interest in mysticism and a friendship with Nehru and his sister. He plies Nehru and other Asiatic politicians with letters and cables advising them on the conduct of affairs.
>
> But the oddest thing about Clifton is that, despite his mysticism he retains a lively interest in the world of business. Outwardly a recluse, he confers constantly with a circle of international business men. They stand in considerable awe of him, and it is an interesting sight to see them agitatedly awaiting a summons to his suite.
>
> Clifton's current business preoccupation is the establishment of a tanning industry in India.

From this we get more evidence of the dream world Harry had created around himself and confirmation of his eccentricity as seen through the eyes of an independent, professional observer. It also shows how successfully he had built up the impression of big business and his importance as a commercial potentate whose opinion might rock the markets of the world or influence the politics of Asia!

Had Sam White investigated the backgrounds of the international businessmen 'agitatedly awaiting a summons to his suite', he might have been considerably surprised. One such person who wrote to him from New York appears to have been involved in the spirit business in more than one sense of the word:

> My dearest Brother in Spirit,
>
> You have been so very much in my vibration that I am compelled to write you.
>
> I have a client in Toronto, Canada who wanted ten thousand barrels of Rye whiskey so I got in touch with .....

The rest of the letter is irrelevant!

The reference in the newsletter to Harry's occasional heavy gambling, and bearing in mind his lack of success in such a pastime, probably accounts for a considerable part of the money he got rid of.

As he only spent a comparatively short time in India it is difficult to believe that his sensitivity to cold was due to living there.

It is a fact that he was continually writing verse and published several books of his poems, but their sale was almost nil. He wrote on the backs of envelopes, menus, statements of account, the fly leaves of books or any scrap of paper that was to hand when his Muse was upon him. But the critics did not acclaim his work.

Sarah Hurst died in January 1963, whereupon Harry appointed himself joint trustee with Leonard Urry; and when the sale of the estate to Guardian Assurance was completed, I and my staff were kept on by the company. After discharge of the mortgage debts out of monies received from the estate, Harry should still have been a rich man, but it seems he could not get out of the way of squandering his wealth.

One of his most disastrous purchases was land on the coast of Sardinia, for which he paid £300,000. The vendor, who, it transpired after, had paid only £30,000, vanished as soon as the sale to Harry was completed. It was then discovered that the title to the land was bad, the sale illegal, and Harry had lost his money.

Although I was employed by Guardian from May 1963, I continued to look after Lytham Hall until the company bought the house in 1966. After the sale there remained on the premises family portraits and a few pieces of furniture.

One day, one of Harry's henchmen arrived at the estate office and informed me that 'Mr Clifton had sent him to Lytham to see if there was anything left in the Hall or the office that could be sold, as he was in need of money.'

Suddenly I felt a surge of anger amounting almost to fury at the prodigal and stupid waste of a magnificent estate. I pulled open the strong room door and said:

'Look! Here are his father's guns; the furniture, Sotheby's say, should be sold on the premises. Let's put the lot together and have an auction sale at Lytham Hall!'

'My God! The end of the Cliftons of Lytham!'

A picture fell to the floor of the office. I picked it up and turned it over. It was the engagement photograph of John Talbot Clifton and Violet Mary Beauclerk.

Epilogue

West Lancashire Evening Gazette
By Jill Sutton Wednesday, November 28th, 1979.

Mr Harry Clifton, Fylde's most famous landowner, former Squire of Lytham, traveller, gambler and friend of kings has died in Brighton, aged 72,

The white-bearded, nomadic recluse, once one of the richest landowners in the country and until 1937 owner of most of Lytham St. Annes died in hospital yesterday, virtually penniless.

He had been taken ill with a heart attack, the second in a short time, at the Brighton home of his close friend for the last twenty years, Mrs Margaret Kilner, a soothsayer.

Mortem aut Triumphum

The Clifton Family Tree
(abbreviated)

Sir William de Clyfton, 1216-72 =

Gilbert de Clyfton, high sheriff 1278, 1286, 1287, 1289. ob. 1324 =

Sir William de Clyfton, living 1329 =

Sir William Clifton, 4 Edward III = Margaret, dtr. of Sir Robert Sherburne.

Sir Nicholas Clifton, governor of Ham = Eleanor, dtr. of Sir Thomas West, ancestor of Lords de la Warre.

Sir Robert de Clifton, Knight of the Shire, 1382 =

Thomas Clifton = Agnes, dtr. of Sir Richard Molyneux of Sefton

Richard Clifton = Alice, dtr. of John Butler

James Clifton = Alice, dtr. of James Lancaster

Robert Clifton = Margaret, dtr. of Nicholas Butler

Cuthbert Clifton of Clifton, ob. 1512 = Alice, dtr. of Sir John Lawrence

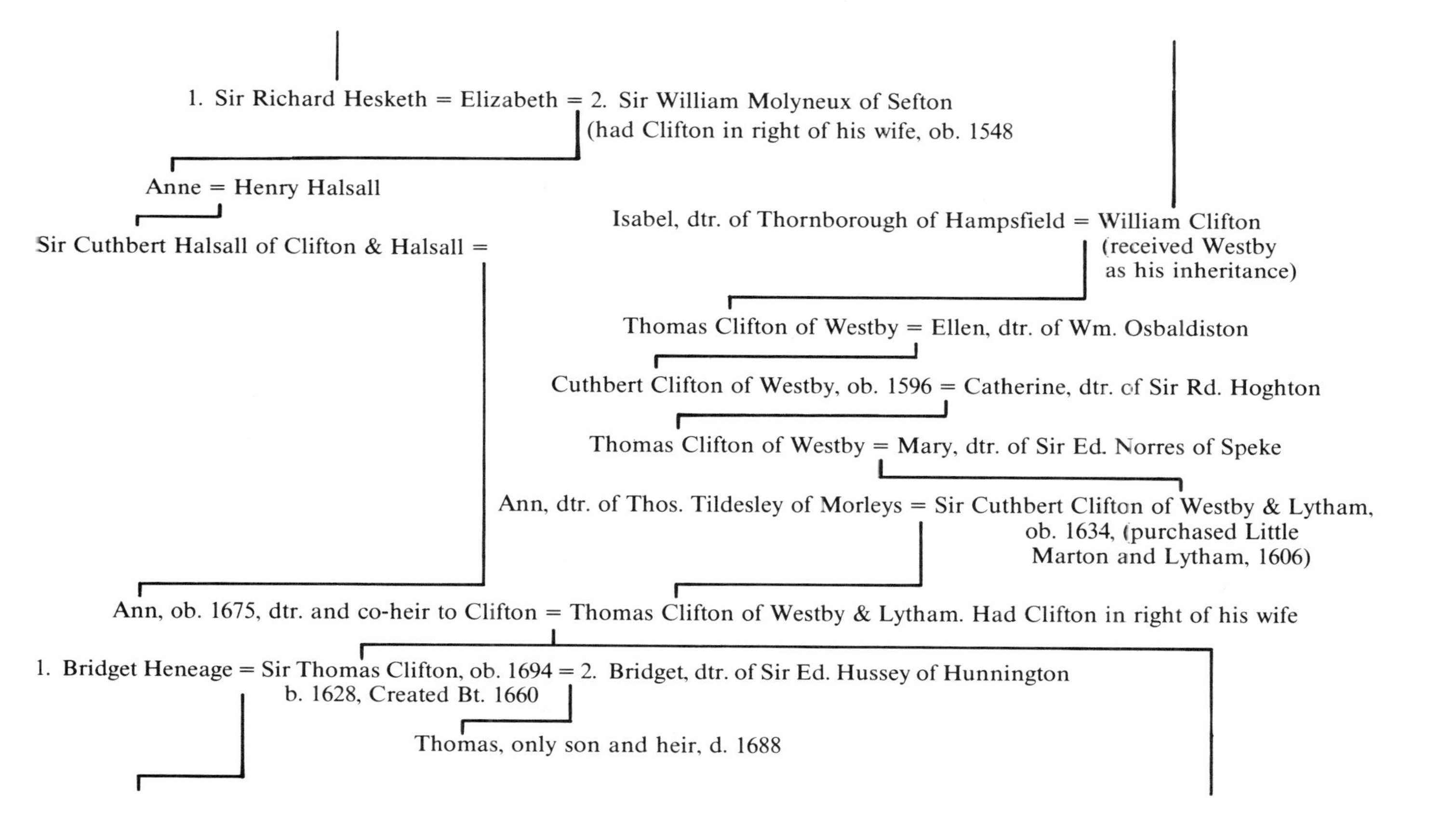
1. Sir Richard Hesketh = Elizabeth = 2. Sir William Molyneux of Sefton
(had Clifton in right of his wife, ob. 1548
Anne = Henry Halsall
Sir Cuthbert Halsall of Clifton & Halsall =
Isabel, dtr. of Thornborough of Hampsfield = William Clifton
(received Westby
as his inheritance)
Thomas Clifton of Westby = Ellen, dtr. of Wm. Osbaldiston
Cuthbert Clifton of Westby, ob. 1596 = Catherine, dtr. of Sir Rd. Hoghton
Thomas Clifton of Westby = Mary, dtr. of Sir Ed. Norres of Speke
Ann, dtr. of Thos. Tildesley of Morleys = Sir Cuthbert Clifton of Westby & Lytham,
ob. 1634, (purchased Little
Marton and Lytham, 1606)
Ann, ob. 1675, dtr. and co-heir to Clifton = Thomas Clifton of Westby & Lytham. Had Clifton in right of his wife
1. Bridget Heneage = Sir Thomas Clifton, ob. 1694 = 2. Bridget, dtr. of Sir Ed. Hussey of Hunnington
b. 1628, Created Bt. 1660
Thomas, only son and heir, d. 1688

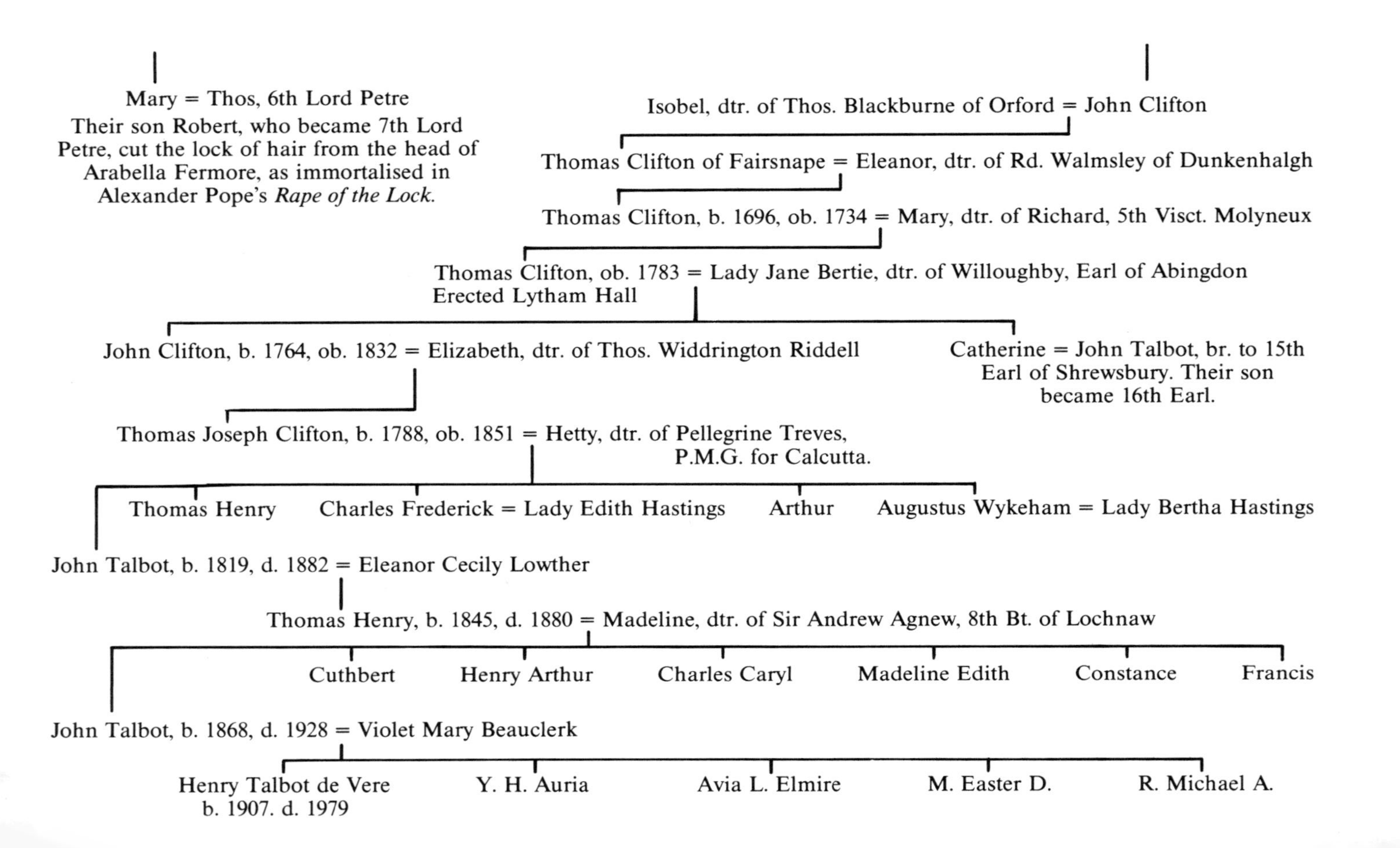

Mary = Thos, 6th Lord Petre
Their son Robert, who became 7th Lord Petre, cut the lock of hair from the head of Arabella Fermore, as immortalised in Alexander Pope's *Rape of the Lock*.
Isobel, dtr. of Thos. Blackburne of Orford = John Clifton
Thomas Clifton of Fairsnape = Eleanor, dtr. of Rd. Walmsley of Dunkenhalgh
Thomas Clifton, b. 1696, ob. 1734 = Mary, dtr. of Richard, 5th Visct. Molyneux
Thomas Clifton, ob. 1783 = Lady Jane Bertie, dtr. of Willoughby, Earl of Abingdon
Erected Lytham Hall
John Clifton, b. 1764, ob. 1832 = Elizabeth, dtr. of Thos. Widdrington Riddell
Catherine = John Talbot, br. to 15th Earl of Shrewsbury. Their son became 16th Earl.
Thomas Joseph Clifton, b. 1788, ob. 1851 = Hetty, dtr. of Pellegrine Treves, P.M.G. for Calcutta.
Thomas Henry
Charles Frederick = Lady Edith Hastings
Arthur
Augustus Wykeham = Lady Bertha Hastings
John Talbot, b. 1819, d. 1882 = Eleanor Cecily Lowther
Thomas Henry, b. 1845, d. 1880 = Madeline, dtr. of Sir Andrew Agnew, 8th Bt. of Lochnaw
Cuthbert
Henry Arthur
Charles Caryl
Madeline Edith
Constance
Francis
John Talbot, b. 1868, d. 1928 = Violet Mary Beauclerk
Henry Talbot de Vere b. 1907. d. 1979
Y. H. Auria
Avia L. Elmire
M. Easter D.
R. Michael A.

Notes on the text

1. Sacheverell Sitwell British Architects and Craftsmen.
2. Fitzhanger Manor, now Ealing Public Library.
3. Henry Cecil Clifton's account of Pellegrine Treves.
4. *Haydock Papers*, (1888), 237.
5. John Porter, *History of the Fylde.*
6. Lord Fitzroy Somerset, Military Secretary to Commander-in-Chief.
7. David Duff, *Eugenie & Napoleon III.* Louis Napoleon stayed at Fentons Hotel in 1831 and 1832, having two floors at the daily rate of £4, which he considered excessive.
8. Lancashire Record Office (hereafter Lancs. R. O.) Report for 1959.
9. Rossall Hall, now the school.
10. The italics are Talbot's underlinings. Lord Lonsdale died on 19th March 1844.
11. Lord Lonsdale having died on 19th March 1844 - a month before the wedding - his eldest son Sir William and brother of the Colonel, succeeded as 2nd Earl and, as he never married, the Colonel was next in line for the title. It was the Colonel's son Henry, however, who became the 3rd Earl in 1872 as the Colonel died before his brother.
12. Violet Mary Clifton, *The Book of Talbot.*
13. Richard Cobden and John Bright, the Lancashire Abolitionists.
14. John Porter, *The History of the Fylde of Lancashire.*
15. James was Fair's son who was also seriously ill.
16. The italics are Hetty's underlinings.
17. Catmose Lodge, Oakham, Rutland.
18. Douglas Sutherland in his book, *The Yellow Earl,* describes Barleythorpe as a hunting box on a princely scale which was to become the hunting headquarters of later generations of Lowthers.
19. Maynooth - a training college for Roman Catholic clergy in Ireland.
20. G. M. Trevelyan, *English Social History,* 516. 'Having been accorded the station of civic equality by the Catholic Emancipation Act of 1829 and being perpetually recruited by Irish immigration into England, the Roman community went on increasing in numbers and

influence. But in 1850 it was still obnoxious to a strongly Protestant nation, as was shown by the misdirected popular outburst against the so-called "Papal Aggression" when the Pope set up territorial bishops in England.'

21. John Porter, *History of the Fylde.*
22. G. M. Trevelyan, *English Social History,* 518.
23. 19 Bruton Street, belonging to Lord Fitzhardinge, second son of the Earl of Berkeley.
24. M.P. for Peterborough, 1841-1859.
25. Talbot did not win and Lord Fitzwilliam retained his seat.
26. Major R. J. T. Williamson, *History of the Old County Regiment of Lancashire Militia.*
27. *Ibid.*
28. *Ibid,* 269.
29. Lord Methuen wrote to John Talbot's agent in 1860: 'I do not like writing at present to Mr Clifton to ask how my oldest friend is - I hear he has been very ill - but is now better - I hope most sincerely he is so - Pray kindly send me a few lines to say that he is - as I am most anxious about him. I have been very unwell myself and my writing is not very distinct - but I hope you can decipher it.'
30. 'Journal of Residence in Africa 1842-1853', vol. i, *The Van Riebeeck Soc.,* (Cape Town, 1961).
31. Extract from diary of Colour Sergeant J. Fisher, 1st Battalion.
32. Henry Clifford VC, his letters and sketches from the Crimea.
33. What the Bishop's account was for is not known.
34. G. M. Trevelyan, *English Social History.*
35. George Augustus Cavendish-Bentinck, Judge Advocate General.
36. Sir Charles Abney Hastings Bart.
37. Lady Edith's younger sister.
38. The eldest son of George and barbara Yelverton became 3rd Marquis but died at the age of nineteen, and was succeeded by Henry, his brother as 4th Marquis, upon whose death without issue, the baronies, by writ, fell into abeyance among his sisters, the Earldom of Loudoun devolving upon Lady Edith.
39. Hugh Clifton, great grandson of Thomas Henry, who also attended Eton writes: 'The Eton Rifle Volunteer Corps was founded in 1860 at the height of a French invasion scare. It is interesting to note that T. H. C. was a corporal. My source, of which more anon, says, "even the corporals were boys of some standing in the school". The uniform is described as "whitey-brown tunic with light blue facings, edged with red cord". On their heads were worn "stiff kepis". Colours were presented to the Corps by the Provost's wife in 1860, and in 1861 they were reviewed by the Queen and Prince Albert. They must have been an extra-ordinary sight, as it is said that hardly any of their uniforms fitted properly! Rev. Russell Day, T.H.C.s housemaster, or more properly, tutor, kept a house called Carter House - a hideous, rambling edifice of great antiquity, whose only claim to fame is that Shelley's wife, Mary, once stayed there in 1797. Day himself was "a little

man with tinted spectacles, slow measured step and quiet muffled voice". The boys, with considerable lack of originality, nicknamed him "Parva Dies". He had "a placidity in his manner which spoke of sufferings patiently borne; but he was by no means a weak master. Shrewd, humorous, methodical in all his arrangements, and quietly firm, he kept his division well in hand . . . [No mean feat – classes often consisted of up to seventy boys!] . . . His ways were . . . winning . . . and he was an entertaining teacher, for his knowledge was extensive and various, and he abounded in anecdotes, sallies and pleasant jests . . . He had few superiors as an instructor. He was an original thinker, and his lessons were always more than mere construings of Latin and Greek." He is said to have hated superstitions and would tell his pupils that any boy who took pains not to walk under a ladder was violating the first commandment. He set "traps" for boys, who were declaiming the Latin verses they had to learn by heart and was "very unpopular for his pains." He also made himself "unlovable" by insisting that boys did not rush out of class as soon as the bell rang (which was invariably the case), but insisted that the exit should only be commenced when he had given the word.' He resigned his post in fury when Dr. Hornby (H.M.) promoted two junior masters over his head!

From James Brinsley-Richards, *Seven Years at Eton, 1857-1864.*

40. He was also commissioned Cornet in the Lancashire Hussar Regiment of Yeomanry Cavalry in October 1870.
41. Violet Mary Clifton, *The Book of Talbot.*
42. Quintin Hogg was a fellow Old Etonian of Lord Kinnaird who became involved in the purchase of the house. Arthur Fitzgerald Kinnaird, Baron Kinnaird of Inchture, Perth, had married Mary, the fifth daughter of Sir Andrew Agnew and was Madeline Cifton's sister. This was the then famous Lord Kinnaird, known as the 'busiest man in London' and regarded as second only to the Earl of Shaftsbury in his humanitarian influence, combining a variety of philanthropic interests with a prominent position in the banking and insurance world, and who gave over fifty years unsparing work on behalf of Association Football, and prowess in almost every form of outdoor sport (Number Three St. James's Street, Autumn 1981, Berry Bros & Rudd Ltd.). His second son, the Hon. Kenneth Fitzgerald, married Frances Victoria, Thomas Henry's youngest daughter and later came into the title.
43. Thomas Fair was a Lieutenant in the Lytham Rifle Corps.
44. Gabriel Harrison, *The Rage of Sand.*
45. He had been appointed a trustee of the settlement.
46. Pierre Sichel, *The Jersey Lily.*
47. Noel Gerson, *The Lives and Loves of Lillie Langtry.*
48. Violet Mary Clifton, *The Book*

of Talbot, 156.

49. The Presumptive Portion was one-sixth of £40,000 with interest at four per cent, in addition from Colonel Clifton's death in April 1882. The portions were made under Lady Drummond's absolute control during her lifetime, with power of appointment, i.e. she need not divide the £40,000 in equal shares, but could give more to one and less to another if she thought proper. Without her full consent Cuthbert could not claim his portion.
50. The estate solicitors.
51. Who the reluctant volunteer was is not known.
52. Violet Mary Clifton, *The Book of Talbot,* 9.
53. Violet Mary Clifton, *The Book of Talbot,* 11.
54. As John Talbot's diary for 1895 is missing, the whole account of his Alaskan journey has been taken from *The Book of Talbot,* and this is a much abridged version.
55. Speaker of the House of Commons from 1905 for sixteen years and created Lord Ullswater on his retirement.
56. An Eskimo female.
57. Private horse-drawn omnibus attached to the estate.
58. He had contracted Black Water Fever and nearly died close to the Mountains of the Moon.
59. Henry, the 15th Duke, married Lady Flora, daughter of Charles Frederick Clifton (Lord Donnington) and Lady Edith, Countess of Loudoun.
60. Churchill, *My Early Life,* 359.
61. Churchill, *History of the English Speaking Peoples,* iv, 298.
62. Starosta - village elder.
63. Shikari - hunter's attendant.
64. To celebrate the Coronation of Edward VII.
65. Geoffrey Moorhouse, *India Britannica,* 157-159.
66. So called after the Eskimo Antonguela saying 'Maoona' - 'which way'.
67. Whilst Captain Voss does not seem to have made a fortune, the sea anchor or drogue is a standard piece of equipment in R.N.L.I. lifeboats, ships' lifeboats and yachts, and its use in small craft for riding out gales or preventing 'broaching to' in a heavy following sea has been proved on countless occasions.
68. Consisting of gold images and plate from Lima Cathedral.
69. Cocos Island lies about 600 miles south west of Panama and 1,500 miles north of Callao.
70. One account says that Captain Thompson died in a London hospital, but before he died wrote directions on a map. *Sunday Pictorial* (26th February 1939).
71. It later transpired that Gray had a twelve month monopoly to search for the treasure.
72. The British Vice Consul.
73. It is hard to conceive a more extraordinary reason for shooting a horse. Ironically, in June Talbot had written to James Fair telling him to send Ashton 'a good hammerless ejector gun as he had been so kind to him.'
74. Violet Mary Clifton, *The Book of Talbot,* 301.
75. *From Piano to Forte,* Cassell & Co. Ltd.
76. *As I Was Going Down Sackville Street* is dedicated to Violet Mary Clifton, and contains

passages describing incidents in Ireland, Lytham and Kildalton when John Talbot and Gogarty are together, and, whilst parts make hilarious reading, his portrayal of Tabot as an extrovert is almost cruelly overdone, although he always makes haste to laud Talbot in some other way. When I first read the book, I mentioned to Mrs Clifton that I had been entertained by Gogarty's description of her husband (whom I had never met) and she was not amused. 'He should never have written what he did', she said unsmilingly, with such depth of feeling that I never referred to the book again.

77. Lady Kinnaird was Talbot Clifton's youngest sister.
78. Violet Mary Clifton, *The Book of Talbot,* 336.
79. Violet Mary Clifton, *Notes to the Book of Talbot.*
80. Gertrude Bell, the noted traveller and writer.
81. Violet Mary Clifton, *The Book of Talbot,* 358.
82. Violet Mary Clifton, *The Book of Talbot,* 369.
83. *As I was going down Sackville Street.*
84. At his baptism the sponsors were Henry, Duke of Norfolk and Lelgarde, Lady Bellingham.
85. The quotes in inverted commas are from an essay on Oxford written by Harry Clifton.
86. Richard Michael Alleye, born 13th February, 1917, the younger son.
87. His twenty-first birthday.
88. The Clifton colours.
89. R. G. Leigh of the Foreign Office wrote to Lord Ullswater re Harry calling on Consul General at Saigon, 3rd September 1930.
90. He later engaged the Colonel to train his horses at Lytham.
91. Kildalton was not subject to the settlement.
92. Avia was the second daughter, who suffered from TB and, as transpired, was not cured.
93. Easter Daffodil, the youngest daughter.
94. Clifton; sable on a bend argent three mullets gules. St. Albans; Quarterly, 1st and 4th France and England quarterly, 2nd Scotland, 3rd Ireland (being the arms of Charles II) over all, a baton sinister gules charged with three roses argent.
95. Gerald Baird, the Kildalton factor, who later married Easter Daffodil, the youngest daughter.
96. In fact, she returned it.
97. Co-owner and trainer of the horses.
98. Daughter of Prince Paul Galitzin and the Countess Natalie Strogonoff.
99. Col. Paul Rodzianko C.M.G., *Tattered Banners,* Seeley Service & Co. Ltd.
100. Anita Leslie, *The Gilt and the Gingerbread.*
101. Robin Goodfellow (Capt. Eric Pickman) writing in the *Daily Mail,* 10th February, 1936.
102. Now Pontin's Holiday Camp.
110. Rosa Lewis, owner of the Cavendish Hotel, Duke Street, and confidante of kings and princes.
111. The de-frocked Harold Davidson, Rector of Stiffkey, was a crowd-drawing feature of the Golden Mile, appearing

variously as: fasting in a glass case and, previously, in a fiery furnace being prodded with a pitchfork wielded by a crimson-clad, betailed demon!

105. In the circumstances it seems a pity they could not get his name right!
106. *Los Angeles Daily News,* 2nd May, 1938.
107. 'I was invited to give the Lowell lectures in Boston during the spring of 1914, and concurrently to act as temporary professor of philosophy at Harvard . . . At Harvard I met all the professors. I am proud to say that I took a violent dislike to Professor Lowell, who subsequently assisted in the murder of Sacco and Vanzatti. I had at that time no reason to dislike him, but the feeling was just as strong as it was in later years, when his qualities as a saviour of society had been manifested. From *The Autobiography of Bertrand Russell (1872-1914).*

    Sacco and Vanzetti were radical Italian immigrants arrested after a violent robbery in 1927 and Professor Lowell headed a committee that was instrumental in persuading the Judge to pronounce sentence of death.
108. *Daily News,* 1st and 2nd May.
109. *New York Times.*
110. *Call Bulletin,* San Francisco.
111 It was during October 1985 that Dr Hammer contacted me through Lady Virginia Fiennes, asking for information about Harry Clifton, whom he knew in America, and wished to mention in his autobiography, *Hammer, Witness to History*. A few days later the doctor himself 'phoned and said he had 'some sizzling tales about Harry', and we agreed to exchange those parts of our manuscripts which related to him. The next afternoon the London office of Occidental Oil telephoned - would I send my manuscript by British Rail's Red Star delivery arriving Euston at 10.30 p.m. that night to be collected and flown with courier to Los Angeles the next day? This was a typical example of how the Hammer organisation works if he wanted something quickly! In return he sent me nine pages of his manuscript referring to Harry and in writing commented that he thought my story of Harry would make a good television play or series. He said he had taken the liberty of raising the subject with Lady Jane Wellesley of Antelope Films, but regrettably for a number of reasons this proposal quietly died. In his book he refers to Harry and King Farouk of Egypt as two of the strangest customers ever served by the Hammer Galleries.
112. They were large crystal glasses bearing the forty-two Clifton quarterings and crest.
113. 'The Rufford Ghost' was said to be that of a monk.
114. The crest of Savile of Rufford Abbey is an owl affrontee arg. debruised by a bend sinister wavy sd.
115. Telegram from Clifton to Secretary of State for Air, Whitehall.

116. The Archdeacon of Lancaster.
117. The patronage of those holding the Roman Catholic faith is administered by the Universities of Oxford and Cambridge, Oxford being responsible for benefices south of the Trent and Cambridge to the north.
118. After the war, Lord Derby paid Clifton £400, and as the watercourse was taken over soon after by the newly-formed South Fylde Drainage Board, the matter was ended.
119. *Lytham St. Annes Express,* 27th October 1944. Mr Justice Vaisey in his summing up.
120. Statement prepared by Archdeacon Fosbrooke. Estate Records.
121. Latham's Memoranda of Meeting in London, 15th May 1944.
122. Trustees' minutes after William Latham's visit to Dublin, 22nd and 23rd February 1950.
123. Charles Higham and Roy Mosley, *Merle.*
124. Trustees' minutes.
125. *George of the Ritz.*

Bibliographical note

MUCH of the material used in this book has come from the various family papers and diaries to which I have had access, and personal contacts and information which I have gleaned after a long association with the estate and the Clifton family.

Besides these 'original' sources, I have consulted many secondary works, most of which are listed individually in the notes to the text. In addition, there is a large and invaluable archive at the Lancashire Record Office (DDCl) which adds greatly to our understanding, especially of the earlier period.

Acknowledgements

I would like to thank Guardian Royal Exchange Assurance for their support in publishing this book, and for allowing me to use the family papers and John Talbot Clifton's diaries which came into their possession with the house and estate office.

The many family papers, which were loaned to the County Record Office by the late Henry Clifton, were purchased from him by Mr J. C. Hilton of Lytham, and thanks are due to him for thus ensuring that they remain in Lancashire. He also purchased the lordship of the manor of Lytham.

I am particularly indebted to Dr Alan Crosby, who read the manuscript and suggested that the chapter on the ancient history of the Cliftons could and should be amplified; this resulted in the preface which replaced my original, much shorter summary. Dr Crosby also compiled the excellent and useful index.

I am grateful to Dr Armand Hammer who kindly sent me part of the manuscript for his autobiography in exchange for part of my own manuscript.

The inclusion of the Lillie Langtry letters in the story is due to the generosity of Mr J. B. Clarke of Hardhorn, who very kindly sent me photocopies of the originals, which he owns.

For help given, thanks also to Alan Ashton, Lawrence Atkins, John Braes, Barry Dawson, Hugh Clifton, James Disley, Jill Sutton and Edith Tyson.

Due to my 'prairie' education, spelling is not my strongest point, but Doreen, my wife, who typed the manuscript, was my speller and consultant grammarian, as well as my sternest critic! To her, my love and thanks.

John Kennedy

Note on the illustrations

MOST of the illustrations in this book came from the former estate office at Lytham. We are particularly grateful, however, for the kind permission given by Mr J. C. Hilton for the reproduction of the estate plans and early sketch of Lytham Hall. The *West Lancashire Evening Gazette* also kindly allowed us to reproduce several of the photographs from their files. Thank you all.

Index

A

B

C

D

E

F

G

H

V

W